IMAGINATION IN CONFINEMENT

IMAGINATION IN CONFINEMENT

Women's Writings from French Prisons

ELISSA D. GELFAND

Cornell University Press

ITHACA AND LONDON

Cornell University Press gratefully acknowledges a
grant from the Andrew W. Mellon Foundation that
aided in bringing this book to publication.

Copyright © 1983 by Cornell University Press

All rights reserved. Except for brief quotations in a review, this book, or parts thereof, must not be reproduced in any form without permission in writing from the publisher. For information address Cornell University Press, 124 Roberts Place, Ithaca, New York 14850.

First published 1983 by Cornell University Press.
Published in the United Kingdom by Cornell University Press Ltd., London.

International Standard Book Number 0-8014-1543-8
Library of Congress Catalog Card Number 83-7191
Printed in the United States of America
*Librarians: Library of Congress cataloging information appears
on the last page of the book.*

The paper in this book is acid-free and meets the guidelines for permanence and durability of the Committee on Production Guidelines for Book Longevity of the Council on Library Resources.

Never rebellion or depression, but, over all, a great silent laugh
—Albertine Sarrazin

Women's imagination is inexhaustible
—Hélène Cixous

Contents

Preface 9
Acknowledgments 11
Introduction: Premises 15

PART ONE: SOCIAL AND LITERARY CONTEXTS
1. Female Criminality: The Biological Monster 39
2. Women's Prisons: The Social Monster 63
3. Philosophical and Literary Tradition:
   The Intellectual Monster 83

PART TWO: WOMEN'S TEXTS
4. Madame Roland 131
5. Marie Cappelle-Lafarge 153
6. Marguerite Steinheil 176
7. Anne Huré 195
8. Albertine Sarrazin 214
   Conclusion 239
   Bibliography 243
   Index 255

Illustrations

Madame Roland in prison, 1793   130
Madame Lafarge by Chapon, 1836   154
Madame Steinheil, 1908   177
Albertine Sarrazin, 1967   215

Preface

Women who have been judged and imprisoned as criminals have been censured because of their sex more than their crimes. They have been made to answer to and for society's unresolvably contradictory views of women, views rooted in timeless masculine fears and desires and yet, over time, severed from those sexual roots. Criminal women—by their affirmation of self, their singularity, and their distinctly unfeminine comportment—have kept reminding us of those dark needs and fears we would otherwise not choose to think about. Society's contradictory response has been double: condemn these women on sex-specific moral and sexual grounds, and at the same time neutralize and assimilate them into "general" ideas about deviance, thus rendering them invisible.

A few imprisoned women have chosen to assert themselves and their singularity by writing their stories and so have "committed" creative acts analogous to their deviant social acts. Their writing, too, has reminded us that, for both society and the literature that represents society, there exist values and priorities other than the ones in place. And here as well the cultural response has been contradictory: dismiss these female prison works as too particular and subjective, and also absorb them into canonical criteria extolling universality and heroism, thus ensuring critical neglect.

This book explores both these obscure areas—the situation of female criminals and the works they wrote from that situa-

PREFACE

tion—in an effort to connect the structures of their lives with the symbolic structures of their writing. I examine, specifically, the contexts and texts of five women imprisoned in France over the course of the past two hundred years and show the interplay of the forces that shaped their lives and works. These women, in their experience and invention, offer us unusual insight into the cultural processes affecting women: in social paradigms of female normality, we see myths exerting their considerable power, and we see those myths refused, manipulated, or transformed through women's imaginative responses.

These women, despite their different historical moments, speak to the same unchanging concerns; their texts echo across centuries of unquestioned presuppositions about female "nature." They break the silence to tell us about their shared heritage, and they also reveal much about ourselves and our own imprisonment in cultural prejudices.

All translations for which no English title is indicated in the notes are mine.

ELISSA D. GELFAND

South Hadley, Massachusetts

Acknowledgments

In the generally solitary pursuit that researching and writing this book has been, support and help of many kinds have sustained and warmed me.

I was fortunate to have known and worked with the late Reinhard Kuhn, who as teacher and mentor opened the world of prison literature to me. I have received generous financial support, in the form of an Andrew W. Mellon Fellowship for Interdisciplinary Study and a faculty grant, from the Faculty Grants Committee of Mount Holyoke College. Without their help my extended periods of research in Paris would not have been possible. The most productive portion of this research, without doubt, took place at the Bibliothèque Féministe Marguerite Durand, a mine of historical documents on French women. For her interest, invaluable assistance, and remarkable fund of knowledge, I particularly want to thank the head librarian at Marguerite Durand, Yolande Léautey. My thanks also to Julien Sarrazin for giving me access to important manuscripts and for sharing his own insights about and experience of French prisons.

Friends from among the close-knit group of feminist faculty members at Mount Holyoke as well as at Smith College and the University of Massachusetts have offered their comments and encouragement: my thanks to all these women, especially Susanna Barrows, Jane Crosthwaite, Penny Gill, Jean Grossholtz,

Acknowledgments

Fi Herbert, Gail Hornstein, Meredith Michaels, Bonnie Miller, Cathy Portuges, Marilyn Schuster, and Kay Warren.

My thanks to François Geleznikoff for his invaluable overseas assistance.

I have benefited greatly from my discussions of women's issues and women's history with Ellen Rothman.

I have learned an inestimable number of things from Annette Kolodny—and laughed with her all the while.

To Isabelle de Courtivron, for her unfailing friendship and vital intellectual and emotional support, I am, as ever, grateful.

And my loving thanks to Jim Glickman, who has helped me in every way—and who is the nonpareil.

Permission to translate has been kindly granted by the following: Editions André Balland: *Les Ecrivains en cage*, by Françoise d'Eaubonne, © Editions André Balland 1970. Editions Gallimard: *Oeuvres poétiques complètes*, by Paul Verlaine, © Editions Gallimard 1938. Editions René Julliard: *En prison*, by Anne Huré, © Editions René Julliard 1963; *Le Passe-peine: 1949–1967*, by Albertine Sarrazin, © Editions René Julliard 1976. Editions Mercure de France: *Mémoires de Madame Roland*, by Madame Roland, © Editions Mercure de France 1966. Société des Etudes Romantiques: "L'Héritage des lumières: Mythes et modèles de la féminité au xviiie siècle," by Paul Hoffmann, in *Romantisme*, no. 13–14, 1976.

Some material in this book is drawn from the author's articles published in *The French Review*, 51, no. 2 (December 1977); *L'Esprit créateur*, 19, no. 2 (Summer 1979); *Romance Notes*, 20, no. 2. (Fall 1979); *Modern Language Studies*, 11, no. 1 (Winter 1980–81); *Yale French Studies*, no. 62 (1981).

E. D. G.

Imagination in Confinement

Introduction: Premises

> Monstrous: deviating from the norm in appearance or structure; grotesquely unnatural—*The American Heritage Dictionary*

Among the few extant works written in Western prisons since the Middle Ages, there is a remarkable paucity of texts by women. There are as many reasons for the absence of prison writings in general as there are particular political, moral, and social histories in Western culture, but there are also shared reasons. The concept of prison as a place of prolonged confinement, and thus a form of punishment in itself instead of a prelude to execution or torture, appeared rather recently. Only since the second half of the eighteenth century has incarceration signified empty time and not imminent death, with the result that the material and psychological possibilities for writing have undergone a marked change. Also, widespread literacy is relatively recent, and so early prison stories were transmitted orally, not in writing.

A glance at existing collections of prison literature reveals a steady repetition of authors, a literary canon of outcasts: Villon, Cervantes, Pellico, Chénier, Dostoevski, Sade, Byron, Verlaine, Wilde, Genet. And reinforcing this canon are influential studies of prison literature and of "the literature of revolt," including works on the *poètes maudits* of the nineteenth century, Camus's *L'Homme révolté* of the modern existentialist rebellion, and Sartre's *Saint Genet*, which broadened the definition of social "negritude." It is apparent that both authors and critics have been almost exclusively male—and the reasons for this sexual discrepancy in prison literature are in part no different from those that explain the more general underrepresentation of women in creative enterprise.

The first premise of this book is that general factors that impede verbal expression for prisoners have affected imprisoned women as well. Thus such matters as censorship, the inability to write or to obtain paper, authorities' insistence on physical rather than mental effort, and the prevalence of illness are relatively gender neutral. Nevertheless, the effects of these difficulties in self-expression cannot have been the same for men and women because of the additional psychological barriers to writing that have long hindered women. It is clear, for example, that the effect of verbal censorship varies directly with the prisoner's belief in the validity and strength of words. It is equally true that in prison the primacy of physical over intellectual work can reinforce the biological definition of women that persists in our culture. Men and women also differ in their acceptance or rejection of the dependency under which prisoners function: while most women, conforming to the passivity expected of them, seem to adapt to this dependency, most men refuse it, in some cases to the point of revolt. I will be exploring the sex-specific effects of women's imprisonment as they pertain to the works they marked.

Much of the documentation used here is not French—in particular, twentieth-century criminological works that are more empirical than the somewhat abstract French texts but that are nonetheless transculturally applicable. But the authors chosen are all French women who were subject to the evolving, industrial-age, post-Revolutionary French prison and whose writings thus offer possibilities for intertextual comparison. In *Surveiller et punir* Michel Foucault argued that the simultaneous changes from an agricultural to an industrial economy and from a monarchy to a republic transformed the the modes and purposes of punishment. While valid for any Western capitalist system, this most closely translates the modern French experience.[1] Unlike, for example, the American

---

[1] Michel Foucault, *Surveiller et punir: Naissance de la prison* (Paris: Gallimard, 1975). Also published as *Discipline and Punish: The Birth of the Prison,* trans. Alan Sheridan (New York: Pantheon, 1977).

INTRODUCTION

prison experience, which, as H. Bruce Franklin demonstrates, is closely linked to black history and culture,[2] the prison system in France cannot be separated from other institutions of social control such as monasteries, convents, and armies. Prison, says Foucault, is not marginal to French society. These institutions, so crucial in French social and political history, explain the relative ease with which modern forms of punishment—confinement, regimentation, routinization—entrenched themselves in the late eighteenth century. For example, prisons for women bore some resemblance to convents. Since for centuries many women had endured forced exile in convents, the association between confinement and religious orders was strong. The transformation of convents into prisons in the eighteenth and nineteenth centuries and the use of nuns as prison warders were logical developments.

The eighteenth-century demarcation between old and modern concepts of prison is the historical starting point for this study: both the social and literary contexts discussed and the women's texts analyzed date from the eighteenth century on. But we must bear in mind the ambiguity of this chronological boundary. Although the modern prison indeed began taking shape at this time, this signaled more continuity than change. The purpose of imprisonment shifted from temporary containment of the criminal to his or her prolonged separation or "elimination" from society, but the techniques of incarceration perpetuated and intensified methods of discipline used by nonpunitive institutions, blurring rather than clarifying the lines between punishment and social control.

Foucault's ideas on the rise of the prison offer a useful chronological framework for the study of prison authors and also provide a fresh look at an old problem with enormous implications for women. His main thesis is that the evolution of punishment techniques belongs not to the history of law or ideas, but to "the history of the body"—the general ways social control has been exerted on individuals. The body is vested with economic and social value that has changed over time:

[2]H. Bruce Franklin, *The Victim as Criminal and Artist: Literature from the American Prison* (New York: Oxford University Press, 1978).

when punishment was a monarch's personal revenge, the spectacle of physical torture displayed his power vividly; with political and social change, the body as the object of sanction was replaced by the "soul" (in the sense of mind or spirit), and its dispositions now had to be modified. In other words, in the late 1700s imprisonment went from being punitive in purpose to being corrective and normative. With this shift in focus from physical to spiritual and psychological control came a change in the determination of the prisoner's innocence or guilt: confession and punishment itself as proof of culpability increasingly were replaced by the empirical findings of criminologists and psychologists. Thus the prisoner's confined body and mind came under the authority, albeit indirect, of "experts" in what Foucault calls "social control." And at the same time that punishment and modification were being shifted from body to mind, the body was acquiring greater economic value to industry, leading to the introduction of prison labor. The complex issue of the relation between mind and body, which I shall subsequently explore, is crucial to understanding the peculiar situation of the female criminal, since that relation for the imprisoned woman and for women in general has been vastly different than for men.

The consequences of Foucault's theories run counter to long-standing views about "progress" and "humane" reform in punishment. First, says Foucault, the apparent "softening" of punitive methods, especially in the nineteenth century, was an illusion that masked a less visible but equally destructive form of subjection—twentieth-century prison authorities prolong this hidden subjugation of the spirit by consulting "experts" in normative psychology. Also, changing prison conditions, which have always been considered a result of humanitarian reform, were in fact a logical accompaniment to changes in disciplinary institutions such as schools and asylums. In all, says Foucault, punishment moved from a response to a criminal *act* to a way to modify the individual *criminal.*

Surveiller et punir is ardent and persuasive, though its personalized use of Marxian economic terminology clearly situates Foucault's struggle in terms of the concepts bourgeois/popular, empowered/powerless. For him, institutionalization is a com-

INTRODUCTION

plex power strategy, one of whose aims is to hold in check the origin of social struggle. But the limitations of Foucault's analysis for a discussion of women are apparent. While Marxian and feminist politics by no means exclude one another, nowhere in *Surveiller et punir* is the struggle of women mentioned; the book is essentially about the history of male criminals. Nonetheless, Foucault's insistence on the normative function of imprisonment—touching the behavior and not the life of the criminal—conveys the core of the double standard operating in men's and women's prisons, since "normality" is different for each sex. What is more, the depersonalizing of the body into an object in a network of power and economic relations restates the dispossession of the body women have historically endured. Foucault's main contention, while not raised specifically for women, adds a new dimension to a basic tenet of feminist analysis: that the corporeal domain has been the one delegated to women. If the history of the prison is the history of control over the body, and if women have been oppressed by being anatomically defined, imprisoned women have suffered double biological subjection.

My second premise refers to apparent "ghettoization": Why *women* prisoners? In current feminist inquiry as it is pursued in America, one participates at once in rereading established writers and critics, recovering little-known women authors, and articulating new theories about writing. The authors discussed in this book—with the exception of Madame Roland and Albertine Sarrazin—are not commonly known or else are infamous for reasons unrelated to their writing. In reading their memoirs, diaries, and fiction, I had to abandon virtually all the ideas, however noble or stirring, of the most respected students of prison literature. At issue here is what Annette Kolodny calls the "contexts of judgment" or "the adequacy of the prior assumptions and reading habits brought to bear on the text."[3] For example, do the following theories stand up in the face of women's prison writing?

---

[3]Annette Kolodny, "Dancing through the Minefield: Some Observations on the Theory, Practice, and Politics of a Feminist Literary Criticism," *Feminist Studies* 6, no. 1 (spring 1980): 16.

If the mind is strong enough to construct in a prison cell a moral philosophy that is not one of submission, it will generally be one of domination. Every ethic based on solitude implies the exercise of power.[4]

(With the safety dream [in prison] goes) the dream of freedom through transcendence. The spirit wills itself stronger than prison bars . . . The "wings" of the mind make it possible to soar beyond oppressive walls.[5]

Power, domination, transcendence: these are the topoi critics have assumed to be not only the prime characteristics of prisoners' writing, but in fact the very wellsprings of their imaginative production in confinement. Yet there is little evidence in the texts that follow of a will to dominate or to possess; there is at best a sense of weakness inverted into irony (Sarrazin) or solitude glorified as martyrdom (Huré). There is likewise little evidence of triumph over circumstance and, until recently, no evocation of transcendence. The act of creating in a hostile environment like the prison cannot be universalized so long as women's and men's lives in a "normal" environment—which prison in large part reflects—remain radically different.

The absence in women's writing of contestation from what Genet calls the "common ground of audacity" is precisely the point at which literary theory concerning prison writing and texts by women diverge. One reason for the absence of contestation by imprisoned women is simple: to contest, one must be sure of one's foothold in the world; to transcend and offer an alternate vision of society, one must be able to leave that society. Socially and intellectually "earthbound" throughout time, women have generally neither experienced nor expressed transcendence in the same terms as men. To achieve transcendence, as Camus, Baudelaire, and others would have it, one must believe that imaginative liberation is possible in spite of corporeal immobilization. Thus studies of prison literature, like the entire Western philosophical tradition, have always posited

[4]Albert Camus, *The Rebel: An Essay on Man in Revolt*, trans. Anthony Bower (New York: Alfred A. Knopf, 1967), 36. A translation of *L'Homme révolté* (Paris: Gallimard, 1951).

[5]Victor Brombert, *The Romantic Prison: The French Tradition* (Princeton: Princeton University Press, 1978), 6. The author's own translation of his *La Prison romantique: Essai sur l'imaginaire* (Paris: Librairie José Corti, 1975).

INTRODUCTION

a mind/body dichotomy. But these studies have in fact placed value on the first term only: the spiritual has been isolated from the material and has come to dominate it. The imprisoned body has been ignored and engulfed by the superior mind. For imprisoned women, mind and body have never existed in this same relationship; rather, their corporality has been emphasized, as it has been for all women, and their potential for transcendence has therefore been limited or denied.

Further, as Patricia Meyer Spacks points out in *The Female Imagination*, women's "self-awareness" has always been marked by a conflict between feelings of sureness and of inadequacy.[6] Anger that is sure of its target—whether that target is a society that defines outcasts or the ruling power that incarcerates nonconformists—will brandish the same absolute goals that Camus assigns to the literature of rebellion in general: "a *demand* for unity," "a *rejection* of the world," "a living *transcendence*," "desire for *destruction*," or "*rectification* of the actual world" (*L'Homme révolté*). But women have traditionally had difficulty expressing rage directly. The female writer's mind, says Virginia Woolf, "must have been strained and her vitality lowered by the need of opposing this, of disproving that." When she does write with anger, her mind is "harassed and distracted with hates and grievances," with the result that "she will write in a rage where she should write calmly. She will write foolishly where she should write wisely. She will write of herself where she should write of her characters."[7]

Woolf's judgment of women writers' general ambivalence toward rage, though harsh, suggests why their anger is indirect and deflected, why it does not strike at external forces. Likewise, the opposition expressed by the imprisoned women in this study is personal, not absolute—it contests how they as individuals are viewed in contrast to their own sense of themselves. Françoise d'Eaubonne, who purposely omits women from her study *Les Ecrivains en cage*, makes the point that her chosen writers are rebellious "liberators" because of the ques-

[6]Patricia Meyer Spacks, *The Female Imagination* (New York: Alfred A. Knopf, 1972).
[7]Virginia Woolf, *A Room of One's Own* (New York: Harcourt, Brace, 1929), 95–96, 101, 120–21.

21

tions they ask: Villon, Genet, and others work in the domain of "the world as it ought to be," challenging the status quo. Working from their own codes of outrage, they push toward the periphery that is social containment:

> A prisoner of high quality seeks to define, in the midst of silence, deprivation, and the reduction of man to his simplest elements, the metaphysical essence of what might possibly be Good, or Evil, without relating these essences to the judge's or criminal's use of these same terms.
>
> The cursed ... bore witness against their own era in the name of the succeeding one, which era held the promise of death for contemporary values.[8]

Women's testimonies do not fit d'Eaubonne's description. Even in their modern fiction, imprisoned women have presented, if not the social, certainly the psychological obstacles with which they still must wrestle.

New theories are needed about women writing from prison, since universalizing ones do not work. By studying texts from a feminist perspective ("women's writing"), one automatically retains a mind/body connection. But, far from generalizing the "human" aspirations of imprisoned women, I instead search here for new ideas based specifically on their mental and physical experiences in confinement. This focus is, I believe, the most fruitful for understanding women in society (authors/prisoners) and women in texts (characters/prisoners). When we utilize gender specificity and the idea of mind/body split, there is of course danger of appearing to affirm the old sexual dichotomies that Cixous, Derrida, Irigaray, and others have exposed as mechanisms of hierarchy. It is true that in a world without gender-distinct prisons, sex-biased suppositions about men's and women's criminality, and lopsided literary canons, universal and polyvalent points of view would hold. But the authors discussed in this book wrote in historical, criminological, and literary climates that marked them as individuals and shaped their works. For, as Annette Kolodny reminds us, cre-

---

[8]Françoise d'Eaubonne, *Les Ecrivains en cage* (Paris: André Balland, 1970), 209, 225–26; my translation.

INTRODUCTION

ation "consists not of ghostly happenings in the head but of a matching of the states and processes of symbolic models against the states and processes of the wider world."[9] Understanding these processes allows for a different kind of reading of texts and an end to the obscurity of the authors or their assimilation into the general category of "outcasts." Further, establishing the threads that connect women's texts through time makes visible a tradition of motivation and realization, strong and identifiable in its own right.

My method in this book, with its goal of illuminating the relation between social structures contemporary with a text and the system of values implied by the text's problematic character, is a socioliterary feminist criticism.[10] Whereas establishing this relation between society and text is usually difficult for women as literary subjects, the corpus of female prison works offers uniquely discernible evidence of this interplay. Isolating most women's distinctive place in social organization at a historical moment has been complicated by women's social dispersion among men and by their conceptual assimilation to men in cultural systems and theories. But, because most women's prison texts were written under explicitly sex-specific conditions, they evince a clear and dynamic interchange between context and text—between social and literary representations of the cultural myths surrounding women.

An analysis of the homologies between conceptions of female deviance and their reflection in women's literature partakes of the nature and danger of myth itself: for if definitions of "deviant" and "outsider" in fact result from a *process* of judgment—that is, from a *dynamic* involving the judger, the judged, and the terms of judgment—myths are static, antidialectical *descriptions* that focus on the designated individual only.[11] Myths

[9]Kolodny, quoting Clifford Gertz, *The Interpretation of Cultures: Selected Essays*, her p. 4.
[10]See Christiane Makward, "La Critique féministe, éléments d'une problématique," *Revue des sciences humaines* (December 1977), 619. This article is an excellent overview of the varying approaches to and problems raised by a feminist criticism. See also my article, "Imprisoned Women: Toward a Socio-literary Feminist Analysis," *Yale French Studies* 62 (1981): 185–203.
[11]Howard S. Becker, *Outsiders: Studies in the Sociology of Deviance* (New York: Free Press of Glencoe, 1963); my emphasis.

about deviant women, whether their underpinnings are biological, psychological, or sociological, remove women from social context and social responsibility and reify their abnormal status. And removing women from social processes, aside from fixing their role as the dichotomized "other," also eliminates from the discussion of deviance the power differentials that determine who makes the rules about conformity and nonconformity.

Women who are writers as well as criminals are marginal in another way that reinforces their social exclusion: they are part of the dynamic of literary exile or eccentricity. Recent feminist thought in France and America has shed light on the historical marginality of the woman writer in general; applied more literally, this analysis can illuminate the situation of the imprisoned woman writer. Germaine Brée, in her historical discussion of important noncriminal French women authors, makes the point that these authors, far from adapting to accepted models of the "mythic Frenchwoman," were geographic, economic, or sexual "outsiders" whose rejection of myths was "inherent to the situation of their lives."[12] In this way Brée links the social context of all women to their writing, relating their lived experience to their imaginative rendering of it. Brée's reference to the fruitfulness of analyzing women's narrative structures along with the "situation of the woman writing,"[13] when applied to criminal or imprisoned female authors, helps us appreciate the rejection of myths in both life and art. Criminal women's refusal of imposed cultural models and their literary recasting or redefining of social structures are especially apparent. For the deviant woman's crime is by definition an overt social rebellion against her mythified role, and her creative act of writing, with its subversive textual strategies, is a "covert resistance" to imposed definitions of her identity.[14]

[12] Joan I. Roberts, quoting and summarizing Brée's ideas in "Pictures of Power and Powerlessness: A Personal Synthesis," her introductory essay to *Beyond Intellectual Sexism: A New Woman, A New Society*, ed. Joan I. Roberts (New York: David McKay, 1976), 38. Brée's article, "French Women Writers: A Problematic Perspective," appears on pp. 196–209.
[13] Brée, "French Women Writers," 203.
[14] Expression used by Roberts in "Pictures of Power and Powerlessness," 37, to describe women writers' general recourse to indirect or coded forms of criticism in their texts.

INTRODUCTION

Women's relationship to, and rejection of, cultural myths in their lives and writing is currently being explored somewhat differently by French and American feminist critics. My approach in this book, by its empirical nature, is squarely in the American feminist tradition of textual exegesis. Some of my theoretical underpinnings, however, owe much to the radical inquiry into myth, language, and power that French women have been undertaking. The French feminist reevaluation of men's and women's relation to "discourses," or systems of representation, underscores both the force of the cultural paradigms under which the women studied here lived and the significance of their textual responses to those models.

French feminist theoreticians, whatever their specialized perspectives on women's issues, share the belief that the male "voice" has dominated Western culture.[15] This hegemony of "the master's discourse"—a phrase indicating not only the pervasiveness of masculine values in all systems of representation but also the superiority they have enjoyed—is, these women believe, the strongest and most insidious perpetrator of women's oppression. The visible forms of economic, political, and social domination are only extensions and reflections of the deeply entrenched and intransigent forms of repression and oppression that are present in the unconscious. Specifically, the feminine libidinal forces in us all have been squelched, silenced, and absorbed by the appropriative and univocal force of masculine desire. And language, written and spoken, conveys these naturalized power configurations of the psyche.

For the women discussed here, these mutually reinforcing kinds of domination in the social and psychological spheres have been particularly focused. The male voice has articulated the prescribed monolithic model of female normality, whose very terms spring from the unquestioned authority of myth. Masculine psychic configurations alone have determined the

---

[15]See, for example, Catherine Clément and Hélène Cixous, *La Jeune Née* (Paris: UGE 10/18, 1975); Hélène Cixous, Madeleine Gagnon, and Annie Leclerc, *La Venue à l'écriture* (Paris: UGE 10/18, 1977); Luce Irigaray, *Ce sexe qui n'en est pas un* (Paris: Minuit, 1977); Julia Kristeva, "Pratique signifiante et mode de production," in *La Traversée des signes*, ed. Julia Kristeva et al. (Paris: Seuil, 1975), 11–30, and "Le Texte clos," in her *Sēmeiōtikē: Recherches pour une semanalyse* (Paris: Seuil, 1969), 113–42.

appropriateness of women's social comportment. And, as is true for all cultural myths surrounding women, the fundamentally sexual nature of the fears from which those configurations arise has been obfuscated by layers of institutionalization and mystification. For that reason the possibility of feminine cultural models rooted in a different, feminine imagination not only has never been realized, it has never even been conceived. The feminine imagination is the unthought and the unspoken.

Women have historically had to speak and write in a language alien to their own experience. Their relation to the codes of domination under which they have lived has of necessity been one of polarized choices: either they adopt the prevailing discourse or they remain silent; either they cast themselves and their lives as the ruling powers see them or they remain invisible. And most women have kept their stories within them. But where women have spoken of themselves, we have an opening into their own perceptions of their experience, which traditional history and criticism have viewed through androcentric lenses. Through these lenses, the preoccupations transmitted by women's texts appear too personal and particular to be of central importance, the self-image too small to inhabit any space but the margins.

Feminist readings move that image to the center and affirm rather than distort women's experience. If the women's texts studied here transmit the same circumscription that has characterized women's lives in the world, that constraint is viewed as a springboard for response, not as naturalized fact; it is seen as the material for dynamic textual strategies, not as static, unquestioned necessity. The central concern of this book is this dual phenomenon, which existing scholarship on prison literature fails to address: the social reality of the woman criminal and the literary fact of imprisoned women's writing. Women's writing in general and women's prison literature in particular, when seen as forms of "subversion," "implied criticism," or the "undermining" or "undoing" of imposed social and literary paradigms, take their rightful places as vital creative traditions.

The material that follows is divided into two parts: contexts and texts. The various contexts are those forces that defined the peculiar situations of women prison writers at certain times

INTRODUCTION

in French history. Incarceration affects women differently from men: (1) society views female and male criminals in dissimilar ways; (2) definitions of and methods of achieving "normality" for women and men diverge; (3) conditions within men's and women's prisons vary. Two other factors regarding the situation of the woman prison writer in particular are important: (4) the French philosophical tradition as it concerns women's intellectual potential; and (5) the French literary tradition as it affects women's writing. These interconnected domains are the contexts for the small corpus of important women's prison texts that has survived.

The areas of criminality, penal history, and literary convention interpenetrate. Believing, as does Raymond Williams in *Marxism and Literature*,[16] in the intellectual life's necessary connection with society and history and in literature as social process rather than as hardened forms, I would add that, for women, all spheres of social and personal life have been parallel and mutually reinforcing. Thus, for example, the eighteenth-century medical view of the normal female constitution as vulnerable to the senses had as its "psychological" correlative the idea of the female deviant as "desensitized." Likewise, in literary expression of the time, the recognizable "feminine quality" was sensitivity. More recently, early-twentieth-century explanations of female criminality as the result of somatically induced "hysteria" are mirrored in the penal categories of the time ("hysterics," "hypersuggestives," "liars") as well as in judgments of women's writing as more or less "sincere" and "authentic."

The second part of this book, texts, will focus on the work of five imprisoned women whose writing reflects the forces that shaped their lives. It is impossible to say that these women—Manon Phlipon (Madame Roland), Marie Cappelle-Lafarge, Marguerite Steinheil, Anne Huré, and Albertine Sarrazin—are "representative" of French women since the eighteenth century who have been imprisoned. Indeed, by education and circumstance they were in many ways different from their fellow pris-

---

[16]Raymond Williams, *Marxism and Literature* (Oxford: Oxford University Press, 1977).

oners. In relation to the general prison population, these women were exceptionally literate, motivated, and active. Yet if as individuals they depart from the mass of incarcerated women, their experience is strongly emblematic of the lives of women in general: like all women, though in a more focused way, they were marked by the codified and proscribed feminine models of their time. They all internalized those models to some extent as measures according to which they could speak of themselves: by at once accepting and rejecting external views, they perforce defined themselves by those views.

Most imprisoned women have ostensibly extolled social conformity. However, their texts carry an implied criticism of that conformity. At the same time that they subscribed to conventional femininity, these women—consciously or not, both in their lives and in their writing—adopted a form of "unfeminine" comportment. Claudine Herrmann, in *Les Voleuses de langue,* establishes for all women the "supreme feminine opposition" between conformity and eccentricity or between the acceptance and the refusal of virile values.[17] As a way out of this oppositional impasse, most women writers—including the authors studied here—wrote "coded" or "subversive" books. Thus, for example, the principal characters in women's texts, while apparently following the tenets of expected behavior, may in fact switch sexually assigned roles. The texts of Madame Roland, Marie Cappelle-Lafarge, and other prisoners are also "coded": while apparently drawing themselves, either as first-person memoir narrator or as third-person fictionalized self, in terms that reconfirm conventional imagery, these women use strategies that counter that self-presentation.

The most frequent psychological strategy apparent in women's prison texts is the use of solipsism. This solipsism, not the empty, "feminine" narcissistic psychological prototype, is active and assertive. As a parallel to women's historically circumscribed status, of which actual imprisonment is an extention, women prison writers have been thrown back upon the self, and the periphery against which they have pushed is the imposed definition of their identity. Female criminals, dealing

[17]Claudine Herrmann, *Les Voleuses de langue* (Paris: des femmes, 1976), 38.

INTRODUCTION

and mother to write, act, and speak out. It is no small paradox that Roland, accused of no specific act of deviance or harm, was the one most explicitly denounced as a "monster" and the only one of the five to be executed. She wrote several texts, both before and during her incarceration, but the one I will examine here is her complete *Mémoires* of 1793. Roland's memoirs, which are already studied for the history of the French Revolution, are also an essential text for understanding women's confessional literature of the prison.

The one writer from the nineteenth century, Marie Cappelle-Lafarge, was, like Roland, from a sheltered bourgeois background and relatively well educated. Also like Roland, Cappelle-Lafarge revealed an unusual independence of spirit and strength of will. Having also chosen to marry late and out of "reason," Cappelle-Lafarge soon tired of Charles Lafarge, a prosperous forge owner, and of life in the Corrèze region. Her relations with her in-laws, which typified the Paris/province split, were strained. When Charles Lefarge died in 1839 soon after eating a cake his wife had sent him, his mother accused Marie. Although the precise cause of his death is uncertain, Marie Cappelle-Lafarge was condemned for poisoning him. Her trial and appeals lasted a very long time and reveal the unsettled and arbitrary nature of justice at the time. She ultimately spent twelve years in prison, at Tulle and Montpellier, was freed by Louis Napoleon, and died soon after.

Though, in contrast with Roland's case, justice was precise in its charges against Cappelle-Lafarge, her punishment was remarkably unfocused and indeterminate. Unlike Roland's summary sanction, Cappelle-Lafarge was left to waste away, socially and civilly "dead," in a penal limbo that mirrored her era's protracted vacillation between the goals of elimination and rehabilitation. Individuals certain of her innocence sought to exculpate Cappelle-Lafarge early in this century; she was finally exonerated in 1979 when it was decided that Lafarge had died from typhoid. Cappelle-Lafarge wrote two long works in prison: her witty, vital *Mémoires* of 1841–43, which have affinities with Roland's memoirs, and her reconstructed, less successful *Heures de prison* of 1841–47 (published in 1854).

Less compelling but as historically important as those of Roland and Cappelle-Lafarge are the memoirs of Marguerite Steinheil. Now obscure, Steinheil was best known at the turn of the century as the mistress of President Félix Faure; she was in fact present at, and briefly implicated in, Faure's mysterious death in 1899. The daughter of wealthy factory owners, like Roland and Cappelle-Lafarge she had been educated at home. Also like them, she married relatively late and her husband was an older man, in this case Adolphe Steinheil, a little-known painter who was himself involved in shady dealings, perhaps espionage. Both Adolphe Steinheil and Marguerite Steinheil's mother, Madame Japy, were strangled in 1908. Marguerite Steinheil, who was sleeping in the same house that night, was suspiciously unharmed, and she eventually was arrested after giving several conflicting versions of the events.

For reasons that remain unclear, Steinheil, unlike the other women studied here, was found innocent; she was detained in Saint-Lazare prison while awaiting trial. Also unlike the others, Steinheil wrote her memoirs after her incarceration, using notes she had kept in jail. Nonetheless, her *Mémoires* of 1911–12 help us understand the link between nineteenth-and twentieth-century forms of punishment for women and evolving theories of female criminality. Steinheil's text stands at the juncture of physiological and psychological explanations of female criminal behavior, and its superficial aesthetic judgments and preoccupations parallel the ease with which one criminological lexicon replaced the other. Her memoirs also reveal the first conscious striving for literary effect by a woman prison writer.

Anne Huré, born in 1918, has now essentially disappeared from the French literary consciousness, though her novel about monastic life, *Les Deux moniales* (1962), was well received when it appeared. As a young woman, Huré became a Benedictine nun; after a crisis of faith she broadened and intensified her spiritual and intellectual inquiry and eventually left the order. Considerably more educated than most women prisoners, she pursued a doctorate in theology, became an ardent follower of the philosopher Husserl, and later applied her own intellectually elitist interpretation of Husserl's epistemology to all her novels. A series of robberies and bad checks brought repeated

INTRODUCTION

arrests until as recently as 1970; in between were several well-publicized suicide attempts. Since 1971 there has been silence.

Huré's autobiographical novel *En prison* (1963) is a terse, abstract, and ascetic account, in the third person, of her internment at la Roquette and Haguenau prisons. Along with Albertine Sarrazin's *La Cavale*, it signals the advent of the use of fiction by a woman prison writer, a distinctly late-twentieth-century innovation. And yet, despite its new genre, *En prison* is in content a profoundly conservative text. Its heroine denies her imprisoned womanhood and opts for the illusory asexuality of metaphysical concerns, with the result that she neither confronts nor reshapes her experience but is instead shaped by it. Though she pushes to the limit the feminine topos of solipsism, Huré's disincarnate self-affirmation is finally ineffectual. For all her intellectual strength, Huré, of the women studied here, is perhaps the most victimized by and passive in the face of external judgments and events.

A contemporary of Huré's, Albertine Sarrazin (1937–67) chose a literary response to prison that is radically different in power and approach: reshaping and reinterpreting events through fiction. Yet it is just recently that Sarrazin's writing has received the attention it deserves, for only the sensational aspects of her life—prostitution, robbery, imprisonment, escape, a love affair with a fellow prisoner, premature death, and a widely publicized postmortem inquest—are familiar to most French people. In prison Sarrazin wrote two novels, *L'Astragale* (1964) and *La Cavale* (1965), poems, and several diaries.

Of particular interest for this study will be her *Journal de prison 1959* and her fictionalized fresco of prison life, *La Cavale*, the former for its continuity with preceding generations of women's confessional literature, the latter as the first truly successful prison novel by a woman. Sarrazin's writing, insisting on authorship over notoriety, signals a significant change in the female prison tradition even while it reveals ties to its literary heritage. And Sarrazin's use of fiction for her own ends connects her writing to contemporaneous events in women's literature in general, events involving experimentation with and critiques of language and representations of the feminine in fiction.

33

There are other names one associates with crime and prison accounts in France: the women recorded in the Bastille archives; the Marquise de Brinvilliers, who in the 1660s and 1670s experimented with various poisons on her father, siblings, and husband and whose hair-raising confession was followed by a less-than-convincing Christian conversion; the Mancini sisters, involved in the intrigues of Cardinal Mazarin; Madame de Staal-Delaunay, implicated in the treasonous political machinations of her employer the Duchesse du Maine (1718); the Comtesse de la Motte of the 1785–86 royal scandal, the "affair of the necklace"; the novelist Claudine de Tencin, whose lover committed suicide in 1726 and blamed her; the convicted murderess of the late nineteenth century, Madame Weiss; Gabrielle Bompard, a prostitute and convicted murderess who became the archetype of feminine degradation (1880s); Henriette Caillaux, who shot the director of *Le Figaro* for the sake of her husband's political career and was acquitted; Madame Bessarabo, the poet and feminist activist Héra Mirtel, who was condemned for killing her husband in 1920; Marthe Hanau, a financial genius imprisoned for fraud in 1928; Sylvie Paul, first a German prisoner of war, later convicted as a murderess in 1951; Gabrielle Russier, whose love affair with a seventeen-year-old male student led to her imprisonment for "corruption of a minor," her persecution, and her suicide; Nicole Gérard, who killed her husband to keep her child; and others.

Since the eighteenth century, women like these have been studied for their monstrousness. Reasons for their behavior have been argued everywhere from specialized studies to tabloid newspapers. Like monsters, these women are at once a "compound of elements from various human or animal forms"—that is, an amalgam of the contradictory opprobria heaped upon unconventional women—and "an animal . . . having structural defects or deformities"[18]—that is, a type easily identifiable by its deviation from a strictly defined standard.

As lawbreakers, then as prisoners, and finally as authors,

---

[18] *The American Heritage Dictionary of the English Language,* ed. William Morris (New York: Houghton Mifflin, 1969).

Introduction

these women committed both literal and figurative crimes. Criminological and creative models of women's normality and abnormality reinforced each other: the moral and social deviance that characterized the female criminal and prisoner has been explicitly articulated in law, judicial processes, penal codes, and criminological treatises. The transgression of the woman writer, though less apparent because not explicitly defined, was nonetheless the real "crime" of stealing education, culture, and ultimately the written word itself. Even with the legitimization of the prison writer in modern times, beginning with last century's cult of the heroic criminal, women authors have remained outcasts from the now-established male prison tradition. On a very basic level, then, the constructs that explained women's deviant behavior in all spheres—constructs that were never of their own making—were homologous and importantly determinant. It is to these normative views of their behavior that women's texts respond, and at the same time *from* these views that the texts' narrative, lexical, and thematic elements arise.

Part One

SOCIAL AND LITERARY CONTEXTS

1

Female Criminality: The Biological Monster

Recent work by feminist criminologists has attempted to remedy what Carol Smart describes as the overwhelming neglect of female criminality by scholars and penal officials.[1] Before and since the dawn of criminological discourse in the late nineteenth century, when theoreticians began speaking of the criminal rather than crime, female criminality has been either subsumed by male criminal behavior or isolated in caricatures of women's own behavior. The female criminal has been either invisible or too visible—as a monster of nature. The silence surrounding female delinquents has been defended on the grounds of their statistically small number even though, as Marie-Jo Dhavernas observes, statistics themselves are "a reflection of social control more than a measure of transgression."[2] That is, statistics reflect the application of laws to individuals, which in turn depends on the rights and duties attributed to them. Statistical discourse reflects "the obsession of a society" or its ideology, not actual behavior.[3]

[1] Carol Smart, *Women, Crime and Criminology: A Feminist Critique* (London: Routledge and Kegan Paul, 1976).
[2] Marie-Jo Dhavernas, "La Délinquance des femmes," *Questions féministes* 4 (November 1978): 55.
[3] Michelle Perrot, "Delinquency and the Penitentiary System in Nineteenth-Century France," in *Deviants and the Abandoned in French Society: Selections from*

39

Statistics are questionable as an indicator of differences in men's and women's criminal behavior not only because "ideological modes" influence research questions and methods, but also because it is difficult to determine sexual differences for such an issue.[4] The distinctions between men's and women's criminality were long attributed to biological dimorphism and then, by mid-twentieth century, were laid to cultural and environmental differences. Yet as recently as 1978 a scientific study of sexual differences, *Le Fait féminin*, again evoked this unresolved problem of natural versus cultural causes of behavior. Though they are feminists who reject purely sociobiological theories of men's and women's "natural" determination, as scientists the contributors could not ignore certain experimental observations of differential comportment. One such area of observed differences directly concerns this study: aggressive behavior. One American contributor, Eleanor Maccoby, remarks that, even if aggression is learned, its much greater occurrence in boys suggests that they possess a biological predisposition toward it.[5] Another American scholar of psychology, Zella Luria, likewise refuses both absolutist positions—genetic determinism and total environmentalism—as partial and as stemming from the two "extreme . . . image[s]" we have of "the nature of sexual differences."[6] Though a seemingly simplistic and overconciliatory description of the current state of natural versus cultural difference theory, Evelyne Sullerot's statement is nonetheless comprehensive: "Everything is not genetic, everything is not hormonal, everything is not environmental, everything is not social, everything is not political."[7]

The continuing scientific debate about aggression and sexual

---

the *Annales Economies, Sociétés, Civilisations*, Vol. 4, ed. Robert Forster and Orest Ranum, trans. Elborg Forster and Patricia M. Ranum (Baltimore and London: Johns Hopkins University Press, 1978), 219. Translation of January–February 1975 issue.

[4]Evelyne Sullerot, commentary, in *Le Fait féminin: Qu'est-ce qu'une femme?* collective work directed by Evelyne Sullerot and Odette Thibault (Paris: Fayard, 1978), 311.

[5]Eleanor Maccoby, "La Psychologie des sexes: Implications pour les rôles adultes," in *Le Fait féminin*, 251.

[6]Zella Luria, comment in debate, "A propos de la psychologie différentielle des sexes," in *Le Fait féminin*, 277; my translation.

[7]*Le Fait féminin*, 311.

specificity is too complex to present here, but it does reveal that criminological statistics are radically insufficient to "describe" women's and men's behavior. Scholarly and penal neglect of the apparently small number of deviant women therefore cannot be justified. And, as Ann Jones argues persuasively, the absence of research on female criminality reflects the more general historical ignorance about women, perpetuated by men's fear of confronting unsettling dilemmas:

> The intimation that women are less violent than men by *nature* leads to disquieting conclusions about the innate moral superiority of women, conclusions that men are no longer willing to accept; and the alternative suggestion that women may be less violent because of their socialization raises even more unnerving possibilities to improve society by bringing up men to be more like women.[8]

In spite of—or, more accurately, in keeping with—this incuriosity about female criminality, theoreticians have on occasion addressed the question. Most relevant to the responses of imprisoned women is the positivistic way their criminality, when treated separately, has always been described. Crime has been attributed to their "nature," with differences only in the definition of what that nature is: biological, psychological, or sociological. That prevailing criminological theories both influenced and were influenced by their epochs can be seen in the newspapers and literature of their times; that they inhabited the collective unconscious stems from their general "commonsense" appeal, which has its origin in accepted philosophical, medical, and social thought. Both the positivistic treatment of criminality by specialists—the after-the-fact "observation" of certain criminological characteristics—and the general public acceptance of such explanations point up the essentially revisionist, as opposed to exploratory, nature of criminological thought. That is, female offenders were condemned for their social or moral "abnormality" *after* the crime. Such easy discernment of "causes" of female criminality also clearly shows

---

[8]Ann Jones, *Women Who Kill* (New York: Holt, Rinehart and Winston, 1980), 5; original emphasis.

the link between criminal and noncriminal women; for, if all women's lives were biologically determined, the deviant woman's act stemmed from a deviation from that expected sexual schema. This revisionist, highly conservative approach to female criminality, despite evolving lexicons for the characteristics "observed," has not altered. In this chapter I shall trace the overall apparent shifts, since the 1700s, in criminology's focus on women, while bearing in mind that the positivistic underpinnings of this criminological theory have remained unquestioned and unchanged.

Although there is a dearth of documentation on imprisoned women before the eighteenth century, certain observations can be made: crime in general was almost synonymous with poverty, and women's crime was synonymous with poverty, vagabondage, and prostitution. Patterns in female crime reveal it to be domestic or economic in nature. There was what Arlette Farge calls a "reciprocal influence" (*aller et retour*) or interdependency between situations that provoked female criminality (economic instability, the need to defend a household, unwanted childbirth) and situations that involved aggression against women (rape, abandonment, adultery).[9] It was therefore generally lower-class women who were arrested for crimes. Female criminality was not, however, considered much of a danger, except insofar as invasion by the poor was the real fear within the rising bourgeoisie. With the growing consolidation of the couple and the definition of feminine honor in terms of conjugal fidelity, notions of a "dangerous" or "suspect" woman centered on her family role: "Once outside of the familial context, she possessed great freedom of word and act, and thereby became more than anything the target of scornful judgment."[10] Thus widows, orphans, and vagabond and exiled women, by their rootless sexual status, were the most vulnerable to accusation and the most severely punished. Such women threatened

---

[9]Arlette Farge, "La Femme criminelle et agressée," unofficial copy (from a course, "Delinquency and Repression," taught by Arlette Farge and Michelle Perrot, Jussieu-Paris 7, 1978–79), 33.

[10]Nicole Castan, "La Criminalité familiale dans le ressort du Parlement de Toulouse 1690–1730," *Cahier des Annales*, special issue, "Crimes et criminalité en France, xviie–xviiie siècles" 33 (1971): 95, 107.

the model of family sexual stability that Rousseau and other eighteenth-century philosophers developed into paradigms of social utility and general welfare. Not surprisingly, the word "honor," referring to sexual and maternal roles, reappears in women's prison texts of that century.

The class differences that determined the accessibility and desirability of conjugal stability in the eighteenth century were accompanied by educational differences. The poorest women—those most often accused and imprisoned—were also the least educated, making the percentage of illiteracy higher among prisoners than among the general population. A study of literature from the prison must therefore take into account this obstacle to writing, at a time when prisoners were allowed to write. The few women of the seventeenth and eighteenth centuries whose texts we have—Madame de Staal-Delaunay, the Duchesse de Duras (Louise), Mademoiselle de Pons, the Comtesse de la Motte, Madame Roland—either were from privileged milieus or enjoyed the unusual luxury of an education. It is significant that these few women writers were all imprisoned for "political" or politically related crimes, for it points up the correlation between civil crimes, low socioeconomic status, and high likelihood of arrest.

The late eighteenth century, in particular the Revolution, was a watershed for all French ideas and institutions, including gender roles. The rise of individualism and the pre-Romantic tradition it spawned influenced men and women differently: if assertion of individuality was admired in men, in women it was perceived as threatening. As a result, submissiveness became the most valued sign of female normality. And a criminal act, seen as the strongest form of self-assertion, was considered the complete refusal of women's passivity and the denial of their assigned role. A brief comparison of the best-known women criminals of the seventeenth and eighteenth centuries, the Marquise de Brinvilliers and Madame Roland, will illustrate the marked change between the centuries in views about female violence.

Brinvilliers had more humble origins than her later counterparts Roland, Staal-Delaunay, and Duras. She was sentenced to death for poisoning and "dictated" her memoirs to her confessor, Edme Pirot, since she herself was "almost completely untutored."[11] The memoirs reveal more about Pirot's (and society's) judgment than about the marquise: she was viewed as weak and scandalous, but unquestionably dangerous. It was believed that her lover and accomplice, Sainte-Croix, had incited her to violence and made her the "instrument" for his evil alchemical experiments. Brinvilliers's noble status, acquired through marriage, made her crimes all the more shocking. But the overwhelming evidence of her guilt outweighed any extenuating considerations, and she received the full punishment of imprisonment, torture, and execution. Violence in women was acknowledged and dealt with severely before the Revolution.

With Roland one sees the emergence of powerful new social norms that located female honor in domestic happiness. As women in general experienced increasing moral and social repression, it became more and more inconceivable that they had a potential for violence. Certainly Rousseau's views of women reveal a mythification in which female violence cannot even be contemplated: women's "modesty" will always contain their desires, as will their natural "taste" for "honest things."[12] The collective view of female criminals was articulated by Rétif de la Bretonne: "If virtue in a Woman can never be as meritorious as in a Man, a criminal Woman is also less guilty."[13] Roland's political and intellectual activism, as an expression of her individualism, threatened the newly entrenched standard of female submissiveness, a standard to which Roland insists she has conformed. Her story took place at the crossroads of the diverging views of women's violence—acknowledgment of that violence versus denial. Her contemporaries' judgments focus squarely on Roland's departure from expected female behavior, thus diminishing her potential for individual expression; yet these same contemporaries had no difficulty condemning and exe-

---

[11]Jacques Saint-Germain, *Madame de Brinvilliers* (Paris: Hachette, 1971), 33; Edme Pirot, *La Marquise de Brinvilliers, récit de ses derniers moments* (Paris: A. Lemerre, 1883).

[12]Jean-Jacques Rousseau, *Emile; ou, De l'éducation*, book 5 (Paris: Garnier Frères, 1964), 448.

[13]Rétif de la Bretonne, *Les Gynographes; ou, Idées de deux honnêtes femmes sur un projet de règlement proposé à toute l'Europe, pour mettre les femmes à leur place, et opérer le bonheur des deux sexes* (1777), quoted in Perrot, "Delinquency," 243.

cuting her for her violent act, as Brinvilliers had been dealt with more than a century before.

Thinkers like Rétif de la Bretonne had their counterparts among doctors and moralists of the time, whose understanding of the physiological and psychological functioning of women not only reinforced the bourgeois family ethic but also constituted the dominant theory of female deviance. Pierre Roussel's *Système physique et moral de la femme, suivi du système physique et moral de l'homme* (1775)— with "moral" meaning psychological—reflects the influential "animist" tradition that was to blossom fully in the nineteenth century.[14] Roussel, using Stahl's theory of "temperaments," claims that psychological traits are explained by physiological phenomena. Organs and humors account for the various character types (sanguine, phlegmatic, bilious, melancholic) as well as for individual capacities for thinking and feeling. Roussel's title itself shows the male/female duality that was at the heart of animist medicine: women and men, by their dissimilar constitutions (the woman's being "weak" by definition), respond differently to sense impressions and to mental operations. For men sensations and movements are more marked in the region of the head, thus empowering them to seize vast, universal principles; women's "sensibility" is both stronger and more diffuse than men's, and the "tyranny" of sensations binds them to the ordinary world, making them unable to aspire to noble conceptions. The combination of weaker organs and more active sensibility in women has several by-products: strong intuition and acute appreciation of nuance; inconstancy; inability to grasp abstractions; timidity; and modesty.

The persistence today of ideas like Roussel's is evident. At the time such a view of women was considered holistic, since it linked all their habits and characteristics, "with woman's body as the center." Normality for woman was a "sanguine temperament," whose manifestations were rosy cheeks, gaiety, light-mindedness, and capriciousness. A "sanguine" personality reflected a unity and harmony between the physical constitution

---

[14]Pierre Roussel, *Système physique et moral de la femme, suivi du système physique et moral de l'homme*, 6th ed. (Paris: Caille et Ravier, 1813).

and moral inclinations. The theme of self-unity, of wholeness, is recurrent in women's texts of the time. Further, external occupations, it was believed, could affect women's character, necessitating "the uniformity of their activities."[15] In 1775 one can already see the nineteenth-century ideal woman, confined and immobilized, sanctified by medical knowledge. One also sees the basis for Lombroso's later "anthropometry," in which criminality is anatomy.[16] Finally, one sees estimations of women's creative ability as limited by their despotic senses and uncontentious minds. It is no wonder that Madame Roland, for example, fears "defeminization" for having acted politically, paints a portrait of herself as round and healthy, and evokes the importance of "sensation" in presenting her character. Likewise the Duchesse de Duras continually affirms her love and concern for her parents, legitimizing herself through family identification. Even earlier, the Marquise de Brinvilliers was called both a "denatured" woman and her "natural" evil self when she confessed her crimes.[17]

The nineteenth century, an extremely complex period both in its multiplication of social norms and in its increasing number of delinquents, nonetheless saw diffuse ideas shaped into rigorous positivistic theories of criminality. Statistics were vested with the stature of objective truth. The first statistics of the "Compte général de l'administration de la justice criminelle" appeared, and, with the increasing use of empirical methods in criminological research, even humans could not escape being typed and categorized (Balzac's *La Comédie humaine* is just one literary example of this tendency). Crimes were labeled as against property or person, and criminals were grouped by geography, sex, and age. For women the virtue of family intimacy reached its height, constricting their role not only within the bourgeoisie, but in popular milieus as well. Thus H. A. Frégier, chief of the Seine Préfecture in 1838,

[15] Ibid., 37.
[16] Roussel's "Essai sur la sensibilité," in *Système physique*, also prepares, indirectly, Lombroso's ideas about the "insensitivity" of women, and particularly of women criminals. For Roussel, "Insensible bodies . . . are . . . passive and indifferent; they offer as the only resistance to external forces that of their mass" (p. 342). Lombroso in part explains women's deviance in these same terms.
[17] Pirot, *Marquise de Brinvilliers*, 118.

designated as "vicious" and "suspect" those women all through the social hierarchy who chose a life of "scandal" rather than "a pure and retired life."[18] Now more protected and separated from encounters with the outside world, women became the object of a special morality dictated by both church and state. Religion, family, and—emanating from the two—presumed social good were the core of their normative behavior. Equally significant for women and for the articulation of views on their delinquency was the general increase in hostility toward all criminals, which Michelle Perrot dates from the 1840s. Certainly a less tolerant overall climate may have somewhat attenuated the earlier refusal to acknowledge female violence. But it is likely that the expanded participation of women in the labor force, coupled with the even stronger correlation made between the working-class poor and crime, also drew attention to female criminality. Last, it has been pointed out that reforms for general social equality, particularly in education, encouraged the belief that criminality, if it persisted, had to be innate, not cultural.[19]

It is no surprise that, given the prevailing adverse climate, few prisoners wrote of their experience: "The shame, the social stigma inflicted by the prison, repressed any desire to give testimony.... In a hostile world, only hardened revolutionaries or those condemned to the hardest prison term dared to speak up."[20] Balzac's novels and the legendary Lacenaire bear witness to the century's cult of the "great criminal." And the woman of this time whose prison works are not only the most impressive but also the only published ones was, not coincidentally, the center of one of the century's greatest murder trials: Marie Cappelle-Lafarge. Accused of poisoning her husband Charles Lafarge, Marie Cappelle endured the worst aspects of the new adoption of scientific experts by judicial process. She—who the record now proclaims is innocent—was convicted of poisoning when the great medical chemist and showman Orfila found a harmless, almost undetectable quantity of arsenic in the corpse.

[18]H. A. Frégier, *Des classes dangereuses de la population dans les grandes villes et des moyens de les rendre meilleures* (Paris: Institut de France, 1838), 11.
[19]Perrot, "Delinquency," 215, 231.
[20]Ibid., 215.

The prosecutor in the Lafarge trial, Odile Barrot, labeled the accused woman a "monster."[21] Cappelle-Lafarge's *Mémoires* and *Heures de prison* contain a rich mixture of responses to the coexisting views of the woman and the criminal: detailed analysis of the crime's events, which reflects the highly empirical nature of judicial "fact" at the time; a clear affirmation of the woman-at-home morality, much like Madame Roland's; increasing religiosity; irony against public judgment; and presentation of the self as having purely virtuous character traits.

Women like Cappelle-Lafarge were in essence burdened with the contradictions of their era in the way that all women, as Simone de Beauvoir shows in *Le Deuxième sexe*, have been saddled with humanity's unresolvable oppositions. Certainly the polarization of ideas on female sensuality and sexuality between Roussel and the nineteenth-century criminologist Lombroso—with Roussel affirming women's hypersensitivity, Lombroso their insensitivity—passed effortlessly into the public consciousness. The words of a nineteenth-century prison reformer, Pauline de Grandpré, voice the dualities upon which criminal theory for women was based:

> There is a great preoccupation with woman in our century... some blame her, others praise her; perhaps no one knows her well. She is a deep nature that is hard to define, sometimes devoted to the point of sublimity, sometimes egotistical to the point of absurdity. She is a being who is troubled, capricious, full of fantasies, charm, sweetness, energy, abnegation. Sometimes weak as a child and, when sustained by enthusiasm, stronger even than man.[22]

Women such as Cappelle-Lafarge and her fictional counterparts, the sadistic and "virile" heroines of Romantic literature, "corresponded to fears and fantasies that were becoming prevalent in the society of their time."[23]

---

[21]Léon Abensour, *Le Féminisme sous le règne de Louis Philippe et en 1848* (Paris: Plon-Nourrit, 1913), 208.

[22]Pauline de Grandpré, *Les Condamnées de Saint-Lazare: Mémoires par Madame * * * * (Paris: F. Curot, 1869), 16.

[23]Isabelle de Courtivron, "Weak Men and Fatal Women: The Sand Image," *Homosexualities and French Literature: Cultural Contexts/Critical Texts*, ed. George Stambolian and Elaine Marks (Ithaca: Cornell University Press, 1979), 213.

FEMALE CRIMINALITY

Thus the nineteenth century saw articulated a typology of the female offender. Yet there was by no means a break with the medical body/machine model; on the contrary, all the classical studies of female lawbreaking rest on the same biological determinism: woman's body is the key to her normality, and hence her abnormality. Despite the appearance of scientific rigor and empirical "proof," the "new" typologies perpetuate the same eternal presuppositions about women. The many nineteenth-century treatises on female criminality vary only in their terminology; all reaffirm—whether as "perversion," "moral insanity," or "mental degeneration"—the noncognitive and "natural" source of female deviance. For the sake of the survival of the species, women must be less criminal: imprisonment would endanger procreation. But women's physiological divergence from men must also be a sign of their inferiority, as Roussel's treatise had already shown and Lombroso's chilling thought echoes: "Woman is intellectually and physically a man who is arrested in his development."[24] Therefore when a woman is criminal, she is that much more perverse and cunning than a man.[25] These views of women's sadistic criminality—the symbol of which was the chosen "feminine" crime, poisoning—lasted well into the next century.

Perpetuating the eighteenth century's understanding of "moral" as psychological or characterological, Pritchard and Esquivol set criminality in direct relation to "perversion," attributing crime to "moral insanity" and "malicious" dispositions. Roussel's model still prevailed, but it now served to explain pathology rather than health. The alienist Morel, who in the 1860s was highly influential in this current of crime-as-madness, called the criminal a mental "degenerate."[26] However,

[24]C. Lombroso and G. Ferrero, *La Femme criminelle et la prostituée*, trans. from the Italian by L. Meille (Paris: Félix Alcan, 1896), xiv; my translation. The English version, *The Female Offender* (London: T. Fisher Unwin, 1895), lacks the preface and the section "The Normal Woman" that appears in the French edition.
[25]What was labeled as "cunning" and "perversity" was in fact the necessarily more hidden quality of female criminality at the time. Since women were more isolated and protected than before, it is understandable that their wrongdoings would be less visible.
[26]Cited in Georges Heuyer, *Les Troubles mentaux: Etude criminologique* (Paris: Presses Universitaires de France, 1968), 5, 19.

Morel made a sexual (in fact biological and moral) distinction concerning innate degeneracy: whereas for men the highest deterioration was crime, for women it was prostitution. As early as 1845, Joséphine Mallet, a prison reformer, wrote *Les Femmes en prison*, rightly claiming that "among the numerous writers who have been concerned with the penitentiary system as it applies to prisoners in general, not one has concerned himself specifically with women convicts." Unfortunately, her reason for assuming the task herself is "to make known the general and specific causes of vice and crime among women, who are so different from men by their constitution and by their moral habits."[27] Mallet, imbued with a Rousseauesque sensibility about social responsiblity and also about women's family/social role, never questions existing views of women. Instead, she asserts woman's "natural" weakness, her modesty, and her vulnerability to passion that only maternal love and religion keep in check. Mallet at least acknowledges that sex and class differences in education and social position exist, but for her they are criminogenic in the same way as geography and age.

Cesare Lombroso dominated late-nineteenth-century criminology, which he called, tellingly, "criminal anthropology." Though contested by the growing current of sociological thought and now long discredited, Lombroso's theories enjoyed hegemony well into the twentieth century. He devoted much serious, if misplaced, study to women, but his uncontrolled positivism had devastating effects. Also, his "social Darwinism,"[28] which established a hierarchy within the human species based on race and sex, foreshadowed social thought for decades to come and is still echoed in chromosomal explanations of deviance.

The essence of Lombroso's reasoning regarding women, developed in *La Femme criminelle et la prostituée*, is as follows: woman's body is the key to her lesser criminality, since her role as reproducer makes her naturally more conservative than man. Also, since she withstands the pain of childbirth so rou-

---

[27]Joséphine Mallet, *Les Femmes en prison: Causes de leurs chutes, moyens de les relever*, 2d ed. (Paris: P. A. Desrosiers, 1845), viii, xi.
[28]Smart, *Women, Crime, and Criminology*, 27–37.

FEMALE CRIMINALITY

tinely, she must be less sensitive to pain—that is, insensitive (whence her frigidity and indifference to sexual pleasure). Because of the antagonism in women between their reproductive and intellectual functions—intelligence being by nature "virile"—they are also finally too unintelligent to commit crimes. Like children, whom they resemble anatomically, women respect the law not out of any superiority but, rather, out of "moral deficiency." Because they are less intelligent and less active, women also resemble one another: "All women fall into the same category, whereas each man is an individual unto himself; the physiognomy of the former conforms to a generalized standard, that of the latter is in each case unique."[29]

How, then, does Lombroso account for women who do commit crimes? He was, in fact, ultimately unable to explain female criminality, except to say that the deviant woman was in most respects a man. He makes a distinction between the "occasional" criminal (the majority) and the "born" criminal (a rarity). The former is like all women anatomically and intellectually, and so her crime is a function of such "natural" feminine characteristics as suggestibility, temptation, passion, and lying; the latter is abnormal by her "masculinity," both anatomical (quantity of hair, skull size, voice) and intellectual (inventiveness, cleverness). Thus the born female criminal is that much more cruel and sadistic than the male.[30] Again, Lombroso: "She tends to make her victim suffer, to kill him little by little. Man is more fierce: he kills and slaughters without pity; but he is less well versed than woman in the art of prolonging suffering and of making a man endure the maximum degree of pain that is humanly possible."[31] As is true for all the positivistic explanations of women's criminality, Lombroso "finds" the biological abnormality he is seeking after the fact. For her biological abnormality, the female offender is condemned socially; for her criminal offenses, she is condemned legally. Thus she is twice

---

[29] Lombroso and Ferrero, *Femme criminelle*, 168.
[30] Poisoning, for example, was considered the quintessential feminine crime, whence the celebrity of Marie Cappelle-Lafarge's arsenic trial. Commonsense images of the "woman poisoner" dominated the press at the time.
[31] Michelle Perrot, "Sur la femme délinquante et criminelle au xixe siècle," unofficial copy (from course "Delinquency and Repression"), quotes Lombroso; her p. 40.

51

guilty: "As a double exception, the criminal woman is consequently a *monster*."[32] The few of his contemporaries who disagreed with Lombroso did so on the grounds of his discussion of men, for none of them doubted his deterministic view of women. Henri Joly begins his treatise by saying that men and women share the same human nature (passion and egoism) but not the same social opportunities, thereby making them react differently to criminogenic influences (such as illegitimate birth, abandonment, or poverty). But in his attempt to introduce social factors to counter Lombroso's belief in biological determinism, Joly falls into assumptions about women's "lying" and superstitious tendencies, which only motherhood can overcome. As ever, women are better or worse than men.[33] Gabriel Tarde seeks to be a "philosophical statistician" in his analysis of criminal types, claiming there are flaws in Lombroso's criminal pool. Tarde concludes, however, with a disappointing reversal: since, as he believes, practicing crime leads to physical and moral anomalies (the "moral sense" is for him a cerebral organ), then there results a resemblance between male criminals and all women, in terms of their anatomy and degree of vanity.[34] The sociological point of view, represented by Caignart de Mailly, claims that Lombroso and his disciples should study the offender in his milieu rather than in some abstract typology, since crime is "an antagonism between the individual and society."[35] Caignart de Mailly sees the criminal as antisocial, not as incurably ill. He does not, however, contest the definition of "social utility." Because for social positivists such as Caignart de Mailly crime is a normal fact of any society, their response is to substitute "rehabilitation" (read normalization) for isolation as the true goal of punishment, which has had different effects for women and men.

Press clippings from the nineteenth century give some idea of

[32]Smart, *Women, Crime and Criminology*, quoting Lombroso and Ferrero, her pp. 34–35; my emphasis.
[33]Henri Joly, "La Criminalité féminine," in *Le Crime: Etude sociale*, 2d ed. (Paris: L. Cerf, 1888), 250–76.
[34]Gabriel Tarde, *La Criminalité comparée* (Paris: Félix Alcan, 1886).
[35]M. P. Caignart de Mailly, *L'Evolution de l'idée criminaliste au xixe siècle et ses conséquences* (Paris: Secrétariat de la Société d'Economie Sociale, 1898), 19.

the public perceptions under which accused women such as Marie Cappelle-Lafarge were judged and incarcerated.[36] Well-publicized trials make clear the highly prejudicial climate women faced: as Mary Hartman says, "It is striking that the actual situations of the accused women, which can be reconstructed with some confidence, coincided so rarely with the ways in which the courts and press perceived them." The accused women are invariably described physically, as if their appearance offered the possibility of empirical verification of their criminality. In a series of five pieces about vitriol disfigurations and murders by women, it is clear that jealous revenge by a woman against her female rival was met with light punishment or acquittal, whereas poisoning a husband brought severe punishment. This suggests that jealousy was considered a "normal" part of the female character, while aggressive refusal of the family role was deviant, and that more profound sexual judgment was passed on these women for having transgressed codes of moral respectability.[37] Coverage of the famous Weiss affair, in which the accused had allegedly tried to poison her husband and then kill herself, echoes Rétif de la Bretonne's much earlier contradictory view of women: "There is in female murderers in general a thoroughly delightful mixture of poetry and arsenic, of sentimentalism and rat poison."[38] Thus Weiss was a "monster" by her mixed nature, her coexisting passion and reason. Lombroso's idea of the nonindividuality of women is also visible in coverage of this case: "All the women of this stamp are the same. It is they who first formulate plans for the crime, which they encase in the sweetest of words; then when the police come, they say they have been hypnotized by the man whom they were obeying."[39] Because Weiss refused to become hysterical during her trial, she was all the more monstrous. Yet another article describes Weiss as a true hysteric: neither a "scoundrel" nor a

---

[36] For nineteenth- and twentieth-century press clippings, see the "Dossier-criminalité" at the Bibliothèque Féministe Marguerite Durand, Paris 5ᶜ. All translations of articles are mine.
[37] Mary S. Hartman, *Victorian Murderesses: A True History of Thirteen Respectable French and English Women Accused of Unspeakable Crimes* (New York: Schocken Books, 1977), 8, introduction.
[38] Henri Rochefort in *L'Intransigeant*, June 1891.
[39] Ibid.

"victim of social conventions," she was one of the "great hysterics" who were all "the same woman, but with different appearances." "Hysteric" at this time meant deficient in some way and referred to "incomplete individuals characterized by arrested or deviant intellectual development."[40] In closing, the journalist says that Weiss and other "unbalanced women" "join together all contradictions" and are a "strange amalgam" of charm and perverseness. Another commentary on Weiss in the same dossier asserts: "When women start creating tragedies, you never know where they will stop."[41] Both impressionable and autonomous, irresponsible and responsible, maternal and sadistic, hysterical and cunning, feminine and virile, the woman criminal of the nineteenth century faced the impasse and the silence such conflicting opinions imposed.

Little changed in criminological theory with the turn of the century; if anything, the vigorous feminist activity of the time aroused even harsher judgments of women offenders. When Freudian theory made available a new discourse on feminine "nature" and on normal and abnormal motivation, criminologists had only to shift from a biological to a psychological standard of normality, since the two were inextricably linked. Also, with increasing numbers of "masculine" crimes being committed by women, criminological theory had to explain this in terms other than simple family role dysfunction. The resulting plethora of interpretations of female criminality produced a variety of forms of treatment through the century.

In January 1900 *Le Matin* ran a series of articles on "feminine crimes" that purported to explain the motives for and types of female delinquency. The causes were: "love, jealousy, the desire to possess the loved one completely, the revenge upon a woman rival." These were the visible motives, behind which was "[the woman's] deeper concern for her dignity, for the reputation she must preserve, for the position in the world she must maintain." All crimes, from fortune-telling and blackmail to crimes of passion, continued to be interpreted according to notions of women's "duties." Another article from 1901, by Georges

---

[40]Madame Ratazzi in *La Nouvelle Presse libre*, September 1891.
[41]Article in *XIXᵉ siècle*, October 1891.

Clarétie, gives evidence for the persistence of Lombrosian thought in the public mind: "In the preparation of a crime and in the refining and organizing of its details, women excell.... Most crimes committed by women are 'beautiful crimes.' "[42] The same piece claims, "The feminine crime is somehow unusually odious and perverse." Like his criminologist contemporary Camille Granier, the journalist here subscribes to the belief in "predispositions" that partake of both physiological and psychological determinism.[43] Using famous scandals of his time, Clarétie makes the distinction between Parisian and provincial criminals, claiming that the former have less time to commit their crimes (and therefore use revolvers) and also less burdensome husbands (and therefore commit fewer murders), whereas the latter suffer unending boredom (and therefore choose slow poisoning) and have fewer lovers (and therefore commit more crimes). Finally, newspapers of the time are filled with stories about the "apaches," male gangs whose members mirrored Vautrin and Gide's reform-school boys. To harass the bourgeoisie, they paraded their violent marginality. Apaches could only be male: their women prostituted themselves to feed the gang. Groups like the apaches reveal the ongoing correlation in the public consciousness between crime and social condition: violent and idle males aroused fear; females remained subservient and invisible.

Belief in individual "instinctive perversions" survived with Dupré (1912), for whom malicious moral and social acts stemmed from the "constitutional anomalies of the individual's tendencies."[44] With psychoanalysis came consideration of the individual's emotional and family milieu during childhood, and this blossomed with Alexander and Staub's Freudian approach to criminal behavior. Believing that both "psychoneurosis and criminality are defects in one's social adjustment," with differences only in their "psychological dynamics," Alexander and Staub posited mankind's "instinctive criminality."[45]

[42]Georges Clarétie in *Journal*, July 1901.
[43]Camille Granier, *La Femme criminelle* (Paris: Octave Doin, 1906).
[44]Cited in Heuyer, *Troubles mentaux*, 5.
[45]Franz Alexander and Hugh Staub, "Id, Ego, and Superego," taken from *The Criminal, the Judge and the Public*, reproduced in *Law and the Lawless*, ed. Gresham M. Sykes and Thomas E. Drabek (New York: Random House, 1969), 172.

This approach also led to the theory of the "claim to virility" that presumably was behind female delinquency. While such psychoanalytically based theories finally acknowledged that dangerousness was given criminal expression because of external factors (psychological trauma, social conditioning, and brain disease, for example), they unfortunately opened the way to views of women as pathetic, uncontrolled victims of their sexuality.

"Hysteria" and "hypersuggestibility" were the key words of the time. The use of these terms, particularly "hysteria," was extremely loose: it referred to many illnesses, often contradictory, including everything from an organic dysfunction of the uterus, to a neurological disorder, to hyperemotionality. The recurrence of the terms "hysteric," "hypersuggestible," "somnambulist," and "mythomaniacal" since the 1900s, and most strongly in the 1920s and 1930s, reveals a particular view of the personality of female criminals. One Dr. Paul Voivenel, in a newspaper article from 1927, attributes poisoning to the mythomaniacal, morally insensitive, and neurologically unsound "character" of hysterics.[46] He and others believed that all the great female poisoners in history (Brinvilliers, Jegado, Weiss, Cappelle-Lafarge) resembled one another in heredity and anatomy, and also "morphologically" in the sense that their character traits stemmed from their anatomy. There is a clear linguistic shift from Lombroso's medical typology, with its "zones" and "lesions," to intangible but verifiable "psychologizing" categories. A 1933 piece on a study of young women imprisoned in Fresnes presents the findings of a "psychiatric examination" administered to the prisoners. The majority (55%) were found to be "feebleminded," "unbalanced," "mythomaniacal," "perverse," and "above all, above all, *hysterical, hypersuggestible women*."[47] The "cures" recommended for those women sought particularly to repress the symptoms they were thought to display. Thus, for example, the rule of silence, formerly believed to induce the prisoner to meditate, was now imposed to eliminate the manifestation of mythomania and hysteria: women's

[46]*La Rumeur*, December 1927.
[47]"La Criminalité de la jeunesse féminine," clipping from September 1933; emphasis in original.

speaking. In all, the relation between criminological theory and penal policy at the time mirrored the perceived relation between "illness" and "cure" or, in terms of prison, "rehabilitation." Thanks to a shift in emphasis from nineteenth-century beliefs in predetermined, group-identifiable behavior to modern individually rooted pathology, there was also a movement toward belief in the nonresponsibility of the criminal. For women the loss of responsibility for their actions only served to reinforce their perceived passivity and their lack of capacity for violence.

As was the case for Lombroso's "perversion" and for our contemporary "role socialization" theories, the frequent appearance in the press of "hysteric" and similar terms shows that specialized research filters down to other strata and informs commonsense perceptions. One of the few prison texts by women of the early twentieth century, the memoirs of Marguerite Steinheil, reveals the power of attributing traits to women criminals. Steinheil, accused of killing her husband and mother, repeatedly defends her innocence against charges that she was a hysteric, a liar, and a somnambulist. Newspapers of the time called her version of the crime's events, her defense, a "hallucination." Steinheil responds in two ways to the charges that mental alienation caused her criminality: first, she recounts, often and in great detail, the events surrounding the murders, as if attention to observed fact could demonstrate the equilibrium of her reason. Second, she discusses at length the literary and artistic salon she had conducted for several years so as to prove her direct familiarity with authentic imaginative production, as opposed to the vain and unproductive fantasy of which she was accused.

A prison text from the 1940s to 1960s, Sylvia Paul's *Ne me jugez pas!*, also reflects the movement toward personality modification as the goal of institutional rehabilitation.[48] Paul describes the characterological classifications of prisoners that existed at Rennes prison during her confinement: hysterics, incorrigibles, the retarded, prostitutes, and abortionists, among others. As was the case for prevailing psychiatric definitions of

---

[48]Sylvie Paul, *Ne me jugez pas!* (Paris: Gallimard, 1962).

normality, these categories were grounded in presuppositions about female sexual normality and adjustment. Prison cures, which Paul says frequently involved the use of bromides, clearly envisioned passivity and resignation as goals. Paul's text itself is marked by a striking numbness, a dullness that in no way reflects her dossier's personality label of "incorrigible."

The most influential criminologists of the 1920s to 1950s continued to make assumptions about women's inherent "nature." W. I. Thomas, for example, representative of the early liberal tradition in criminology, believed in individualized "socially induced pathology" as the cause of deviance;[49] thus, offenders are "sick" and poorly adapted. Individual pathologies are linked to the subject's "wishes," which are grounded in sexual and affective desires. These wishes, when confronted with a particular social situation, will account for adjustment or maladjustment. For Thomas, however, men's and women's wishes differed: "Men crave excitement," whereas women "are supposed to possess 'originally, from childhood to death, some interest in human babies.' "[50] For Thomas, the concept of a "defective self" rather than faulty social structures underlies failures of social and moral conformity. Women need only readjust to their traditional feminine role.

Otto Pollak, more directly deterministic in his theories, revived the traditional theological belief in women's basic evil nature, though he did take social factors into account. More precisely, his "cultural" description of women is in fact a biological and psychological stereotype. Pollak's ideas seem a throwback to nineteenth-century beliefs in women's "perversion": "It is Pollak's contention that women are the masterminds behind criminal organizations; that they are the instigators of crime rather than the perpetrators; that they can and in fact do manipulate men into committing offences whilst remaining immune from arrest themselves." Also, says Pollak, "Man's complaint about woman's deceitfulness is old.... The characterization of greater deceitfulness is, however, by no means confined to criminal women."[51] As a result, says Pollak,

[49]Smart, *Women, Crime and Criminology*, 37–46.
[50]Cited in Jones, *Women Who Kill*, 7.
[51]Smart, *Women, Crime and Criminology*, 46–53.

female criminality is more "masked" than men's, the strange proof of which, for Pollak, is the absence of data about women.[52] Pollak also stresses the criminogenic influence of women's "generative" phases—menstruation, pregnancy, and menopause—all of which make them prone to lying. With Pollak's theories, one sees a return to nineteenth-century views of women's nature, proof once again of the unchanging basis of criminological thought about women.

In the 1960s an esteemed French student of deviance, the psychoanalyst Georges Heuyer, had the merit of placing the psychology of the "normal" individual, the delinquent, and the mentally ill individual on the same plane; for him the same intellectual and affective mechanisms were at work in all cases, though they were exaggerated in the sick individual.[53] But this is where Heuyer's egalitarianism stops. Implicitly describing all males in his generalizing view, Heuyer goes on to set apart women on purely genital and endocrine grounds. Heuyer's words speak for themselves:

> Masculine criminology is motivational in focus: robberies, murders, rapes; feminine criminology is sexual: sexual in mental illness and also sexual in misdemeanors and in crimes, in infanticides, in poisonings, in anonymous letters, in violence, in prostitution. (p. 10)

> There is, in feminine delinquency and criminality, an affective, sexual, hormonal character, which is more or less evident but constant, variable according to the age of the delinquent, from prepuberty to menopause and old age. (p. 320)

> Female [criminal] typology is subject to the evolution of her genital life. (p. 332)

> The delinquent or criminal woman always manifests an abnormal affective state. (p. 337)

So strongly does Heuyer believe in his hormonal model that he urges the establishment of an "Institute for Feminine Criminology" to study "totally scientifically" the relationship between

---
[52] Jones, *Women Who Kill*, 7.
[53] Heuyer, *Troubles mentaux*.

endocrine disorders and women's crimes (p. 337). The application of Heuyer's ideas to an actual judicial situation requires knowledge of the offender's personal history, and such exposure has generally been very harmful to women on trial. Although Heuyer's institute has never been built, penal institutions have nonetheless operated on paternalistic assumptions about proper affective and sexual behavior for women: for a woman who has "brutally broken away from her role as mother or wife by killing her child or her husband, the fact of being a woman is no longer an advantage."[54] That is, the apparent leniency of the judicial system toward women—apparent because it belies a denial of female violence—ceases once women reject hyperemotionality, passivity, and dependency. As Carol Smart points out, even contemporary nonbiological role theory explanations of female criminality—those that point to the differential socialization of girls and boys—are incomplete because they neither seek the causes of dissimilar role expectations nor interpret deviance from them. A recent compilation of biological and sociological theory about women, Le Fait féminin, reveals how still vastly underexplored is the area of aggression and violence in relation to gender.

Even more disturbing is the response to current feminism of some criminologists who, like their predecessors, present " 'scientific' conclusions firmly mired in the prevailing cultural stereotypes."[55] For example, Freda Adler, in Sisters in Crime, links the apparent increase in female crime to the renewed women's movement and to a desire to emulate men. Though Adler's attempt to understand female criminal behavior as "a natural extension of normal female behavior"[56] is an essential goal, her anxiety about and women's activity and her dismissal of it are an unfortunate throwback.

In sum, women's crime has been treated as a moral and social offense, whereas men's crime is considered only antisocial behavior. Lawbreaking, hardly an imitative "virilization" of a woman, serves to marginalize her all the more. It is no wonder

---

[54] Josyane Savigneau, "La Femme délinquante ou les bienfaits ambigus du sexisme," Le Monde (March 4, 1977).
[55] Jones, Women Who Kill, 5.
[56] Freda Adler, Sisters in Crime (New York: McGraw-Hill, 1975), 3.

FEMALE CRIMINALITY

prison writers of the past twenty years, including Albertine Sarrazin, Anne Huré, and Nicole Gérard, all insist in some way on their affective and sexual identity: Sarrazin reaffirms passion and heterosexual love and dependency; Gérard describes in detail the affective climate in her prison; and Huré very obviously avoids any reference to sexuality by dwelling on "eternal" spiritual issues. Unlike Genet's hostile rejection of society, Wilde's evocation of his formerly respectable self, or Boudard's presentation of a "manly" male inmate culture, these women's texts contain little questioning of political, social, or legal processes. The realities upon which their imaginations focus are internalized ones; as such, their writing lends credence to Smart's observation that criminals' common recourse to available pseudopsychological (that is, normalizing) explanations of their own acts may lead the offender to believe her behavior is beyond her control and may reinforce existing attitudes toward that behavior.[57] This observation is borne out by a recent report on women's attitudes toward penal justice in general: "Women more than men tend to view justice as a mechanism that is autonomous, ahistorical, independent of the social context, and not 'political.'"[58]

There has been relatively little criminological scholarship in France in recent years—that is, scholarship of the American empirical kind—for reasons about which students of the French intellectual heritage can speculate. It is my guess that two factors may contribute to the paucity of such studies: first, there is the ongoing politicization of the French intelligentsia, which implies placement of an issue such as criminality within the author's larger social analysis. Michel Foucault and the leftist collective authorship of the juridical journal *Actes* are but two examples of criminological theorists whose politics are integral to their analysis. Second, there has been the development of a broadly "structuralist" penchant in recent French thought, a penchant that, by its ahistorical and abstract nature, is incompatible with circumstantially bound approaches.

---

[57]Smart, *Women, Crime, and Criminology*, chap. 5.
[58]Claude Faugeron and Dominique Poggi, "Les Femmes, les infractions, la justice pénale: Une Analyse d'attitudes," *Revue de l'Institut de Sociologie* 3–4 (1975): 376.

Whatever the reasons, case studies of French prisons and prisoners are rare.

With the French prison revolts of the early 1970s, press coverage and testimonies by former inmates began systematically to unveil some of the problems—in men's prisons.[59] Since women did not rebel, "silence, ignorance, and myths continue to surround them."[60] It is also true that the current women's movements in Europe and the United States have driven a wedge between the tradition of biological determinism in criminological theory and the feminist reevaluation of all social structures. Rather than seeking the causes of criminality, many feminists, particularly in England and America, try to illuminate the assumptions underlying legal and judicial definitions of crime—for example, the assumption that prostitution, according to law, is almost always a "woman's crime" or that rape implicates the victim as well as the assailant. The relativity of notions of legality is also being scrutinized, as is evident, for example, in the case of abortion as a reflection of the interplay between law and theories of biological determinism.[61]

There is also, particularly since the prison riots of the 1970s, increasing awareness of the dynamic between women's prisons and women's lives in the larger society. For centuries there have been studies of the social organization within men's and women's prisons. Until recently, however, such studies have been merely descriptive and uncritical of the views of women that they in fact perpetuate. Because of the interchange between criminological theory and penal policy contemporary with it, we must now consider this dialectic and its historical evolution.

---

[59]See, for example, Serge Livrozet, *Aujourd'hui, la prison* (Paris: Hachette, 1976); *Les Prisons, un bilan: Témoignages de fonctionnaires pénitentiaires sur l'évolution du régime carcéral depuis 1945 et les causes du malaise*, special issue of *L'Action pénitentiaire* 96 (n.d., app. 1973); Syndicat de la magistrature, *Au nom du peuple français*... (Paris: Stock, 1974).

[60]Catherine Erhel and Catherine Leguay, *Prisonnières* (Paris: Stock, 1977), 7.

[61]See, for example, Smart, *Women, Crime and Criminology;* Hartman, *Victorian Murderesses;* Jones, *Women Who Kill;* and Rita James Simon, *Women and Crime* (Lexington, Mass.: D. C. Heath, 1975).

2

Women's Prisons: The Social Monster

Whether or not one believes prison is a true microcosm of society, the relation between prison and societal structures is tight. As Michelle Perrot puts it, prison is "a broken mirror that reflects our image at the outer limit of experience."[1] Prisons have always confirmed the position of women in the outside world: they have particularized conditions for women along the lines that prevail in the culture at large. Thus class distinctions, operative in defining crime and criminality in the seventeenth and eighteenth centuries, also functioned within prison systems. Likewise, the nineteenth-century preoccupation with bourgeois morality determined the conditions suitable for the female offender—that is, convents and, within them, strict segregation of prostitutes. And the more recent belief in the psychological forces behind deviant conduct has greatly influenced the idea of "treatment" as reinstilling "normal" feminine behavior. Women entered prison carrying social baggage and, inside,

---

[1] Michelle Perrot, "Delinquency and the Penitentiary System in Nineteenth-Century France," in *Deviants and the Abandoned in French Society: Selections from the Annales Economies, Sociétés, Civilisations*, Vol. 4, ed. Robert Forster and Orest Ranum, trans. Elborg Forster and Patricia M. Ranum (Balitmore and London: Johns Hopkins University Press, 1978), 213. Translation of January–February 1975 issue.

that burden was reaffirmed, "precisely because of their being women, as if women's condition in some way *redoubled* the circumstances of life within prison."[2]

The conditions under which women have been incarcerated have evolved in accordance with definitions of their "dangerousness" and with changing purposes and methods of punishment in general. Sources for this information vary with each period: during the Old Regime, when prisons were only one of a number of forms of punishment and were used only to house those awaiting judgment, execution, or exile, few official documents of prison life were kept.[3] Prisons were called "refuges" or "keeps." Prisoners, however—particularly those of quality and therefore probably of education—frequently wrote memoirs, such as those in the vast Bastille archives series. Women who were of bourgeois background and had been educated at home (for example, Madame Roland, Madame de Staal-Delaunay, and Louise de Duras) also responded to their imprisonment by writing. These educated bourgeois women, along with imprisoned noblewomen ("king's prisoners" or political prisoners of high birth and wealth), unlike the mass of poor inmates, were generally involved in political intrigue. These women—particularly the nobles active at court—also had enjoyed relative social and intellectual freedom before the Revolution. The absence in Revolutionary prisons of obstacles to writing fostered women's production of memoirs and journals.

Although these texts vary in their information about prison life, they all reveal certain general features of imprisonment at the time: prisoners were treated differently according to class and court rank, reflecting the Old Regime's dislike of uniform laws.[4] Also, various structures were used as prisons, including chateaus, convents, and hospitals. Men guarded women, since women were considered too weak and too easily influenced to be effective. All classes and ages and those suspected of all sorts

[2]*Sorcières: Les Femmes vivent,* issue on "Prisonnières," no. 6 (n.d.), 5; my emphasis.

[3]See Mireille Vincent-Cassy, "Prison et châtiments à la fin du Moyen Age," in *Les Marginaux et les exclus dans l'histoire,* Cahiers Jussieu no. 5 (Paris: UGE 10/18, 1979), 262–74.

[4]See Frantz Funck-Brentano, *Légendes et archives de la Bastille* (Paris: Hachette, 1902).

of crimes were mixed in the same prison, and men and women were separated only by easily penetrable fences. Prisoners paid entrance and exit fees as well as all jailing costs, and money could buy anything, including a private cell, or *pistole,* food from outside, a mattress, music, and heat. Madame de Staal-Delaunay, imprisoned for eighteen months in 1718 for her presumed complicity in the Duchesse du Maine's attempt to overthrow the regent, presents herself as well treated, even happy, in the Bastille. However, Henri Petitfils's contention that women were allowed servants, sewing needles, and pets in prison to indulge their "coquettishness" is obviously an inadequate explanation.[5] In fact, Staal-Delaunay, she herself says in her "Mémoires," received less severe treatment than men because the authorities hoped she would denounce other conspirators.[6] Since prisoners enjoyed freedom of movement as well as the proximity to the other sex, liberal visitation rights, and access to good food and clothing, amorous adventures were common. It is not surprising that Staal-Delaunay recounts at length her own "carte du tendre" romance with the Chevalier du Mesnil. This affective fulfillment, possible for many women only through the communication of the sexes in prison, is part of Staal-Delaunay's sense of happiness, and it echoes Roussel's notion of the "sanguine," healthy normal woman. But Staal-Delaunay also notes that in prison she is free from responsibilities (p. 89), indicating that in the 1700s the burden of family and religious duties, which dominated nineteenth-century correctional reforms, had not yet been incorporated into punishment.

Corporal punishment prevailed through the eighteenth century, as vengeance or appeasement for the ruling power, and it culminated in the bloodbath of the Terror. Staal-Delaunay tells us she fears physical pain much more than imprisonment (p. 85). As late as 1786 the Comtesse de la Motte, the central figure in the "affair of the necklace," was sentenced to be whipped and branded while confined at Salpêtrière pris-

[5]Jean-Christian Petitfils, "Les Femmes à la Bastille," in his *La Vie quotidienne à la Bastille du Moyen Age à la Révolution* (Paris: Hachette, 1975), 110.
[6]Madame de Staal (Madame Delaunay), "Mémoires de Madame de Staal, écrits par elle-même," in *Oeuvres,* 1: 1–339 (Paris: Renouard, 1821).

on.[7] One can fully appreciate the kinds of torture performed on women before the late 1700s by looking back a century at the case of the infamous Marquise de Brinvilliers. Found guilty of numerous actual and attempted poisonings, she was sentenced in 1676 to be tortured, beheaded, and burned. This torture consisted of *la question* (forced swallowing of water to induce confession), *l'amende honorable* (public confession and begging for pardon), and *le feu* (burning in infamy).[8] Over the half-century between de Brinvilliers and Staal-Delaunay, one sees a growing reluctance to punish women physically as moral conversion increasingly becomes the goal of discipline.

During this period there was also a change in the educational background of women prisoners. The Marquise de Brinvilliers had had only the barest "literary" instruction and remained essentially illiterate, and so her direct experience of punishment is recorded only in her confession as written down by Father Edme Pirot in the *Récit de ses derniers moments*, plus a few comments in the correspondence of her contemporary Madame de Sévigné:

> She entered the place where she expected to have been put to the torture, and seeing three large vessels of water, "This," said she, "must certainly be to drown me; for, considering the smallness of my size, they can never pretend to make me drink so much." She heard her sentence read without the least token of fear or weakness; and towards the latter part of it, she desired them to begin it again, telling them that the circumstance of the cart had struck her so much as to divert her attention from the rest. On her way to execution, she desired her confessor to place the executioner before her, that she might not see that rascal Desgrais, who had taken her. Desgrais preceded the cart on horseback. Her confessor reproved her for the sentiment, upon which she asked pardon, and submitted to endure the disagreeable sight. She

---

[7] De la Motte, a confidante of Cardinal Rohan and then of Queen Marie Antoinette, was accused of stealing a valuable pearl necklace in a scandal of huge political implications. Apparently caught in the crossfire between Rohan and the queen, and perhaps between rivaling Austria and France, she fell completely from royal favor and was sent to the Bastille, then to the Salpêtrière prison.

[8] Edme Pirot, *La Marquise de Brinvilliers, récit de ses derniers moments* (Paris: A. Lemerre, 1883), 160.

mounted the ladder and the scaffold alone, bare-footed; and the executioner was a quarter of an hour dressing, shaving, and preparing her for the execution: this caused a great murmur among the crowd, and was certainly cruel. The next day her bones were gathered up, as relics by the people, who said she was a saint.[9]

This long passage, along with Le Brun's painting of a radiant marquise, bears witness to the public ambivalence toward female criminality. Madame de Sévigné's near admiration for de Brinvilliers's resolution and strength, as well as the people's superstitious confusion of ignominy with sainthood, reflect a recognition of female assertiveness, in this case in the form of extreme deviance. Later, such acknowledgment of female violence and the capital punishment it engendered diminished.

The marquise's limited education is apparent in her handwritten "personal confessions," compiled before her arrest. They are a catalog of her sins in which poisoning, incest, and adultery mingle with calm indistinguishability. They are given not even the merest narrative shape. For de Brinvilliers imprisonment (at la Conciergerie) was not a sustained loss of freedom, as it was for women of succeeding generations, but a brief prelude to execution. There is therefore no evocation of the prison itself, except for occasional references to eating and sleeping. The events of de Brinvilliers's last day, including a detailed description of her punishment and an account of her religious "conversion," are the entire substance of Pirot's text.

If one bears in mind Foucault's thesis that the history of punishment is the "history of the body,"[10] one finds a paradoxical equality between men and women in this early period of corporal punishment. Since in fact the crime and not the criminal was being sanctioned, the prisoner's sex was secondary in determining modes of punishment. The spectacle of physical torture, in which the public could play its supporting role, served to avenge, not to rehabilitate. Sexual distinctions did

---

[9]Madame de Sévigné, *Letters of Madame de Sévigné to Her Daughter and Her Friends* (New York: E. P. Dutton, 1937), 233. A selection from the English translation of the 1806 French edition (London: J. Walker, 1811).

[10]Michel Foucault, *Surveiller et punir: Naissance de la prison* (Paris: Gallimard, 1975). Also published as *Discipline and Punish: The Birth of the Prison*, trans. Alan Sheridan (New York: Pantheon, 1977).

underlie the frequency and occasionally the forms of revenge used (dismemberment was not performed on women), but until prison became a punishment in itself, differences in treatment were based largely on class rather than sex.

A further equalizing force in early imprisonment was the judicial emphasis on confession: "Only the spoken word proves guilt . . . but the prisoner's confession is of value only if it is made freely."[11] Confession, rooted in medieval canon law's emphasis on repentance, provided the prisoner his or her only active role in the civil punishment process. Repentance as evidence of modification of the soul, however, not only flowered in the nineteenth century, but also acquired sex-specific forms in keeping with the dominant morality. The particularly strong attachment of imprisoned women to confession, both as Christian rite and as literary expression, is doubtless linked to the powerful association between their social deviance and their perceived straying from Christian duties. In fact the parallels between prison life and convent life in the eighteenth century are striking, as seen, for example, in Diderot's *La Religieuse*. The convent is male centered—with Christ as the ultimate male authority—and the women are kept dependent and ignorant.[12] Further, both institutions are "denaturing" and "desocializing," as Diderot's Sister Suzanne explains: "Man is born for society. Separate him, isolate him, his ideas grow disconnected, his character becomes twisted, and a thousand ridiculous affections grow in his mind, like roots in uncultivated ground."[13] And both the prison and the convent induce desensitization, as when Suzanne says, "I saw and heard nothing and was quite brutish" (pp. 15–16), and elsewhere, "I understood nothing of what was being said around me. I had become practically an automaton. . . . I was what is called physically alienated" (pp. 44–45).

Like all victims of this attempt to eradicate political and class privilege, women imprisoned under the Terror experienced

[11]Vincent-Cassy, "Prison et châtiments," 270.
[12]See Ruth P. Thomas, "Montesquieu's Harem and Diderot's Convent: The Woman as Prisoner," *French Review* 52, no. 1 (October 1978): 36–45.
[13]Denis Diderot, *Memoirs of a Nun* [*La Religieuse*], trans. Francis Birrell (London: Elek Books, 1959).

unknown and indefinite jail sentences. Two such victims, whose stays in Chantilly's Collège du Plessis (specifically designated for "counterrevolutionaries") overlapped, were the Duchesse de Duras (Louise) and Mademoiselle de Pons. Their journals reveal many of the same observations about their confinement: overcrowding and forced contact with women of other "tastes";[14] private and costly cells for the wealthy; relative ease of correspondence, though such privileges diminished under Robespierre; and free movement within the prison. The prison ambience—at least for those of privileged background—reflects the "uniformity" and "happiness" that Roussel prescribed for women, though Duras and Pons respond quite differently to it. Pons, who was young and protected by Duras herself, speaks more like an unreflective, spoiled participant in the prison's frivolity; Duras, separated from her parents and her son, is much more concerned with the life she has left and so conforms more closely to Roussel's suggested family preoccupations. Thus constraints on writing frustrate Duras's family ties all the more. The frivolity of the other prisoners in the face of daily death warrants is incomprehensible to her. The confiscation of her money and jewels, a forerunner of the modern search frisk and consignment of property, is in fact theft that leaves her unable to resume normal life afterward. By her attachment to Mademoiselle de Pons, Duras reconstructs some affective bonds, which sound the only positive notes in her melancholy story.[15] Women's poems and texts in the Bastille archives series generally recount the pain of separation from family and the intolerability of prison's unknown, unpredictable elements at that time, including sentence length and even the precise offense in question.

The best-known woman prisoner of the period, Madame Roland, echoes in her *Mémoires* much of the same atmosphere of

---

[14]Mademoiselle de Pons (Augustine), *Un Épisode du temps de la Terreur* (Paris: Librairie d'Auguste Vaton, 1857). See also Charles A. Dauban, *Les Prisons de Paris sous la Révolution, d'après les relations des contemporains* (Paris: Plon, 1870), in which the spectacle of prison's chaotic mixing of people is evoked from documents of the revolutionary period.

[15]The Duchesse de Duras (Louise H.), *Prison Journals during the French Revolution*, trans. Mrs. M. Carey (New York: Dodd, Mead, 1891). Also contains memoirs of Madame Latour.

libertinism, corruption, and promiscuity for the Abbaye and Sainte-Pélagie prisons.[16] Like Duras and Pons, she refuses any solidarity with other women because of their vulgarity. According to Louis-René Villermé, a physician who inspected French prisons in 1820, Sainte-Pélagie was the worst in terms of poor hygiene, lack of light and air, inactivity, and overcrowding.[17] But Roland, who wrote long and well-crafted memoirs, goes even further than Duras and Pons, who both essentially resign themselves to prison life. Roland transforms confinement into a structure of her own making, choosing to reduce her food and amenities to those of the poorest prisoner. As will be seen in the discussion of Roland's memoirs, this stoicism is part of her more general affirmation of her "true" self in the face of prison's depersonalization.

By the 1790s, as imprisonment became a mode of punishment in itself, the present system began, slowly, to be created. Increasingly specialized institutions appeared, embodying variations in sentence length and in internal regime. Nonetheless, the continued refinement in theory and in penal reforms concerned the punishment of men only. Women—who were legally and penally equivalent to children—were increasingly punished through isolation, which was indistinguishable from protection by religious congregations.[18] It was axiomatic that Christian values were the only possible climate for women's rehabilitation. Like children, imprisoned women were kept in an arrested and dependent state. This institutional control, a natural extension of Roussel's recommended uniform inactivity for women, paralleled their more general domestic isolation and immobilization. Further, the long-standing practice of exiling young women in convents, as well as their frequent self-exile, greatly eased the transition to prison-convents. And the primary goal of imprisonment at the time—reflection and repentance—was encouraged by the activities normal to convent life.

[16]Madame Roland, *Mémoires de Madame Roland* (Paris: Mercure de France, 1966).

[17]Louise-René Villermé, *Des Prisons telles qu'elles sont et telles qu'elles devraient être* (Paris: Hachette Microfiche, 1971; originally published 1820).

[18]See Henri Gaillac, *Les Maisons de correction 1830–1945* (Paris: Cujas, 1971), especially chapters "Bons Pasteurs et refuges du xix^c siècle" and "Les Sections féminines de préservation."

Documents of the time show that, with the exception of institutions for prostitutes, whose "viciousness" and disease justified specialized treatment, conditions for women were not the focus of penal reforms.[19] It is therefore impossible to trace uniform changes in prison conditions for women except to designate the 1830s as the time when congregations became entrenched, replacing male guards;[20] the 1840s as the beginning of some separation of prisoners as accused or condemned and by crime; and the 1870s as the period when legislation began to segregate prisoners by sex and age. Otherwise class distinctions within the prison remained dominant, though there were few rich persons left in prisons by late in the century.

Among the general reforms that affected women, albeit differently from men, were those that marked the change of goal from exclusion to rehabilitation. Initial isolation was now used to induce the prisoner to repent. Women were automatically examined for pregnancy. Silence was introduced in the 1840s to impede contamination between prisoners. If men responded to silence by developing a "deceptive private language,"[21] women frequently became aphasiacs. Marie Cappelle-Lafarge describes one such woman prisoner, Mademoiselle Grouvelle, an outspoken political activist who became mute and finally went mad. The paucity of texts by nineteenth-century women prisoners may in part be due to such a loss of the capacity for expression.

Education entered the prison, though with clear sex and class differences: women's instruction was almost exclusively religious, since too much knowledge was considered dangerous; working-class prisoners were generally taught to limit their needs rather than to aspire to more. Domestic work such as

---

[19]Villermé, *Des Prisons*, and B. Appert, *Rapport sur des prisons, des hospices, et des écoles des départements de l'Aisne, du Nord, du Pas-de-Calais, et de la Somme* (Paris, 1824).

[20]Gaillac, *Maisons de Correction*, chap. 3.

[21]Perrot, "Delinquency," 216, and also mentioned in Henri Joly, *Le Crime: Etude sociale*, 2d ed. (Paris: L. Cerf, 1888), 268. This male "argot" is associated with the tradition of popular literature by *mendiants* ("*littérature de la gueuserie*") of the seventeenth and eighteenth centuries. Prison tales prolonged this literature of the poor criminal hero (See Roger Chartier, "La 'Monarchie d'argot' entre le mythe et l'histoire," in *Marginaux et les exclus*, 275–311).

sewing and weaving was deemed the best way to keep female prisoners in check, in the absence of what many considered a surefire solution to criminality: maternity. Work was generally believed to be less important for women than for men, however, and was therefore frequently absent in women's prisons.[22]

All texts by prison reformers of the time cry out against prison's rampant "unnatural vices," including masturbation and women's "monstrous marriages."[23] Men are not uniformly seen as endangered by the corruption of fellow prisoners or the evils of prostitution. Only women, by their affectional wants and natural weakness, are prey to such dangers and in need of safeguards. Thus prostitutes, believed the basest of female deviants, were set apart from other women. The introduction of work as part of the prison regime was a logical consequence of the country's economic course. For men and women alike, work in prison was insufficient and badly paid, and training was nonexistent. The seeds were sown, however, for what has been an ongoing sex-specific division of prison workshops: women prepared fabrics, wove, tressed, and sewed, while men worked with wood and stone.

All these reforms had implications for women's lives after prison, and the reforms were both product and perpetrator of their living conditions. The circumstances in women's prisons, combined with prevailing views of the female criminal as at once cunning and weak, led to contradictory beliefs about the consequences of imprisonment: women would be corrupted by prison's environment even while religious instruction would win out; women would fall victim to hysteria and nervous disorders[24] even while they would rise to heroic acceptance and Christian remorse; melancholy and nostalgia would sap the energy they needed for social reintegration even while religious and moral teachings would set them on the right course. What could an imprisoned woman say about herself? Surely these double binds, which closed around all women at the time, also help explain the virtual absence of prison manuscripts during the nineteenth century. Cappelle-Larfarge herself expresses

[22] Appert, *Rapport sur des prisons*, and Villermé, *Des prisons*.
[23] Villermé, *Des prisons*, 96.
[24] Ibid., 91.

well the contradictory expectations under which she had to function:

> When I was strong, when I had courage, and when I dared to struggle alone against calumny, the world said I was impudent, a hypocrite, a heartless woman. Now that my suffering cries out, that the world hears it and sees it bleed, it accuses me of weakness and mocks my tears.[25]

Cappelle-Lafarge, convicted almost simultaneously of poisoning her husband and of stealing a friend's diamonds, smuggled out two manuscripts from the prisons at Tulle and Montpellier. So sensational was the 1840 "affaire Lafarge" that even her publisher René was in danger of legal action for defending her. Cappelle-Lafarge's *Mémoires* and *Heures de prison* are extraordinary historical and literary pieces. Though she in fact describes her state of mind more fully than the state of French prisons, Cappelle-Lafarge nonetheless offers much detail by discussing prison life in relation to herself. Before her conviction and transfer to Montpellier, she was treated with a "certain leniency" in the provincial jails of Brives and Tulle.[26] We learn that she was able to read, write, and embroider at peace and in the company of her maid and cousin. Cappelle-Lafarge, like Duras, Roland, and others before her, shuns the "vulgarity" of her sister prisoners, though she chooses to protect certain individuals. Once at Montpellier, however, she loses her companions, her frequent family visits, and the privacy of her mail. In fact, Cappelle-Lafarge's sixteen years of prison, unlike her predecessors' experience, is a prolonged nightmare. One senses barriers closing in on her until her complete legal "death" and social oblivion. Cappelle-Lafarge first had to fight the ministry's edict that she wear the coarse penal robe, since she refused to accept any external badge of guilt.[27] She also struggled

---

[25]Madame Lafarge, *Heures de prison*, 3 vols. (Paris: Librairie Nouvelle, 1856), 194–95. See also the *Mémoires de Marie Cappelle (veuve Lafarge) écrits par elle-même*, 4 vols. (Paris: A. René, 1841–42).

[26]See "Dossier Marie Lafarge" at the Bibliothèque Féministe Marguerite Durand, Paris 5ᵉ.

[27]Writers such as Pauline de Grandpré, *Les Condamnées de Saint-Lazare: Mémoires par Madame * * ** (Paris: F. Curot, 1869), who attribute women's refus-

through a judicial process that denied her the right to offer evidence in her defense during the preliminary hearing: at that time only evidence for the prosecution could be presented during hearings; the defense could offer evidence only at the trial. At Montpellier Cappelle-Lafarge lost her stove, her decorated cell, and her furniture, apparently owing to administrative inconsistency and an arbitrary policy regarding prisoners' possessions. In this period of both perceived softening and individualization of punishment, she wrote a rich, often painful, sometimes ironic response to the pressures she encountered during her long trial and imprisonment. Her texts bear witness to Foucault's denunciation of "reforms," since they resulted at best in irreconcilable and unlivable contradictions and at worst in total moral and legal repression.

The century ended with a famous trial whose publicity tells us less about conditions within prisons than about the hegemony of deterministic theories of criminality and the increasing importance of psychologizing explanations of crime. Gabrielle Bompard, first imprisoned as a young prostitute in Valenciennes, fell into worse error, as her contemporaries' hindsight determined. She and a male companion, Michel Eyraud, were convicted in 1889 of robbing and murdering a sheriff's officer. The psychiatric examination to which Bompard—but not Eyraud—was subjected reveals the presuppositions surrounding women criminals and the unsettled state of their diagnosis and treatment. Bompard is characterized as having "a complete absence of moral sense," "easily changeable feelings," "violent appetites," and "hyperesthesia" of the erogenous zones, and of being "hysterical," "hypnotizable," "unbalanced," and "desensitized."[28] Because it was believed that her intelligence was intact but her mind unbalanced, Bompard was considered both re-

---

al to wear the coarse prison sackcloth to the uniforms' being neither "elegant" nor "poetic," overlook or deny the deeper symbolic value of these clothes.

[28] Gabrielle Bompard, *Les Confessions secrètes de Gabrielle Bompard,* transcribed by Rémy de l'Aulnaye (Lille: Librairie Populaire, 1890). These "confessions" are as suspect as those of de Brinvilliers recorded by Pirot. De l'Aulnaye changes from a first-person to a third-person speaker, undermining the "fidelity" he vaunts. The same judgment of Bompard can be seen in Marcel Nadaud and André Fage, *Les Grandes Drames passionnels de Casque d'Or à Mata-Hari* (Paris: Georges-Anquetil, 1926).

sponsible and not responsible for her acts. She fell in the twilight zone between being unquestionably guilty and deserving exile and being pitiful and suggestible, according to the period's definitions of psychiatric disorders. Bompard served fifteen years of hard labor in Clermont-Ferrand prison while long remaining the object-lesson "type" for criminal studies. She was the most reprehensible and dangerous of female criminals as well as the most passive and impressionable of female victims.

Whereas most information on prison life in the nineteenth century comes from texts by theorists and reformers (prisoners' manuscripts, which were already few, were either seized or hidden), the next century saw a resurgence of memoirs and, later, fictionalizations from the prison experience. Almost all these women describe their lives inside prison, and, as varied as these lives may be, they reveal clear trends in notions of the "improvement" and "rehabilitation" of the offender.[29] Marguerite Steinheil, accused of murdering her husband and mother, and Henriette Caillaux, accused of shooting a newspaper editor, traveled in powerful political and cultural circles. Both are now seen as reflections of the *belle époque* brand of "aristocracy": Steinheil conducted a literary and artistic salon and was an intimate of President Félix Faure; Caillaux was the wife of the minister of finance. Both were acquitted. Both were among the last famous prisoners to occupy Saint-Lazare's remaining private cell, and they bought fine linen and clothes, candles and wood, and gourmet food. Both were separated from the other women, who worked in the prison workshops making paper flowers, toothbrushes, and linens. Confusing class with intelligence and money with education, Steinheil justifies her own desire for comfort by the bourgeois belief that the poor need less. She considered the other prisoners pathetic "degraded women," and they inflamed her anger by in turn disdaining her.[30] Likewise, Caillaux's adversaries were indig-

---

[29]The exception, Marguerite Steinheil, is the only one of the women in this study who was acquitted, though she spent one year in preventive detention. Steinheil's *Mémoires* provide a last glimpse of the kind of "privileged" incarceration of prestigious figures that virtually ended with World War I.

[30]Marguerite Steinheil, *Mes mémoires* (Paris: Edmond Ramlot, n.d., app. 1911–12).

nant about her special treatment in prison. It should be noted, however, that the apparently lenient treatment of Steinheil and Caillaux arose as much from complexities of the judicial system as from class advantage. As René Floriot points out, juries of the time frequently acquitted criminals they might otherwise have convicted because the court, not the jury, handed down firm sentences. The jury could not know if a guilty verdict would entail imprisonment for five years or perpetuity.[31] Also, preventive detention, on the average, lasted over a year. Until its destruction in the 1930s, Saint-Lazare, built in the eighteenth century, earned a steadily worse reputation for decay, filth, dampness, and vermin.[32] Nonetheless, three thousand women continued to be confined there, and no changes were made.

A dry and direct presentation of women's prisons between and after the wars is seen in Sylvie Paul's *Ne me jugez pas!*[33] Paul, first imprisoned as a juvenile in the early years of Fresnes's "observation center" for minors, was saddled with a "personality dossier," only recently outlawed in France. She was labeled "incorrigible" for life, but, if her memoirs are any indication, prison helped undo that aggressivity. Paul, who was moved from Fresnes to Cadillac (known for its corporal punishment), to Clermont (designated for "troublemakers"), to la Roquette (for robbery), to Cherche-Midi (as a war prisoner), and eventually to Haguenau (for murder), describes her punishment with a dullness, a numbness, that bespeaks anything but rebellious incorrigibility. With the goal of personality alteration in prison, bromides and straitjackets replaced the earlier chains and handcuffs, which were outlawed in 1922.

The categories used in women's prisons in the 1930s also show the confusion between morality and personality in the goal of "rehabilitation." At Rennes, for example, one finds prisoners classified as prostitutes, abortionists, murderers, hysterics, the

[31] René Floriot, *Deux femmes en Cour d'Assises: Madame Steinheil et Madame Caillaux* (Paris: Hachette, 1966), 175.
[32] The famous financial wizard and criminal Marthe Hanau spent sixteen months there in 1928–29 and described the terrible conditions in her newspaper, *Forces*. See also Dominique Desanti, *La Banquière des années folles: Marthe Hanau* (Paris: Fayard, 1968).
[33] Sylvie Paul, *Ne me jugez pas!* (Paris: Gallimard, 1962).

retarded, incorrigibles, and spies. Clearly, presuppositions about female sexual normality and adaptation still determined evaluation and punishment. Heuyer and others were later to echo the opinion that classification of women by character was more important and useful than professional identification and work-oriented therapy.[34] The pervading theme in Paul's story is her attachment to her children, a common reaffirmation of "normal femininity" among imprisoned women. But there is in Paul's case a striking contrast between her determination to secure custody of her children and her passivity toward their conception and birth.

In the following decades, because of the changed profile of criminology, sociological biases overtook psychological ones in determining prison's internal social organization. These biases, which classified prisoners in terms of their capacity to readapt to external social structures, were functionalist in outlook. Thus the different prison regimes corresponded more or less to the systems of reward and punishment, of exchange, and of communication that existed outside. In 1958 legislation that codified the previously stated purpose of confinement—moral amendment and social reintegration of the prisoner—sanctioned gender differences that already existed. That is, the revamped French Code of Penal Procedure merely hardened the existing double standard. Differences between men's and women's prisons were codified not by prescription, however, but by omission. The codes simply ignored gender-distinct conditions in educational programs and in vocational training and so in effect maintained the status quo. In the three pages of his discussion devoted to the prison regimes suitable to women— and these pages, not coincidentally, are in the same section as the rules for children and the mentally ill—the former director of the Penitentiary Administration, Robert Schmelck, posits that women's physical constitutions and personalities justify their differential treatment. Two of these three pages concern the pregnant woman and her child.[35] Schmelck calls women's

---

[34]Georges Heuyer, *Les Troubles mentaux: Etude criminologique* (Paris: Presses Universitaires de France, 1968).
[35]Robert Schmelck and Georges Picca, *Pénologie et droit pénitentiaire* (Paris: Cujas, 1967).

treatment soft, an appraisal that women's texts seem to contradict. As before, the specific situation of women in prison is either dismissed or assimilated to men's needs.

For reasons doubtless related both to the growing dissatisfaction of prisoners that was to explode in the early 1970s and to the rising number of women writers in general who were published in the 1960s and 1970s, we have several contemporary texts from women's prisons. Two of the writers, Albertine Sarrazin and Anne Huré, were or became established novelists; Nicole Gérard, Paulette Veiber, and Gabrielle Russier, for different reasons, wrote testimonies rather than novels, Gérard and Verbier in their journals and Russier in her letters.

Although their crimes and prisons varied, these women all were confined under similar conditions, which Erhel and Leguay outline in *Prisonnières*.[36] The resemblances between women's lives inside and outside prison are evident. Once condemned, all save Huré worked in prison workshops at traditional female occupations (feather crafting, sewing) analogous to those that prevailed outside. The virtues of hygiene and good homemaking skills were not only encouraged, but inculcated as personal qualities. Until conditions were changed in the 1970s, the "progressive regime," a vertical structure of reward and punishment, encouraged conformance to "proper" emotional responses. The prison's "educators," women hired to individualize rehabilitation and serve as models, were nonetheless of a different economic and educational background than most prisoners. The writing of letters was, until 1974, limited to one page three times a week, and the contents are still read and censored. Until 1973 silence remained the rule in prisons, though it was not enforced.

The effects of prison's deprivations vary, depending on a woman's previous life. Since the 1960s there have been numerous studies in America and England of the effects of and responses to imprisonment among all prisoners. The general losses and deprivations experienced were definitively presented by Erving Goffman in his theory of the "mortification of the self." Examining each stage of imprisonment for its particular

[36]Catherine Erhel and Catherine Leguay, *Prisonnières* (Paris: Stock, 1977).

consequences in this "abasement" or "degradation" of self, Goffman speaks of a "disculturation" that renders the individual incapable of "managing certain features of daily life" after release.[37] According to Goffman, the pain of imprisonment begins at admission, when the inmate loses self-identification, property, and name. The replacement of individual belongings by standard prison issue engenders a "personal defacement" or loss of chosen appearance. The "lowly postures and stances" imposed represent an indignity incompatible with the individual's conception of self. Then, says Goffman, the loss of "normal" roles such as that of heterosexual partner leads to a "disidentification." With prolonged incarceration, the prisoner experiences "contaminative exposure" or loss of personal space because of forced contact with fellow prisoners. Finally, there is a disruption of the usual relationship between "the individual actor and his acts," meaning a loss of efficacy, economy, and autonomy in action. The inability to speak freely, for example when receiving orders, will reinforce this loss of self-determination. In her study *Le Froid pénitentiaire,* Simone Buffard echoes Goffman's conclusions and adds some social effects to the individual ones.[38] She claims there is no possibility for solidarity among prisoners in the "collective resignation" that makes prison a Sartrian hell. She evokes class differences between the prisoners and their doctors or psychiatrists as deterring a convict's own positive judgment of himself. Finally, says Buffard, the value of work as important in itself declines as time—pure duration and wait—becomes the prime preoccupation.

While there is no question that men and women suffer comparably, many of the losses will affect them differently because of the differences in their previous lives. The harshest deprivations for women have traditionally been considered to be the loss of sexual identity, the loss of privacy coupled with forced intimacy with other women, the loss of choice and initiative,

[37]Erving Goffman, "On the Characteristics of Total Institutions: The Inmate World," in *Perspectives on Correction,* ed. Donal E. J. MacNamara and Edward Sagarin (New York: Thomas Crowell, 1971), 31–61.
[38]Simone Buffard, *Le Froid pénitentiaire: L'Impossible Réforme des prisons* (Paris: Seuil, 1973).

and the denial of self-labeling personal belongings.[39] Equally difficult for women have been economic dependency and poor work conditions (and frequently unemployment) and constant exposure as objects to be observed, in searches and in surveillance. As Erhel and Leguay, two former prisoners, put it, "The administration appropriates our bodies. Our bodies were open to the [guards'] 'right to view.' . . . A female prisoner is forced to offer herself as a permanent spectacle."[40]

Representative of contemporary French feminist concern with women's "desire," or their autonomous expression of their own sexuality, Erhel and Leguay go on to describe the sex-specific effects of imprisonment on women. If all women's sexuality has been appropriated and redefined in terms of masculine and heterosexual needs only, in prison, say Erhel and Leguay, that appropriation and repression are complete:

> It is very difficult to feel desire in prison. . . . You need an enormous vitality to have your desire "live," rise up, and manifest itself as true desire. . . . The fact of feeling desire in prison already represents a form of resistance to the prison machine.
>
> Since heterosexuality is the social norm, a woman prisoner no longer has any sexuality. This principle does not apply in men's prisons because the male prisoner, like all men, exists for himself and in relation to other men, whoever they may be, through his sex.[41]

Since social norms have repressed women's expression of their own, as opposed to prescribed, desire, those norms conform both in and out of prison to an imposed image of women's sexuality. Prison's negation of women's expression of their autonomous desire therefore appears to society to be a "natural" extension of that negated sexuality. Thus imprisoned women find themselves in a double bind: prison not only redoubles the forces that alienate women from their authentic sexual identity in the society at large, it also suppresses the expression of any

---

[39]Rose Giallombardo, *Society of Women: A Study of a Women's Prison* (New York: John Wiley, 1966).
[40]Erhel and Leguay, *Prisonnières*, 84–85.
[41]Ibid., 134, 141.

true autonomous desires that might arise in the prison itself. Although men too undergo a powerful loss of sexual identity in prison, the positive and assertive male sexual definitions that exist outside are also perpetuated inside. In prison men generally reaffirm for one another their sexual self-images, whereas women are encouraged to mutually reinforce self-denial.

Traditional studies of the pains of imprisonment for women do not generally question the assumptions underlying women's sex-specific responses to confinement. They attribute the harshness of the loss of sexual identity, of privacy, and of self-identification respectively to women's sexually defined role in society, to their mistrust of other women, and to their expected search for self-display. One can and should argue with each of these perceived losses from the standpoint of the presuppositions they indicate about women's lives—for example, the presupposition that women shun the company of other women or that the loss of heterosexual relations is necessarily a deprivation for women and not, as it sometimes is, either irrelevant or a relief from subjection or violence. However, many of these traditionally perceived losses are felt and expressed by imprisoned women. Albertine Sarrazin, for example, in her novel *La Cavale* dramatizes some of these sociological findings. She presents herself in prison as isolated from the man who had "made her a woman" and as forced to cohabit with the collective incarnation of the "eternal feminine," clearly an indication that she has adopted popular mythology.[42] These women's texts ask us not to reevaluate the women's response they transmit, but to rethink the social structures from which they arise.

Another area of inquiry in contemporary Anglo-Saxon studies of prisons has been patterns of response and adaptation in inmate social systems. Studies of women's prisons are few; as is true for studies of men, they are made up of opinions involving the source and nature of inmate systems: the belief that the systems arise solely from prison's peculiar arrangements; the belief that systems are exclusively imported from the world at large; or, most persuasive, the belief that systems arise from

---

[42] Albertine Sarrazin, *La Cavale* (Paris: J.-J. Pauvert, 1965). Also published as *The Runaway*, trans. Charles Lam Markmann (New York: Grove Press, 1967).

both of the above combined with individual prisoners' particular needs. However they are viewed, prison systems all make use of the elements at hand to create a substitute for the universe that is lost. Thus one generally finds in all prisons an informal network of economic relationships, based on scarcity, barter, and wealth. One also finds in women's prisons reconstituted "family groups" or "kinship ties"—with or without sexual intimacy—based on the model of the traditional heterosexual nuclear couple and the extended family.[43] While such systemization results as much from the observer's imposition of structures as from their true existence, prison texts such as Sarrazin's *La Cavale* or Nicole Gérard's *Sept ans de pénitence* do clearly evoke an affectively based network of relationships.

The existence of communities of women within prison, which is documented in sociological studies and in literature, gives rise to a kind of tension that is particularly relevant for the women studied here. Those communities create strains between collectivism and individualism, between identification with the group and separation from it. And these strains remain largely unresolved in women's stories. The authors in this book most often present their fellow-prisoners as a single faceless collectivity with which they at times interact, but which generally remains a foil for their own self-identification or aggrandizement. Moving in and out of prison's social structures, these women at once participate in and observe them.

Writing fiction has allowed Sarrazin and Huré more flexibility of perspective than their autobiography-bound predecessors—that is, without the strict rendering of events found in memoirs, fiction's rearrangement has made for more active and better-defined heroines. For all writers, however, the context of prison has been overwhelmingly constrictive. If women's writing in general has presented heroines of limited autonomy, women's texts from prison have given concrete form to those obstacles to writing.

---

[43]See Giallombardo, *Society of Women*, and Freda Adler, *Sisters in Crime* (New York: McGraw-Hill, 1975). Both studies, especially the latter, are quite traditional, but they offer important details on internal organization in women's prisons.

3
Philosophical and Literary Tradition: The Intellectual Monster

The Imagination

My final premise is that women have always existed in a peculiar relation to thought and the expression of thought—to the philosophical underpinnings of culture and the tools and products that express them. Indeed, the whole French intellectual tradition, which is embedded in the relation of thought to its representation—language in its broadest sense—is now under attack by the most radical French feminist critics. Women like Hélène Cixous, Luce Irigaray, and Julia Kristeva share the realization that language not only is "always, implicitly or explicitly, a definition of human beings in the world,"[1] but also constitutes and perpetuates the power and powerlessness of human beings. Whichever way one chooses to dismantle the way we speak and write—from a psychoanalytic, linguistic, or materialist perspective—one must first posit that degrees and forms of articulation reflect the nature of one's presence in the world.

Of this immense area of inquiry, women prison writers in France have been affected by that part that has delimited women's intellectual capacities (their participation in thought)

---

[1] Raymond Williams, *Marxism and Literature* (Oxford: Oxford University Press, 1977), 21. For an excellent overview of contemporary French feminist analysis of women, language, and literature, see Elaine Marks, "Review Essay: Women and Literature in France," *Signs* 3, no. 4 (summer 1978): 832–42.

and circumscribed the manifestation of their capacities (their participation in expression). In France, particularly since Descartes, philosophy and literature have overlapped and have informed the same intellectual tradition. What has become known as the French "literary canon" was in effect a hardening of the exchange of thought and expression in the form of particular representative works. And women all along have been excluded on both ends. They have been excluded from the process of thinking and creating, through lack of education and therefore of the necessary creative tools, through social pressures against intellectual development, and through dismissal or segregation of ideas they have expressed. And they have been excluded from participating in the "highest" literary forms by a hierarchy of genres, by the opposition of the universal to the particular or the external to the internal, and by the definition of the "imaginative" versus the "practical."[2]

French philosophical and literary traditions have viewed man and woman oppositionally: she is the "other," the "non-Man," that is, all that man is not and thus potentially nonhuman, inhuman, or monstrous.[3] When she thinks and writes, she is even more unnatural and teratological. And when she expresses herself from a position of social and moral ignominy—like the women studied here—she is even more monstrous. After a brief perusal of the French philosophical underpinnings of the mind/body—and, from that, the male/female—dichotomy, I shall turn to its implications for imprisoned women authors.

The issue of mind and body has always informed European philosophical, literary, and medical thought. As both a physical and a metaphysical problem, study of the mind/body relation has at once shown little direct interest in women and yet has been profoundly detrimental to them. That is, the molders of great thoughts have spoken for man and only occasionally (e.g., the diversionary "Querelle des femmes," in which women's "nature" was debated) have entertained the possibility of other relations between individuals and the world. At the same time, prevailing definitions of the mind/body link, and specifically of

[2] See Williams, *Marxism and Literature,* part 1, chap. 3.
[3] Simone de Beauvoir's analysis of woman as "other," developed in *Le Deuxième Sexe,* is the classic text on the subject.

PHILOSOPHICAL AND LITERARY TRADITION

the imagination as a manifestation of that link, have been the basis for defining female normality and abnormality in the domain of creativity. It is clear that medical and psychological concepts also defined creativity and, at least in France, structured literary conventions. The nature of women's imaginative potential—and its manifestations in genre, theme, and diction—have been as strongly determined as women's biological and social identities.

In *L'Imagination,* Sartre traces the term "imagination," in its original ontological meaning of the representation of things, since French classicism.[4] While Sartre's purpose, to show that thinkers have always identified object with image, is not exactly relevant to this discussion, his treatment of images as belonging to the material, objective, corporeal realm and as interrelating with thought (the intellectual, spiritual, subjective realm) is relevant. Thus Descartes radically dissociated the body-mechanism from the soul-ideas, believing that pure thought (the domain of truth) could substitute itself for images (objects that act on our body via the senses and that incite error). Pascal more decisively called imagination "the madwoman in the attic" and "that proud power, which is reason's enemy and which delights in controlling and dominating it."[5] While Cartesians do not claim that the mind has a sex, they nonetheless associate disturbed reason ("passion") with "femininity": "Femininity is a mechanical [versus logical] mode of being."[6] Only Poulain de la Barre, espousing the same intellectual asexuality at which Descartes had hinted, spoke out in favor of women's equality.[7] One

---

[4]Jean-Paul Sartre, *Imagination: A Psychological Critique,* trans. Forrest Williams (Ann Arbor: University of Michigan Press, 1962). Translation of *L'Imagination* (Paris: Presses Universitaires de France, 1936).
[5]Cited in Henri Joly, *L'Imagination: Etude psychologique* (Paris: Hachette, 1883), 4–5. See also Joseph Chiari, *Realism and Imagination* (London: Barrie and Rockliff, 1960).
[6]Paul Hoffmann, "L'Héritage des lumières: Mythes et modèles de la féminité au xviiie siècle," *Romantisme: Mythes et représentations de la femme au xix^{e}siècle,* nos. 13–14 (1976), 9.
[7]See Poulain de la Barre, *De l'égalité des deux sexes* (1673). Earlier philosophy was not anthropocentric in its views of the imagination. Plato distrusted the imagination as "madness" in his ideas on "corrupt" art. The Middle Ages saw imagination as tied in with the superhuman, which could only be described, not explained.

can see the rising star of the "feminine-imaginary-abnormal-mad" cluster that permeated medical and literary ideas, a cluster of terms that has only recently been renamed in positive ways for women by such thinkers as Irigaray, Cixous, and Leclerc. Thus Le Brun's painting of the Marquise de Brinvilliers on her way to her execution portrays her as "blazing" and "illuminated" with the passion of her "bad instincts."[8] Her confessor, Edme Pirot, calls her the "madly submissive instrument" of her lover, Sainte-Croix.[9] He also quotes her as saying, "My imagination is filled with a thousand things that I must tell you and that I cannot say to others" (p. 110). Pirot clearly subscribes to the century's view of the imagination as shameful.

The eighteenth century saw a widening of the gap between women and reason, culminating in Rousseau's devastating blow to intellectual equality. Sartre, continuing his topos of the two modes of knowledge—image and thought—describes Leibniz's attempt to join the two by calling them both intellectual operations, differing only in clarity.[10] Leibniz's influence on Voltaire, coupled with the general preference of the *philosophes* for the rational, made for an intellectual equality between men and women in theory that was not carried into practice. According to Paul Hoffmann, both the *philosophes* and the influential medical theorists of the time projected an ideal of "coherence," of a union of the soul and the body that was identified with both a medical norm and a natural law. But the body remained the sticking point concerning women: for the medical establishment, the clear, empirical, and thus "factual" physiological differences between women and men made for different models of possible "coherence." From these different models came different expectations of behavior: "All forms of behavior are acceptable insofar as they conform to an organic male or female specificity."[11] Thus the dynamic between body and soul was associated with masculine and feminine "natures": "Femi-

[8]Frantz Funck-Brentano, *La Marquise de Brinvilliers, d'après de nouveaux documents* (n.d.), 389.
[9]Edme Pirot, *La Marquise de Brinvilliers: Récit de ses derniers moments* (Paris: A. Lemerre, 1883).
[10]Sartre, *Imagination*, 10–13.
[11]Hoffmann, "Héritage des lumières," 13.

ninity was therefore defined as a collection of desirable ends, to which particular organs contributed and corresponded" (p. 14). Also, says Hoffmann, "Woman's happiness was the reward for and the sign of her perfect conformance to the model [of femininity]" (p. 15). If one remembers that, according to Roussel, woman had a potential for being "tyrannized" by her corporeal senses—as opposed to man's possession of a cerebral or intellectual center of sensitivity—one understands why female "coherence" depended on the woman's uniform activity and immobility, not on the exercise of her powers.[12]

By their normative models, medical thinkers such as Stahl and Roussel exerted a countervailing force to the intellectual egalitarianism of the *philosophes*. For Roussel, the "imagination" was anything that diverted women from their biologically determined state of happiness; it encompassed all areas, mental and spiritual, beyond women's specific anatomy that were sources of illness, hysteria, and therefore unhappiness: "[Woman's] happiness is more secure than man's provided she has learned to protect herself from her imagination."[13] The Goncourts echoed this negative association between the imagination and women in their exaggerated and misogynist opinion of women's political power in the eighteenth century: "It is women's imagination that is seated at the [king's] council table. Women dictate internal and external politics according to the fantasy of their preferences, of their sympathies or antipathies."[14] For Roussel, the imagination gave rise in extreme cases to "hysteria," which was the manifestation of internal scission. By equating internal unity with rectitude, Roussel and others prepared the way for later correlations between hysteria and deviance.

Medical thinkers found their spiritual spokesman in Rousseau, who, at the same time as he departed from his contemporary *philosophes* succeeded ingeniously in providing a metaphysical dimension for medical atomistic and animistic models. building on prototypes of women's behavior and temperament,

[12]Pierre Roussel, *Système physique et moral de la femme, suivi du système physique et moral de l'homme*, 6th ed. (Paris: Caille et Ravier, 1813).
[13]Hoffmann, "Héritage des lumières," 8.
[14]Quoted in Léon Abensour, *La Femme et le féminisme avant la Révolution* (Paris: Ernest Leroux, 1923), 71.

Rousseau went a step further: he posited that woman's specific character, her "frailness," "the promptness of her reactions to internal or external impressions," her "extreme sensitivity to pleasure," were "the transcription onto the organic plane of a spiritual design."[15] Thus woman could, while remaining true to her specific nature, also assume the best of mythified human nature, which nature was neither historical, social, nor empirical. Woman, now accorded a metaphysical vocation, was sure to find happiness by simply letting her own sensibility reign.[16]

The profound effect Rousseau had on Madame Roland has been a frequent subject of study.[17] Her *Mémoires* strongly reaffirm her sensitivity, as she answers attacks that she was "denatured" by her crimes. Her detractors saw her as a "defeminized" monster: for them she had broken with her feminine "unity" by adopting the "virile" values of courage and firmness and by being intellectually and politically active. A newspaper of the period, *Le Moniteur universel*, describes Roland as follows:

> That woman Roland, who fancied herself a great mind with great plans, a philosopher, was in every way a monster. Her disdainful attitude, her proudly opinionated replies, her ironic gaiety... [prove] that she was devoid of any grief. And yet she was a mother, but she sacrificed nature.... The desire to be learned led her to forget the virtues of her sex and such forgetting, which is always dangerous, brought her to perish on the scaffold.[18]

Roland responds to such attacks in her memoirs. In general she counters accusations of "defeminization" by claiming that her life has been faithful to her heart and senses. The awakening of her senses is equated with the discovery of her body, both of which presumably are the true sources of knowledge for women. At the same time, Roland obeys Rousseau's spiri-

---

[15]Hoffmann, "Héritage des lumières," 15.
[16]Rousseau's ideas are most clearly articulated in *La Nouvelle Héloïse*, book 5 of *Emile*, and his *Lettre à d'Alembert*.
[17]See Gita May, *Madame Roland and the Age of Revolution* (New York: Columbia University Press, 1970), and Gita May, *De Jean-Jacques Rousseau à Madame Roland: Essai sur la sensibilité préromantique et révolutionnaire* (Geneva: Droz, 1964).
[18]*Le Moniteur universel*, 29 brumaire an 2, cited in Benoîte Groult, *Ainsi soit-elle* (Paris: Grasset, 1975), 46.

tual dictum by her modesty: her sensual awakening remains shrouded in mystery. For Roland, the senses also remain linked to the imagination. If, however, the former are autonomous, the latter, she claims, is subject to her control. Roland in effect contradicts Roussel's and Rousseau's ideas: she claims to have "captivated [her] imagination by studying."[19] Thus Roland's *Mémoires* reflect, in both theme and lexicon, the prevailing Rousseauesque concept of feminine happiness. It is therefore only partially valid to speak of them as echoes of Rousseau or as precursors of Chateaubriand. They are the response of a woman to the sex-related stigmas of "defeminization" and "denaturization."

The connection that has generally been made between Rousseau and the succeeding Romantic generation holds for the mind/body relation, though perhaps the Romantics held exaggerated expectations for these two instruments. In very general terms, one could say a dialectic developed in the early nineteenth century that functioned under the aegis of a highly spiritual, antimaterialist view of human potential: the Romantics, along with an exaltation of the senses and, ultimately, a desire for the infinite, experienced a consciousness of limits and a nostalgia for past happiness. Without Rousseau's idea of social responsibility to counterbalance the individual experience, however, this later generation pushed further in the direction of pure subjectivism. The subject's state of mind—as seen in the prevalent Romantic themes and topoi—was preeminent. Women, who never enjoyed a real role in the social order and whose so-called universal utility lay in their remaining true to their prescribed internal selves, were understandably drawn to Romantic predilections. The novels of Madame de Staël and George Sand, among others, manifest these preferences, which were also societally approved. The memoirs of the prisoner Marie Cappelle-Lafarge likewise essentially present her state of mind, with little reference to external details of prison life. The memoirs constitute a spiritual autobiography that traces the personal history of Cappelle-Lafarge's "virtues" and culminates

---

[19]Madame Roland, *Mémoires de Madame Roland* (Paris: Mercure de France, 1966), 346.

in her intense religious devotion. They also, with a weary nostalgia, describe the past as the only time of happiness, since the present brings the death of pleasure and desire.[20]

But if Cappelle-Lafarge stuck largely to the subjective arena to which women were by now consigned, she was also writing at the time when the decline of the Romantic vision met the rise of anti-individualistic and positivistic values. The imagination, so prized by Romantics, was simultaneously associated with 'perversion."[21] In a sense Cappelle-Lafarge, like George Sand, was caught in a void: both conformed to their appropriate philosophical and literary conventions even while those conventions were being devalued. Victor Brombert's study of "the Romantic prison" makes the point in a highly pertinent way: Brombert finds similarities of theme and imagery between Romantic literature and prison texts.[22] By bringing together the intensely individualistic Romantic predilection and the generalized societal views of imprisonment, Brombert also suggests the growing correlation at that time between self-absorption and the status of social pariah, a correlation later borne out by the *Poètes maudits*. From the Romantic period on, the "great criminal" increasingly was viewed as the quintessential individual. Concomitantly, the highly nonconformist and individualistic writer frequently was identified with the scandalous social transgressor. But women's relation to expressions of individualism and immorality was the opposite of men's. Thus both literary and social stigmas were behind judgments of works by Cappelle-Lafarge, Sand, and others.

One can further extend Brombert's comparison between the role of outcast as played by Romantics and the role of prisoner. Women like Cappelle-Lafarge were double exiles in that they played both roles. Cappelle-Lafarge's claim to individual identity in a climate of increasing positivistic typologizing—medical, sociological, and criminological—adds poignancy to

---

[20]Marie Cappelle (veuve Lafarge), *Mémoires écrits par elle-même*, 3d ed., 4 vols. (Brussels: Hauman, 1842–43).

[21]Camile Granier, *La Femme criminelle* (Paris: Octave Doin, 1906), 208.

[22]Victor Brombert, *The Romantic Prison: The French Tradition* (Princeton: Princeton University Press, 1978). The author's own translation of his *La Prison romantique: Essai sur l'imaginaire* (Paris: Librairie José Corti, 1975).

Philosophical and Literary Tradition

her cry from isolation and civil death. And yet, like Roland, Cappelle-Lafarge had no vocabulary with which to present herself other than the polarizing one that Romanticism and positivism made available: "passion/reason," "heart/mind," "moral turpitude," "moral madness," plus the well-delineated faculties of "heart," "mind," "memory," "will," and "madness" (this last term will soon reappear, with psychiatric baggage, as "hysteria," "suggestibility," "somnambulism," and "hallucination"). Like Roland, and because of literary convention that still deemed memoirs the most suitable genre for women, Cappelle-Lafarge disavowed her right to the intellect, since memoirs were supposed to deal with sentiment, not reason. Like Roland, Cappelle-Lafarge sought to counter her criminal stigma by reconstructing the past favorably and her writer stigma by rejecting authorial power and knowledge. And with the rise of positivism, Cappelle-Lafarge could not help subscribing to the woman writer's estate: the inferiority implied by her choice of emotion over logic.

The positivists imposed themselves by introducing rationalistic concepts of necessity into an otherwise unstable France (also by the sheer number of their works). As Raymond Williams puts it, for the positivists " 'the world' or 'reality' is categorically projected as the preexistent formation" to which all behavior is a response.[23] Extending Roussel's concept of the deterministic body-machine, in which the physiological explained the psychological, they added the rigor of a system with its own unchanging laws. The ideas of the leading positivistic theorists in fact differ only in vocabulary, not concept, and that is because the terms they used had an imprecise, floating applicability.

According to Sartre, these positivistic "associationists" adopted and expanded Taine's "analysis," the reduction of systems to their fixed elements: "empirical" analysis revealed the physical movements that produced psychic traits in a strictly determined relation. Sufficient "empirical" evidence of this kind allowed for a categorization, and thus universalization, of personality types. It took only one more step to arrive at the "synthesis" that followed the analysis. And so thinkers like Ribot, Joly, and the

---

[23]Williams, *Marxism and Literature*, 29.

Englishman Tuke all posited a necessary unity of body and mind, based on laws of association between biological and intellectual functions:

> The Principle of Unity: intellectual, emotional, and unconscious [factors] have value only if they are joined and have meaning only if they converge.[24]

> The body is an expression of the soul because the body cannot live without the soul any more than the soul can live without the body under the conditions of present-day life.[25]

> [This book is] a detailed analysis . . . of the effect intelligence and imagination can have on the human body functions. . . . The mind acts on the body.[26]

Pushing these ideas further, one arrives at the concept of "cerebral localizations," or specific sites in the brain where this synthesis takes place. Lombroso's anthropometrics crowned this exaggerated mechanization of temperament by locating "lesions" in the brains of criminals.

For the positivists, the ideals of order and harmony, rather than being grounded in the individual's physical or spiritual constitution, became synonymous with social and moral responsibility and antagonistic to the Romantic individual vision. It is no wonder this generation of positivists nearly killed the imagination: unlike "sensations," "ideas," and "images," the imagination could not be localized and observed. The other faculties, in contrast, were constantly being cataloged and defined:

> Feeling: being more or less keenly affected by impressions that external phenomena make on our bodily organs.[27]

> Knowing: being affected by external objects and examining the objects themselves in order to determine their relationship to other objects and to ourselves.[28]

---

[24]Th. Ribot, *Essai sur l'imagination créatrice* (Paris: Félix Alcan, 1900), 66.
[25]Joly, *Imagination*, 187.
[26]D. Hack Tuke, *Le Corps et l'esprit: Action du moral et de l'imagination sur le physique*, trans. from the English (Paris: J.–B. Ballière, 1886), xvii.
[27]Joly, *Imagination*, 5.
[28]Ibid.

Philosophical and Literary Tradition

Intelligence: a purely intellectual mental operation.[29]

Emotion: a genuine disturbance of the mind that also acts upon the body.[30]

Remembering: focusing one's attention on facts that have already affected one's senses but that no longer affect them.[31]

Madness: the state in which the intelligence is no longer in control of images. . . . Images dominate the mind.[32]

But the imagination came to be associated with disorders and illness. For Joly it was the source of visions and hallucinations that, although sometimes cause for joy as well as suffering, indicated malfunction of the reflective faculty. Ribot, attempting to be more systematic, further classified the imagination so as to make it manageable. He distinguished between "subjective" and "concrete" imagination, the former being an affective state based on unsatisfied needs and desires and the latter being the faculty of giving material form to that personal desire. Like Joly, Ribot saw the morbid potential of the imagination in its unrealized state as "passion" or "fixed emotion." Tuke goes beyond the others to introduce what he calls "psychotherapy" or, in 1886 terms, a moral cure for organic disorders. When the imagination acted on the body without the aid of the intelligence, treatment consisted of stimulating the will and providing regular work. Indeed, the creative signification of the imagination also persisted, and in the 1882 *Littré* one finds the following definition: "The faculty of inventing and conceiving joined with the talent to render conceptions vividly."[33] The imagination itself, however, was suspect without the passage from intuition to praxis—without realization. The implications of this view for women were visible then and continue to be

[29]Tuke, *Corps et l'esprit*, 83.
[30]Ibid.
[31]Joly, *Imagination*, 6.
[32]Ibid., 10. This vocabulary dominates Cappelle-Lafarge's texts, which combine Romantic self-portrait with positivistic terminology. The imprecise meaning of these terms, however, makes for contradiction and lack of clarity in some of her descriptions.
[33]Cited in Jules Guillemin, *Les Oeuvres d'imagination: Essai d'esthétique littéraire* (Warsaw: Joseph Sikorski, 1882), 17.

visible: materialization of the imagination, in any of the expressive forms Ribot lists (plastic, numerical, musical, scientific) requires technical skill as well as confidence that one can externalize one's desires.[34]

Add to this limiting of the imagination the late-nineteenth-century suspicion of nonexternal, nonverifiable experience, and the background for Marguerite Steinheil's *Mémoires* becomes clearer. Steinheil wrote when the identification between the imagination and illness was greatest, when imagining meant "making objects that have never existed live again or come to life for the first time."[35] The terms "hallucination," "somnambulism," "dream"—the key words in the prosecution's case against Steinheil—show that the "imagination" had come full circle back to its seventeenth-century meaning. The 1882 *Littré* further defines the word as a form of hallucination.[36] This definition of imagining, combined with the associationist connection between temperament types and behavior, placed women like Steinheil—women who erred and then attempted to give their own account of events—in the category of "paresthetics." These women, seen as suffering from the medical pathology of "paresthesia," or "disordered or perverted sensation" and "a hallucination of any of the senses" (*Oxford English Dictionary*), strongly recall Roussel's "sensory" victims. And so their "remembering" of events in any form was considered a rendering of what had never occurred.

Steinheil's imagination was called pure fantasy. If, as Claudine Herrmann contends, the search for self is the lot to which women have historically been consigned for lack of any self-acquired social identity,[37] and if madness and dreams have been seen as the progeny of that internal search, then one could say madness, ecstasy, and passion have been the only spiritual domain open to women. Steinheil fights against being seen as a "paresthetic," a "hallucinator," and a "liar" by repeat-

---

[34]See Suzanne Horer and Jeanne Socquet, *La Création étouffée* (Paris: Pierre Horay, 1973), for the way the imagination has been deformed by being classified and compartmentalized.
[35]L. Dugas, *L'Imagination* (Paris: Octave Doin, 1903), 3.
[36]Guillemin, *Oeuvres d'imagination*, 17.
[37]Claudine Herrmann, *Les Voleuses de langue* (Paris: des femmes, 1976), 77.

edly citing the observed events surrounding the murders of her husband and her mother. To prove her familiarity with worthy imaginative production, she describes her conversations with literary and artistic figures of her time: Bartholdi, Gounod, Bonnat, Massenet, Coppée, and Zola. Steinheil's vocabulary is essentially aesthetic: chunks of salon conversation and portraits of guests are rendered in great detail. The tone is strong, judgmental, and self-justifying. Steinheil wishes to make it clear that her senses, far from being perverted or disordered, are refined and verifiably accurate.[38]

Twentieth-century views of the imagination and of thought processes are so varied that it is difficult to describe intellectual climates. Whereas the eighteenth and, particularly, the nineteenth centuries offered entire lexicons based on moral and social frameworks—whence the recurrent use of the term "senses," then of "body," "soul," "heart," and "mind" as established entities—recent periods have not worked within such a structure. For women especially, religious and domestic topoi are visible in all the earlier prison works, as opposed to the male heroic and profane ones. For example, all the eighteenth- and nineteenth-century women studied here express religiousness in some form: Madame Roland, though espousing atheism, refers to God; Marie Cappelle-Lafarge becomes increasingly devout in prison; Marguerite Steinheil stresses her lay charity. Also, in the congregation-run jails in which they were imprisoned, virtually all these women were influenced far more by male priests than by the nuns.

With the exception of Anne Huré, women of our century no longer work within this explicitly Christian framework, though related themes remain. Modern women's relation to morality has changed, in part because, as Françoise d'Eaubonne claims, the twentieth century has accepted prison writers in general more easily than did preceding eras.[39] The development of the novel and the adoption of this genre by more and more women were equally instrumental in this change of moral and literary

[38]Marguerite Steinheil, *Mes mémoires* (Paris: Edmond Ramlot, n.d., app. 1911–12).
[39]Françoise d'Eaubonne, *Les Ecrivains en cage* (Paris: André Balland, 1970). Thus Genet, unlike Sade, is appreciated in his own lifetime.

framework. Women, freed from the direct self-presentation necessitated by confessional genres, were able to impose more form on their experience. And with fiction came the possibility of naming things, which represented a break with the earlier whole-cloth lexicons. This naming of experience can already be seen in Steinheil's personal aesthetic vocabulary. Anne Huré, writing in the 1960s, uses extremely abstract terms from her own Husserlian mysticism. Albertine Sarrazin, the clearest example of an author who names the prison experience, borrows "argot" and bad French from the "underworld" and exploits them to render her imprisonment.

The relegitimizing of the imagination after the rationalistic dichotomy between the physical (real, visible) and the metaphysical (spiritual) that characterized positivism was in large part due to Freud's opening up the psyche as a real world in its own right. Determinism moved from the physiological arena to the unconscious, thus releasing the imagination from its association with organic brain sites. For women, however, this freedom was only apparent: normality, still societally defined, simply shifted from a biological to a psychological base. If femininity was no longer physiologically verifiable, it was impalpable, incomprehensible, essential. The surrealists' and futurists' exploitation of this newly identified "eternal feminine" is but one example of the ongoing, externally imposed definition of the female imagination.

Philosophers of mystical bent, such as Husserl and Hoyack, articulated, in different ways, the experience of the profound spiritual reality that the imagination was now considered to be. Husserl, stressing intuition, spoke of the "privileged experience," or a form of transcendence involving pure thought.[40] Anne Huré, in her novels of the 1960s, adopts Husserl's ideas as she deals imaginatively with reality's limitations. Hoyack, a Christian mystic, gives insight into another powerful force operating on contemporary views of the imagination: modern physics. Energy and matter, no longer the deterministic machines of the nineteenth-century understanding, possessed incomprehensible complexity and were constantly interacting

---

[40] Sartre, *Imagination,* chap. 9.

Philosophical and Literary Tradition

with one another.[41] The intelligence—either as Hoyack's divine faculty or, more recently, as the Veraldis' "freshness of vision" that operates intricate new combinations in the physical and spiritual world—gained hegemony.[42] The sense of infinite possibility encouraged by discoveries in physics, while constantly countered by existential and materialist thought, nonetheless seconded the belief in imaginative conquest of all mysteries.

Yet one must question whether this sort of optimism applies to women's imaginative experience in this century. Patricia Meyer Spacks's point is well taken: a sense of increasing possibility in the society around her may in fact only intensify a woman's awareness of her own inadequacy.[43] Indeed, in writing at a time when the novel is supposed to be either a revolt (Camus) or a "correction" of the world according to our collective human experience (Malraux, H. Bruce Franklin, and others), women like Sarrazin and Huré continue to reveal their feelings of failure and inadequacy.

A novelist like Sarrazin clearly shows the incompatibility between contemporary belief in the power of the imagination and most women's experience with that potential power. Sarrazin's *Journal de prison 1959* and her novel *La Cavale*, though antithetical in focus, embrace the same attitude regarding the imagination: the idea that the intellect is powerful and autonomous but at the same time depends on its possessor for expression and realization.[44] In *La Cavale*, for example—the title is a metaphor for the mythic and dynamic "horse" that is her imagination—Sarrazin pits her bodily self (the prisoner) against her creative self (the author). "Whipping" her slumbering intellect into action is described as an enormous, nearly impossible task indicating her difficulty in undertaking imaginative activity. Likewise in her journal, whose subject is the pulse of her own mind, Sarrazin consistently evokes mental

[41]L. Hoyack, *L'Intelligence créatrice* (Paris: Bibliothèque Chacornac, 1931).
[42]Gabriel and Brigitte Veraldi, *Psychologie de la création* (Paris: Marabout, 1972).
[43]Patricia Meyer Spacks, *The Female Imagination* (New York: Knopf, 1975).
[44]Albertine Sarrazin, "Journal de prison: Le Times," *Le Passe-peine: 1949–1967* (Paris: Julliard, 1976), 102–68, and Albertine Sarrazin, *La Cavale* (Paris: J.-J. Pauvert, 1965); also published as *The Runaway*, trans. Charles Lam Markmann (New York: Grove Press, 1967).

effort as necessitating Cornelian discipline and the "grasping" or "seizing" of her faculties. There is something "unnatural"—against her nature, she says—about her exercise of thought. Anne Huré reveals similar difficulty in spurring the imagination, though she is less explicit than Sarrazin. In her novel *En prison,* Huré's central character, Noëlle, displays this difficulty in the form of stoicism.[45] She is faced with a series of judicial setbacks that test her intellectual resilience and her spiritual endurance. As with Sarrazin, an optimistic extension of her imaginative powers is not Huré's way of dealing with the limitations of reality.

The Literary and Critical Canon

The question of the nature and value of the imagination is unresolvable. Whatever its accepted meaning at a particular time—the reproduction of images; the evocation and arrangement of memories; the creation of new combinations; intuition; a fake perception of a purely fictive object; or fantasy—the imagination manifests itself in certain forms. Its expression will be affected by conventions, diction, themes. Even those who posited a totally autonomous and transcendent imagination, such as the symbolists and the surrealists, addressed considerations of form, if only to explode them. Women writing from prison must be viewed in their literary-historical context as it intersects with the domain of "prison literature."

The way women have historically viewed and taken hold of their experience has in large part accounted for their literary representations of it. Indeed, judgments of women's imaginative capacities have been crucial in prescribing the subjects and forms most suitable to their expression. There has also, however, been give and take between those externally imposed conventions and the private impulses of women. I shall explore two aspects of the literary production of imprisoned women: first, the traditional male prison canon and the ways its well-

[45] Anne Huré, *En prison* (Paris: Julliard, 1963).

springs and characteristics are alien to women; then the common features that unite women's texts into a distinct female prison tradition.

Sartre has called all writers "white criminals" since, by evoking another (whether different or parallel) world in their work, they engage in a form of social opposition. Sartre's thesis embodies an extremely activist and optimistic view of writing, since not all texts have such prophetic importance. The well-known male writers from prison, however, have in fact realized the condition of Sartre's "white criminal": they present, with varying degrees of defiance, their versions of "real life," which to them is absent from the society they live in. They have in common a stance of refusal arising from their dialectic with the powers and values of their times. They share a "refusal to integrate themselves" into the intra- and extramural worlds they inhabit; and accompanying that rejection is a necessary shared illumination of a corrected society.[46]

This active stance and the entire tradition of defiant individualism in male literature are best treated in Camus's *L'Homme révolté*.[47] Camus distinguishes between the "literature of consent" and the "literature of rebellion," the former coinciding with ancient and classical eras, the latter with modern times (p. 258). The novel, a relatively modern literary occurrence, is the most adequate expression of revolt, since it allows for "the construction of a substitute universe" (p. 255) and creates the unity our world lacks. And the sources of this creative exigency are, for Camus, the individual's inexhaustible need to find the appropriate imaginative "formulas" (p. 262).

Many theories have been advanced for this common indignation among male prison writers. For some the literal narrowing of physical space makes for "a hardening and a supreme density" of lucidity,[48] like a reverse pathetic fallacy. Such exceptional rarefication of the prisoner's universe makes for a clear, sure, and directed attack on the social order. For others prison

---

[46] D'Eaubonne, *Ecrivains en cage*, 18.
[47] Albert Camus, *L'Homme révolté* (Paris: Gallimard, 1951). Also published as *The Rebel: An Essay on Man in Revolt*, trans. Anthony Bower (New York: Knopf, 1967).
[48] D'Eaubonne, *Ecrivains en cage*, 11.

is an example of a "hostile space," completely divorced from the "felicitous space" of our intimate being.[49] Thus no imaginative integration of thoughts, dreams, and memories can arise from prison's nonprotective, nonintimate cell: the "corner" is "a symbol of solitude . . . the germ of a room, or of a house" and becomes "a negation of the Universe."[50] And from that negation comes contestation. Still others see prison as a locus of metaphors,[51] because of the long association of prison cells with monks' cells, and thus confinement fosters spiritual questioning. Likewise, in such a "poeticized" space as prison, the prisoner can glorify his own Promethean revolt by inverting the roles of prison and society and of the outlaw and the hero (Brombert). Still others see prison writers as marking a period of social instability and transition. That is, they contest because they anticipate change, and their transgressions will be legitimized by the succeeding generation. Whatever the source of their directed indignation, male prison writers move from the center to the periphery, from the self to the walls and then to the world.

Further reinforcing this commonality of nonconformity and contestation in men's texts are their intertextual resemblances of intention and theme. A brief review of canonical male prison writers will point up those resemblances and reveal how paradoxically incomplete and self-concerned the male vision really is.

The first author of the French prison canon, François Villon, wrote from the context of the fifteenth century. His works reveal many of the qualities prized in great prison literature. The poet was jailed at various times for robbery, murder, and sacrilege. Finally condemned to hang in 1463 after torture, confinements, and a royal pardon, he once again escaped death when his sentence was commuted to banishment.

Portions of his last work, *Le Grand Testament,* were written in prison and, in their deepened anger and satire, contrast with his earlier *Petit Testament.* Most striking in *Le Grand Testament*

---

[49]Gaston Bachelard, *The Poetics of Space,* trans. Maria Jolas (New York: Orion Press, 1964) xxxi–xxxii. Translation of *La Poétique de l'espace* (Paris: Presses Universitaires de France, 1958).
[50]Ibid., 136.
[51]Brombert, *Romantic Prison.*

are its immediacy, its rawness of imagery, its "ready word."[52] Villon makes detailed and virulent judgments of his time through, among other devices, vulgar language ("Quatrain"), slang, mockery of his condemners ("Question au clerc du guichet"), and vivid images of death in life ("Ballade des pendus"). The "Ballade des pendus" is also an example of Villon's use of the poetic device of *enjambements* to express irony. What comes through most strongly in Villon's poems is a direct sense of adventure and the "picturesque,"—that is, the uncertainties and perils that marked both his own shady "milieu" and French society in general. Villon's life of wandering and his experience with death, cold, starvation, and fear supplied the facts of his poetry; they gave focus to the more widespread concerns of his society—family, church, poverty, war, and death.

Ascribing motives to Villon, particularly in view of the obscurity of his short life, is at best speculative. When, for example, he asks himself "Why are you miserable? —Because of my miseries,"[53] the source could be some vice in himself or fate impinging from without. Nonetheless, because Villon was well enough born, was educated, and thus enjoyed a partial clerical status, his life as an outlaw appears to be a chosen one. He possessed

> that spontaneous, unshakable, incorrigible maladjustment . . . that inborn revolt, that incoercible refusal to be in the world. . . . He was careful to satisfy his needs and to preserve his freedom, but in a way that went *against* society, rather than one that was dependent on it.[54]

Through infamy, Villon became a legend in his time; in the historical context of "a moving combination of individual liberties, corporative powers, the crushing of the weak, and a contestation of the strong," he was the transcendent hero.[55] And by

---

[52]William Carlos Williams, in his preface to *The Complete Works of François Villon* (New York: Bantam, 1964), xiv.

[53]François Villon, "The Debate between Villon and His Heart" ("Le débat de Villon et son cuer"), in *The Poems of François Villon*, trans. Galway Kinnell (Boston: Houghton Mifflin, 1977), 201.

[54]D'Eaubonne, *Ecrivains en cage*, 37–39; emphasis in original.

[55]Ibid., 35.

evoking himself in his poems either as a criminal already on the margin of society or as a penitent speaking from the other side of death, Villon assumes his identity and turns to judge his era. André Chénier, though a "political" prisoner in terms of historical events, was, like Madame Roland, guilty more by his social condition than by his acts. He was arrested without a warrant, sent to Saint-Lazare for four months, and beheaded without trial in 1794. If he is at the other end of the poetic spectrum from Villon in his self-conscious search for effect, he nonetheless continues Villon's picturesque, heroic, and satirical responses to imprisonment. For, in spite of essential historical differences and changes in outlook, "the experience of being imprisoned does always have some common features, no matter what the particular historical or individual situation."[56] And those common features, coupled with certain notions of a prison author's "male and profound turn of mind,"[57] have helped codify anger and correction as the authentic reactions.

Chénier wrote *Les Iambes* in prison. He had already written a preface to a play, *Les Initiés,* in which the condemnation of his contemporaries, the special moral vocabulary, and the self-glorification he was soon to intensify are already visible:

> This nation, which in the late eighteenth century produced so many marvels of stupidity and baseness, also produced a small number of men who abandoned neither their reason nor their conscience; witnesses to the triumph of vice, these men remained faithful to the truth. . . . And one A. C. was one of the five or six individuals whom neither the general chaos, greed, nor fear could make bow down before the reigning assassins.[58]

Chénier's best-known poems reveal certain affinities with those of Villon. "Ode: La Jeune captive," in which a female fellow prisoner at Saint-Lazare "speaks" while the poet "records," expresses Chénier's belief in his own transcendence. She is given his qualities:

[56]H. Bruce Franklin, *The Victim as Criminal and Artist: Literature from the American Prison* (New York: Oxford University Press, 1978), 235–36.
[57]Judgment of Chénier by a contemporary, cited in André Chénier, *Poésies choisies* (Paris: Cl. Larousse, 1934), 79.
[58]This fragment appears in Chénier, *Poésies choisies,* 71.

Philosophical and Literary Tradition

> I have wings of hope:
> Having escaped from the cruel bird catcher's nets
> Philomela, livelier and happier,
> Sings and soars toward heaven's open fields.[59]

Though the ode is full of artifice and gallantry, the poet's sense of pride and his confidence in his literary immortality—which, of course, Chénier as "recorder" in the poem guarantees—resound as strongly as Villon's call to an indulgent posterity. The poem "Comme un dernier rayon" is Chénier's strongest assertion of his glory, moral and poetic. The subject of his poem is in fact his "lyre": at first the last rays of his dying day, then his faithful companion at death, and finally his weapon for eternal moral victory, Chénier's poetry conquers "the baseness" and "pretense" of his generation. His pen wages a heroic battle:

> Justice, Truth, if my hand, my lips,
> My most secret thoughts
> Have never knit your fierce brow. . . .
> Then save me, save an arm that
> Hurls your thunderbolts, a lover who avenges you. . . .
> Oh my precious treasure,
> My pen! Spleen, bile, and horror, these are
>   the gods of my life![60]

Moreover, Chénier's verse "transports him" "far from his suffering." There is in the general form of Chénier's works a certain flexibility, a dislocation of rhythm that suggests a formal as well as a thematic break with constraints. With satire and indignation, he exploits France's classical heritage only to throw it in the face of his forgetful, barbaric contemporaries.

The paroxysm of imaginative expansion and hyperbole from the prison is evident in the works of the Marquis de Sade. Like Villon and, even more so, Genet, Sade embraced scandal as a source of knowledge; and like Villon and Genet Sade chose to live and to write in aggressive and angry counterpoint to ac-

---

[59]André Chénier, *Oeuvres poétiques de André Chénier*, vol. 2 (Paris: Garnier Frères, 1889), 283.
[60]Ibid., 302–3.

cepted morality. Sade, of all the prison canon writers, accumulated the most time in prison: thirty years, between 1763 and 1814, for "exaggerated licentiousness" and blasphemy, assault, attempted poisoning, sodomy, and obscene writing. His last confinement, at Charenton, was in fact institutionalization for the "mental derangement" that previous imprisonments had triggered.

Sade's complementary novels, *Justine* and *Juliette*, only recently rehabilitated by the French critical establishment,[61] represent imaginative revolt in its purest form. These works rebel against prison not only by their intolerably immoral subject matter, but also by their sheer epic proportions. In response to confinement and solitude, Sade created a massive universe: it comprises frequently repeated scenes and words, a huge number of characters, and exaggerated horrors. And yet, to be sure his anger would find its target amid this mass of scenes and characters, Sade was careful to tighten and focus his thought: he does so through documentation of the perversion he, via his orators, describes and through the philosophical structure he erects by means of repetition and example. So rigorous was Sade in carrying through the implications of his revolt that, as Genet did later, he condemned any efforts to reform the harshness of prison: "Sade spoke ironically and angrily against the prison reformers Pinel and Esquirol, who sought to separate sick individuals from delinquents and to do away with the troublemakers' chains." For Sade such efforts were merely a further manifestation of "the enormous mystification that was the belief in [human] improvement brought by two thousand years of Christianity."[62] It is doubtless because Sade, in his writing, challenged the entire moral framework of his time that his lived experience of crime and sin seems mild compared with the events he created in his fiction.

Paul Verlaine, though not considered primarily a prison writer, was jailed twice—for firing shots at Rimbaud in 1873 and for attempting to kill his mother in 1885. As a criminal

---

[61]See Groult, *Ainsi soit-elle*, for a discussion of Sade's rehabilitation by the French critical establishment (Leiris, Barthes, and others).
[62]D'Eaubonne, *Ecrivains en cage*, 81, 87.

Philosophical and Literary Tradition

Verlaine sought, in an attenuated way, the transcendence of circumstance he explicitly admired in Villon and Sade:

> I idolize François Villon
> But what must I do to be him?[63]
>
> Prince, oh great Marquis de Sade,
> A smile for your shoot that sprouts
> Proudly behind the stockade fence.[64]

Prison appears to have been beneficial to Verlaine in that it enabled him to write a good deal. Unlike the ancestors he admired, however, Verlaine never adopted a consistent stance in relation to society. Therefore, unlike Villon, Sade, and to some degree Chénier, he did not sustain anger or a corrective vision toward his time. If prison was central to the terms and shape of the other authors' revolt, for Verlaine it was essentially a place of containment and separation from the world.

Verlaine pushed in all directions from his cell at de Mons prison in Belgium. His famous "Art Poétique" of 1874 makes no direct reference to the situation in which he wrote, but its call for a poetics based on nuance, music, and the range of sensations lying between dream and reality is a brilliant flourish of invention. And renovation of poetic sounds and rhythms is indeed a kind of correction of the aesthetic world Verlaine knew. His wish for "winged things," while shared by Rimbaud and other of his contemporaries, takes on deeper meaning from a prison cell. And Verlaine's best-known prison poem, "Le Ciel est, par-dessus le toit," further reflects the will to escape, to take flight, via the banal natural imagery common to prison poetry:

> The sky above the roof
> is so blue, so calm,
> . . . .
> Dear God, dear God, life is there,
> Tranquil and sweet.

[63]Paul Verlaine, "Triolets," in *Oeuvres poétiques complètes* (Paris: Gallimard-Pléiade, 1954), 10.
[64]Verlaine, "Ballade de la mauvaise réputation," in *Oeuvres poétiques*, 381.

IMAGINATION IN CONFINEMENT

Harking to Villon's gentle self-reproach for his misfortunes, Verlaine ends his poem:

> What have you done, you there
>   who cries always
> Tell me, what have you done, you there,
>   with your youth?[65]

Thought not as ambiguous as Villon's attribution of his suffering to his "miseries," Verlaine's query about his lost youth to some extent asks society to answer for his misfortunes.

The poem "Autre" is explicitly about prison. Written in tetrasyllabic verse with regular alternating rhyme, "Autre" evokes the monotony of the prisoners' daily walk to the courtyard:

> There they go! Their poor shoes
> Make a noise that is sharp
> And humiliated
> Cigarettes in their mouths
> Not a word, or else it's the dungeon,
> not a sigh
> It's so hot
> You think you're going to die.
> . . . .
> Let's go, my brothers, good old thieves
> Sweet vagabonds,
> Budding rogues,
> My dear good ones,
> Let's smoke philosophically,
> Let's walk
> It's good to do nothing.[66]

Though reminiscent of Wilde's "Ballad of Reading Gaol," Verlaine's poem has none of its horror. Yet it evokes the penal "fraternity" that will be crucial for modern male prison writers—Genet, Boudard, Serge—a fraternity intent on the noble and the "philosophical." And philosophical thoughts will give way to apparent religious conversion in *Sagesse*. Verlaine

---

[65]Verlaine, *Oeuvres poétiques*, 184.
[66]Ibid., 356.

the sinner transcends his contrition and feels he is "chosen" to love God: "I feel the ecstasy and the terror of having been chosen" . . . "and, trembling, I breathe in [God's voice] / —Poor soul, that *is* what you are searching for."[67] That Verlaine aspires to sainthood is already visible in earlier *Sagesse* poems, and his ascension to the spiritual realm is relatively unimpeded. Like Villon, though with far more audacity, Verlaine looks both across and down at his contemporaries from an exile of his own choosing.

The full legitimizing of the criminal-author—a legitimizing that was previously controversial and almost always posthumous—came in this century with the appearance of Jean Genet. For the first time the extremes of criminal identification (by the author) and establishment acceptance and admiration (by critics) met. What is more, Genet's literary and personal importance have made for a retrospective appreciation of past criminal authors and a hardening of criteria for the prison canon in relation to Genet's qualities. The symbolic act that crowned Genet's designation as ultimate criminal and artist of evil was his official pardon and virtual guarantee of lasting freedom, thanks to the pressure brought by Sartre, Cocteau, and other established writers. Genet's spiritualization of antisocial values is considered the quintessence of revolt; his complete integration of his criminal identity is seen as the mark of his "sainthood."[68]

I do not intend to challenge judgments of Genet's extraordinary work—as poetry, as imagistic beauty, his plays and novels are remarkable. His prison texts, however (only his novels and poems were written in prison), embody to an extreme the "virile" qualities prized in the literature of outcasts, qualities that, for all their power, are not universal. Genet's "complete refusal to complain and to be moved to pity"[69] is embodied in his ascetic, solitary heroes, true "tough guys." These criminal heroes, unable to satisfy their infinite spiritual appetites, first

---

[67]Verlaine, "Mon Dieu m'a dit," in *Oeuvres complètes*, 176.
[68]It would be fruitless to paraphrase Sartre's monument, *Saint Genet, comédien et martyr*. For the best explanation of Genet's metaphysics of evil and its debouching on absolute goodness, see this definitive study.
[69]D'Eaubonne, *Ecrivains en cage*, 199.

transgress in our world, then renounce their search for satisfaction in the face of the absolute nothingness to which their search leads.

Genet's own life until the 1940s and 1950s was spent primarily in the youth colonies at Fontevrault and Mettray and at the prisons of la Santé, Tourelles, and Fresnes. Between imprisonments, he committed the robberies and vagabondage that led to his arrests. So little is known about Genet's life that all efforts to "explain" the criminal—using criminological theories about self-fulfilling prophecy and the destructive effects of juvenile incarceration—have given way to existential mystification: Genet "willed" himself into deserving the name "thief" by which society had initially designated him.[70] This paucity of biographical information, coupled with insufficient explanations for his mastery of French, have further intensified the heroic glorification of Genet as man and as writer.

Miracle de la rose, written from Tourelles prison, describes Mettray and Fontevrault through Genet's embellishment of prison.[71] *Notre-Dame des fleurs,* written from Fresnes, recounts the "secret glory" and the "future glory" of several murderers, of whom Genet says: "It is in honor of their crimes that I am writing my book."[72] Divine, whose martyrdom we follow through the novel, chooses self-destruction after much metaphysical searching. The identification between heaven and nothingness, visible in all Genet's works, is complete. In all his works there is confusion between murderers and saints, hell and heaven, evil and good; like Sade, Genet mourns the reform or closing of prisons as the loss of spawning grounds for society's best enemies. So strong is Genet's challenge to society that he opts to destroy it verbally: he chooses writing to convey his hate, since conventional weapons are too localized and limited. Genet's works, enormous in their power and unlimited in duration, are incandescent. His thoughts, though

---

[70]This theory is likewise developed in Sartre's *Saint Genet.*
[71]Jean Genet, *Miracle de la rose* (Paris: Gallimard, 1951). Also published as *Miracle of the Rose,* trans. Bernard Frechtman (New York: Grove Press, 1966).
[72]Jean Genet, *Our Lady of the Flowers,* trans. Bernard Frechtman (New York: Grove Press, 1963), 61. Translation of *Notre-Dame des fleurs* (Lyons: L'Arbalète, 1943).

Philosophical and Literary Tradition

thoroughly autobiographical in source, escape from prison with the timelessness and freedom of a dream.

Genet resembles all his "virile" ancestors in some way: most directly Sade, for the strong relation between his internment and his writing and, in particular, for the pleasure in abjection he describes; Villon, for his choice of marginality as the only path to satisfaction; Chénier, for his judgment of society as barbarous and for the "classicism" of his style; and Verlaine, for his belief in the superior knowledge provided by homoerotic experience. Genet comprises all aspects of the collective "penal fraternity" in his desire to express utter indignation in the purest and most lethal form. Genet evokes most clearly his own verbal rebellion in his introduction to George Jackson's *Soledad Brother:* prison writers, "starting in search of themselves from that ignominy demanded by social repression, ... discover common ground in the audacity of their undertaking, in the rigor and accuracy of their ideas and their visions."[73] Also, says Genet of written revolutionary enterprise, "We must reject nothing of what makes poetic exaltation possible. If certain details of this work seem immoral to you, it is because the work as a whole denies your morality, because poetry contains both the possibility of a revolutionary morality and what appears to contradict it" (p. 7).

If, with Genet's works, prison writing has reached the point of at once being what it appears to be and subverting that appearance, then canon criteria have reached their ultimate solipsism. This solipsism, by which the material aspects of the prison experience are absorbed into and transcended by the author's spiritual response, is one example of the hierarchy that has underlain all judgments of literature. Prison works, like literature in general, have been viewed through an ideological prism that dichotomizes the spiritual and the material, then sees the spiritual as governing.[74] What is more, the spiritual has been made synonymous with "universal." Women's ex-

---

[73] Jean Genet, "Introduction" to George Jackson, *Soledad Brother: The Prison Letters of George Jackson* (New York: Bantam, 1970; first pub. Coward McCann, 1970), 2.
[74] See Julia Kristeva, "Pratique signifiante et mode de production," in *La Traversée des signes*, ed. Julia Kristeva et al. (Paris: Seuil, 1975), 11–30.

clusion from the cultural processes that inculcate dominance—through acquisition of knowledge and language—is reflected in their preoccupations and in their writing. And judgments of that writing, whether explicit or implicit, have deemed women's viewpoint "particular" and the substance of their writing "domestic" and "quotidian."

The Female Tradition

The indignation common to male prison texts informs that particular tradition. But corrective anger alone has been used to define all prison literature; women's texts, from that perspective, are not commensurable. For the various sources attributed to male anger and correction are irrelevant to most women's lives and texts: rather than engage in an overt dialectic with the values of their times, women, who have never created those values, covertly subvert and contest them; instead of seeking to give wholeness to an incoherent world, women search within themselves for unity; and, far from attempting to conquer hostile space by appropriating it, women generally observe and respect it. Indirection and coded contestation, a search for self, and an acknowledgement of surroundings characterize women's prison writing.

Like those of the male authors, the crimes committed by these women writers vary. Women's texts are joined not by the particular acts of which the authors are accused, but by a commonality of absorption with self. And though women's works are marked by the social and literary influences of their times, they also have strong intertextual ties. In other words, each text serves as a gauge of a portion of cultural history even while the tradition of female prison writing as a whole transcends the specifics of time, place, and crime.

The relation of the female prison tradition to the male tradition is in most ways one of divergence. First, in terms of literary history, one sees how the two traditions split and how male texts gained hegemony, as they did in literature in general. The link between all prison writing and literary forms is the autobiographical narrative, which H. Bruce Franklin traces to the early confessions of real and fictional criminals.[75] It is during this early period of the confessional mode of storytelling that there is the most overlap between men's and women's prison texts. Four factors, however, hinder our ability to compile and compare women's and men's early prison writing: the frequent anonymity of the writers; the predominantly oral transmission of the first stories; the high degree of general illiteracy; and the small number of women in confinement. Nevertheless, early documents such as the Bastille archives show similarity of purpose (confession of sins) and form (often verse) in men's and women's texts.[76] Since the goal of these narratives was initially to reform the listening public, the theme of maternal love in poems that women addressed to their children made them diverge from poems by men. Women showed the dangers of straying from the family model. Another divergence is reflected in Villon's poems, where vivid and unprocessed imagery describes a direct encounter with the world. Although the supernatural still pervades Villon's work, reducing the extent of human activity, one already sees the adventurous spirit that will inform the "literature of *mendiants*" and picaresque narratives by men.

The picaresque tale, whether or not told by a criminal narrator, was the first "novelistic" form and marked the alienation of women from this genre. The life of the self-made man, whose adventures now entertained as much as they reformed the listener, deviated from the experience of women. Since the novelistic genre combined reality and fiction, women were put in a no-win situation in representing what for them was reality: either conform to the genres that convincingly translated their reality or else be doomed to eccentrism or irony by adopting a false authority on their experience. Given the crimes women were most likely to commit and be punished for—quotidian, banal, domestic ones—it was impossible for them to cast themselves in the heroic mold. Thus women novelists like Madame de Tencin, imprisoned for three months after her lover, La Fres-

[75]Franklin, *Victim*, chaps. 1 and 4.
[76]See Frantz Funck-Brentano, *Légendes et archives de la Bastille* (Paris: Hachette, 1902).

nais, killed himself in her salon, triumphed as a writer when her work was most removed from her own life—for example, in the *Mémoires du Comte de Comminges*, which, furthermore, were published anonymously.[77] Tencin's own knowledge of prison is transformed into an episode in the count's life. In this novel cum memoirs, the count is locked in a tower because he refuses to marry the woman his father has chosen. The novel's conflict between religion and love is in fact a common women's theme, transposed to a male protagonist. Likewise, in *Le Siège de Calais* (in *Oeuvres*), Monsieur de Chalons is imprisoned by a jealous Edward II of England. Once again the protagonist is given the internal agitation and contradiction normally reserved for female characters. The only vestige of Tencin's own imprisonment in the *Mémoires* is the count's inner response to his situation—the literal domination by his father as viewed from within the character, or from Tencin's own feelings. Madame de Staal-Delaunay's *Mémoires*,[78] a work judged to be "fine," "small," and "light" by her contemporaries, is equally distant from the heroic mold in confessional literature.[79] Sainte-Beuve claimed the memoirs conformed, in genre and tone, to those "suitable to women."[80] Judgments of Staal-Delaunay's text echo perfectly Roussel's treatise on women's sensibility: critics find in her memoirs a "natural" rendering of the author's lively sensory response to external objects.[81]

The eighteenth century was, paradoxically, a time of literary, if not actual, concern with sexual conflicts, at least on the part of certain *philosophes*. Diderot's *La Religieuse*, which treats the forced confinement of women in convents, paints a horrible social reality. Likewise, though with less horror, Montesquieu's *Lettres persanes* evokes the confinement of women through the exotic metaphor of the harem. Women writers in general were

[77]La Marquise de Tencin, "Les Mémoires du Comte de Comminges" (1735), in *Oeuvres de Mesdames de Fontaines et de Tencin* (Paris: Garnier, n.d.), 117ff.
[78]Madame de Staal (Madame Delaunay), "Mémoires de Madame de Staal, écrits par elle-même," in *Oeuvres* 1:–339 (Paris: Renouard, 1821).
[79]Voltaire and Fontenelle, cited in "Introduction" to Staal-Delaunay's *Une Idylle à la Bastille* (Paris: Bibliothèque Historique Mondiale, 1958), 4.
[80]Portrait cited in "Introduction to Staal-Delaunay," *Idylle*, 5.
[81]See Frantz Funck-Brentano's "Preface" to Staal-Delaunay's *Mémoires* (Paris: Firmin-Didot, 1928), 2–16.

much more prudent and resigned in the kinds of conflicts they depicted.[82] Rather than presenting women as total victims, like Diderot's Sister Suzanne, they conformed to moralizing and noncontestatory narrative structures: "A single mistake, a single weakening of her defenses brought [a woman] the punishment of total unhappiness, as if all of time were suspended just at those moments where she happened to be, moments that seemed located on the path of the great forces that commanded the human condition."[83] Heroines like Tencin's either were extremely strong or were mediocre—in which case they erred and were punished. In opposition to the upward movement found in most men's texts— movement toward spiritual enlightenment or social liberation—the moral and social "fall" that characterizes most women's texts does not reflect the same vision. This fatalistic mode in women's plots ran counter to the heroism that informed men's stories.

Women's prison texts of the eighteenth century are a special case of female writing of the time. Tencin's novels, as well as the memoirs and journals of Roland, Duras, Staal-Delaunay, and others, were cautious in their narrative structures. For these women, however, the imminent and dreaded "single mistake" that could spell their downfall had in fact occurred. They had already lived out a social "fall," and their literary task was not to project the consequences of their "mistake" but to return to its origins. For that reason most women's prison texts of that period recount an initial "flaw" or error in judgment that ran its fatal course. This retrospective and self-reflective mode, common to women's prison texts in general, in part explains why exploration, not defiance, informs the female tradition.

Certainly other forces have made it difficult for imprisoned women to turn their anger outward: the general feminist tradition in literature, which is essentially reformist; literary conventions, which were gender-specific in designating suitability and propriety; the "complex of the woman of letters," which undermined fragile success by its conservative nature, as seen, for

---

[82]See Nancy K. Miller, "Female Sexuality and Narrative Structure in 'La Nouvelle Héloïse' and 'Les Liaisons dangereuses,'" *Signs* 1, no. 3 (Spring 1976): 609–38.
[83]Hoffmann, "Héritage des lumières," 7.

example, in women's shying away from poetry as its formal constraints became more demanding; forced intimacy with the self, which resulted from societal expectations; and the simple nature of the crimes women usually committed, which were related to poverty and survival and were hardly adventurous or dramatic. Papillon's and Belbenoit's daring exploits on Devil's Island stemmed from a direct knowledge of free movement and quest in outer reality. But even when in modern times imprisoned women used the new possibilities for freedom that fiction opened to them, they continued to limit their own transcendence. Their quest for authenticity, for intimate truth, for an anterior identity, betrays their ongoing refusal to contest the external world.

There are very few French prison texts, men's or women's, from the nineteenth century, either because they were destroyed or, more likely, because of the pressures on potential authors. In a century that saw the rise of the novel and the appearance of some important women authors, there were also countervailing forces that stifled expression by society's outcasts. All aspects of the prisoner's life and activities were thoroughly controlled because prison and punishment were, for the first time, taken so seriously. Self-expression—oral or written—was considered detrimental to the process of repentance and rehabilitation that imprisonment was expected to promote. Only silence and isolation could occasion reflection, realization, and remorse. Further, as Foucault documents, physical, not mental labor promised eventual reform of the criminal: optimistic reformers saw manual work as a guarantee of the prisoner's subsequent social reintegration; the real economic and political powers understood the value of this cheap labor resource.[84] Finally, bourgeois fear that the poor would undertake self-improvement beyond their basic needs made cultivation of the mind suspect. Since most prisoners were poor and remained relatively uneducated until midcentury, mental expression was difficult as well as discouraged.

Two other characteristics of the literary climate of the time

---

[84]Michel Foucault, *Surveiller et punir: Naissance de la prison* (Paris: Gallimard, 1975). Also published as *Discipline and Punish: The Birth of the Prison*, trans. Alan Sheridan (New York: Pantheon, 1977).

Philosophical and Literary Tradition

may well have sapped the creative potential of would-be writers in prison. First, as Victor Brombert shows persuasively in *La Prison romantique,* authors of Romantic persuasion developed an image of themselves as "outcasts" or "prisoners" of society. Thus their writing is marked by images of cells and captivity as well as by themes of solitude, deformed time, fatality, and mythification of nature, among others. Literal and factual representations of these themes and images by real prisoners, had they appeared, might well have been devalued for lacking a spiritual dimension as it existed in the works of "free" authors.

"Free" authors also exploited the experience of real captives—exclusively male ones—in their glorification of the "great criminal," the hero of a culture parallel to legitimate bourgeois society. Balzac's Vautrin is the clearest example of this incarnation of pure, unfettered criminal energy who achieves stature and respect in his milieu. The legendary Lacenaire was the ennobled descendent of previous prison hero-writers. Reading about such superhuman masculine embodiments of greatness and intelligence can hardly have encouraged prisoners of either sex to write about their own experience.

As in the preceding generations, women's prison literature of the nineteenth century—and the sample is very small—is a special case of women's writing in general. Marie Cappelle-Lafarge shared with most noncriminal female authors a "modesty complex" that made her deny any pretensions to authorship. Like those of her few women contemporaries who wrote, her texts adopt Romantic topoi but also manifest discomfort with those elements. The familiar Romantic themes and images of solitude, despair, nostalgia, time, pantheism, disillusion, and death dominate Cappelle-Lafarge's memoirs as they do the works of Madame de Staël and George Sand. But these topoi, which in men's texts were mostly abstract preoccupations of the spirit, were too much a real part of women's experience to be used as mere literary figures. Tragic existence and victimization—which, as Brombert shows, male writers so nimbly manipulated as metaphors—were for women much more literal events.

Thirty years before Cappelle-Lafarge, Madame de Staël had created heroines who perpetuated the eighteenth-century narrative structure of feminine failure. Delphine and Corinne, exceptional women, lamented their way toward resignation and death. But if earlier heroines had been victims of a flaw in themselves, de Staël's were thwarted by mediocre men and imposed social conventions. Cappelle-Lafarge does not present herself as strong and talented; she does paint herself from childhood on as a victim unable to control her own destiny. Her story renders literally de Staël's fictional image of women's fate: woman is a "juridical prisoner" who is destined to appear before a "permanent tribunal" for having "wrenched herself from the timidity of her sex." For de Staël, all women are "guilty of having been born."[85] Cappelle-Lafarge's memoirs, increasingly a resigned lamentation, end with the author's own death.

Cappelle-Lafarge, as a character in her own story, most strongly identified with George Sand's Lélia. She too felt herself an outcast, damned for her evil passions yet "sublime" by her spiritual capacity. Reminiscent of *Lélia* and Sand's other novels, Cappelle-Lafarge's sentimental Romanticism is tempered by a tough refusal of social constraints. Her text is not Sand's overt revolt against marriage, but it does call for progress in justice and in women's education, for the same somewhat contradictory reasons: moral "improvement" and family welfare. Both writers seem caught between Romantic individual predilections and rising positivistic emphasis on social dynamics, though Cappelle-Lafarge is more strongly rooted in the earlier tradition. That may well be due to the tight congruity between the facts of her life and the Romantic narrative structures of tragedy and victimization, a congruity more focused than in the lives of noncriminal female authors.

Twentieth-century prison texts by women are more difficult to compare with the texts of contemporaneous noncriminal authors, since the dominant tendencies in female writing are harder to delineate. Marguerite Steinheil's *Mémoires* of 1911–12, for example, cannot really be termed a special case of women's literature, except insofar as her strong aesthetic pre-

[85]Pierre Fauchery, "La Destinée féminine dans le roman européen du xviiie siècle (1713–1807)," thesis (Paris 1970), cited in Maïté Albistur and Daniel Armogathe, *Histoire du féminisme français du Moyen Age à nos jours* (Paris: des femmes, 1977), 248.

Philosophical and Literary Tradition

occupations with form and setting have affinities with those of certain *belle époque* women poets, such as Renée Vivien. And Steinheil's thematic concern with maternal love and family echoes the poems of Anna de Noailles and others. That women writers in general turned to poetry at this time is not a coincidence, since it was then the genre that best maintained their tradition and translated their experience. The currents in men's literature of the period were incompatible with women's stories: futurism, modernism, "unanimism," and surrealism reflected the male concerns of militarism, patriotism, eroticism, and antifeminism. It is no wonder the outstanding female author of the early twentieth century, Colette, wrote completely outside that male tradition. Steinheil's text, by its moralizing self-presentation, is closer to the earlier conventional female tradition, though she does share with Colette the use of theatrical imagery and the theme of women's self-sacrifice. And for Steinheil, as prisoner, literal self-sacrifice and "performance" were demanded by her judicial and penal experience. Steinheil used language and literary effect consciously and thus, as Colette did for all women authors, ushered female prison writing into the twentieth century.

The first novels by imprisoned women did not appear until the 1960s. Anne Huré's *En prison* and Albertine Sarrazin's *La Cavale* are thinly veiled autobiographical accounts. Neither text resembles the important experimental work that such authors as Duras and Sarraute were engaged in at the time, but both are laudable efforts to give form and coherence to the prison experience. There are general thematic affinities between the contemporary works of criminal and noncriminal women—for example, the subjective treatment of time and the presentation of female friendships. Most women authors also draw strong heroines, though the tests they undergo differ. If Rochefort's and Beauvoir's protagonists struggle with social, economic, and emotional constraints, Huré's and Sarrazin's confront physical deprivation and confinement. The affirmation of autonomy joins modern female prison texts to the women's prison tradition of self-exploration and self-presentation and also to the larger corpus of self-aware female literature.

En prison is more difficult to associate with women's writing of this era than is *La Cavale*. Huré's novel is closer to the male philosophical and theological tradition of Claudel, Mauriac, and Bernanos. *En prison* is also, in its prevalence of dialogue over action, more in line with some of Sartre's static and prolix "thesis" or "problem" texts. Huré searches for the formal purity that best complements her ascetic heroine and finds it among the abstract and spiritual male texts with which she identifies. But she paints a universe of proud, intelligent, and articulate women. In this sense *En prison* suggests the individualized and male-identified brand of female resourcefulness and strength that marked the 1950s and 1960s.

La Cavale has recognizable ties with the emerging feminist and socially critical literature of the 1960s, though it is not really feminist in inspiration or message. Sarrazin, like Rochefort and Etcherelli, portrays economic inequities and explores the effects of race and class on social justice. She also draws from firsthand knowledge the intricate world of female prostitution. While she does not, as they do, directly criticize any of these situations in terms of group consciousness, she does evoke the pain they can bring to individual women. *La Cavale* mainly asserts the primacy of the mind and Sarrazin's identity as writer, recalling Beauvoir's and Rochefort's lucid and affirmative presentations of strong heroines. Sarrazin's response to the pull of writing also prefigures contemporary feminist calls for self-expression by all women.

Sarrazin's fiction has frequently been compared with that of Violette Leduc, with some justice. Both women's works were prejudged on the basis of their author's personal backgrounds—their illegitimate births and their prison records. Both women recount, with differing degrees of suffering, the personal stigma of their past. And, in terms of literary innovation, both authors communicate their experience mainly through language, though Leduc pushes much further toward a language of pure pain. Whereas *La Cavale* manipulates borrowed slang and bad French to express its heroine's urge for autonomy, *La Bâtarde* delves inward to the language of obsession and trauma.[86]

[86] Violette Leduc, *La Bâtarde* (Paris: Gallimard, 1964).

PHILOSOPHICAL AND LITERARY TRADITION

But another portion of Sarrazin's writing marks a turning point in women's prison literature. Her *Journal de prison 1959*, though conventional in content, is unusual in form. Its flowing, pulsing style recalls some of Duras's works in which the line between the conscious and the unconscious disappears. Though Sarrazin did not intend to explore the power of language, she was aware that the *Journal*'s completely natural voice, her internal "music," was the most effective one. Also, the highly subjective quality of time in the journal has affinities with the suspension and repetition that pervade the works of Duras, Sarraute, Cixous, and others.

In genre and theme, then, Sarrazin's journals (and her poems) have more in common with the confessional works of her imprisoned forerunners. Her fiction, though not radical in form, breaks sharply with the centuries of prolonged female guilt by drawing unapologetic heroines. If Huré sidesteps her identity as a female criminal writer by adopting certain male conventions, Sarrazin makes that identity her central literary concern. That Sarrazin focuses on herself as prisoner and writer rather than as woman is a measure of her special experience. For all women, coming to authorship has been problematic; for the woman prisoner, Sarrazin tells us, that transition has been nearly impossible.

In spite of the forces that discouraged them, some women wrote. Until the twentieth century, imprisoned women consistently chose confessional genres, a choice that constituted a cornerstone of the female prison tradition and another point of divergence from the male tradition. These women, whose own lives epitomized the moralizing narrative structure of error and fall prescribed for female protagonists, were even more vulnerable than "free" women authors. Their confessions and memoirs perpetuated and validated society's image of women. The bare enumerative form of recorded confessions does not concern us directly, for those from France were not written by the women themselves, who were completely illiterate. The Marquise de Brinvilliers's *Récit de ses derniers moments* of 1676 was reported by her confessor; there is no guarantee of its accuracy and, most likely, it includes only those utterances that Edme Pirot chose to remember and organize. Hundreds of years later, Gabrielle Bompard's confessions appeared: they read like a list of every imaginable titillating taboo, but they have all the stylistic distinction of a recipe. What is significant is the relationship of the criminal to the confessional genre: confession, beyond its goal of reforming the listener, confirms the existing and conventional definitions of crime. The confessions of de Brinvilliers and Bompard—unlike, for example, the complex and ambiguous *Testaments* of Villon—are unidimensional and represent noncontestation at its purest.

This difference between women's and men's choice of genre reflects their diverging relations to self-revelation and its literary opposite, invention. Invention, as a product of the imagination, has historically been defined differently for each sex. The influential medical thinkers of the eighteenth century saw imagination in women as a force that diverted them from their biologically and domestically defined state of happiness. That particular model of nonimaginative happiness, plus the actual facts of women's daily existence, led virtually all female prison writers to work with memoirs and journals. Highly codified genres such as poetry and drama were beyond their pretensions. As the Romantics reinforced nostalgia and subjectivism, women continued to choose confessional genres.

Yet women's choice of the genre "memoirs" was, in imaginative terms, a rich one—not a substitute for the male contestatory habit of mind but the strongest and most apt expression of a different life experience. In this one can see the architecture of a truly female tradition of prison writing. As the artful reconstruction of the story of her "fall," memoirs allowed the author to assume maximum fatalism in her account. Staal-Delaunay opens her *Mémoires* by revealing and acknowledging her prime character flaw, presumptuousness: "One becomes convinced that everything is done for oneself" (p. 7). Thus, her story will follow this preestablished personal "defect" and not from any problem in society. Even Madame Roland, who strongly objects to events of her time, presents from the start her own stubbornness and tenacious need for solitude. Her fate must be understood, then, as a necessary result of the interaction of historical forces with her particular temperament. Madame de Tencin's heroines possess the flaw of ambition that will lead to their downfall. Marie Cappelle-Lafarge's memoirs are the most clearly "reconstructed" and fatalistic account of all: she "discovers" omens, retrospectively, in the misfortune surrounding her own family and in the unpleasant events of her early married life.

Memoirs, unlike novels or the unreworked confessional form of journals, enabled imprisoned women to ask questions about themselves rather than about the world. Women's memoirs, viewed negatively as art removed from social responsibility, corresponded to the lack of moral sense associated with women criminals and, more generally, with the feminine.[87] Viewed positively, women's memoirs reflect their accepting individual responsibility without blaming external forces. One can criticize only the woman herself, not the author.

Memoirs also allowed the imprisoned woman to counter accusations of "desensitization" by showing that, over time, she remained the same woman, unchanged. This chronological framework, based on verifiable past behavior, is rigorously associated with "truth" in women's texts. The woman's "true" identity—and this presentation of self is the prime topos of women's prison literature—did not lie in judicial or criminal labels. Rather, sincerity meant "working . . . to align the personality and the life it leads with a pre-established model."[88] Thus women could show the continuity of inner self and the persistent sensitivity that were part of the feminine model of the time. Whatever the gap between the real person and the created persona who serves as narrator, there is always in women's memoirs an inner truth of motivation, a search for wholeness between past and present. It is striking to see how, centuries apart, Roland, Cappelle-Lafarge, Steinheil, and Sarrazin insist that their words are *true:*

[87]See Lisa Appignanesi, *Femininity and the Creative Imagination: A Study of Henry James, Robert Musil and Marcel Proust* (New York: Vision Press, 1973). Appignanesi discusses the myth that identifies a certain mysterious notion of art and creation with the "feminine." Modern psychoanalysis, she claims, only confirmed this association by its dichotomies of passive/active, internalization/externalization, and anima/animus.
[88]Robert A. Fothergill, *Private Chronicles: A Study of English Diaries* (London: Oxford University Press, 1974), 70.

> Truth! Fatherland! Friendship! Sacred objects, sentiments dear to my heart, receive my last sacrifice. (Roland, *Mémoires*)
>
> I did not ask God to make me eloquent; I prayed that he would put forgiveness and truth in my memories and that he would give my words the power to persuade and convince. (Cappelle-Lafarge, *Mémoires*)
>
> I have written these memoirs, this rigorously exact story of my life. (Steinheil, *Mémoires*)
>
> Focus on the bad parts, transform the painful aspect into the TRUE aspect, that's the rare secret. (Sarrazin, *Journal de prison 1959;* her emphasis)

Accusations of "desensitization" were leveled at women not only for their criminal acts, but also for their written accounts of those acts. Ironically, the audience's expectation of female sincerity, based on certain literary conventions, ran against women's authentic absorption with their true selves. That is, their contemporary readers equated denial of guilt with insincerity, as seen, for example, in judgments of Cappelle-Lafarge's *Mémoires:* they showed "cold correctness" and a "search for the right word" in the author's struggle to establish her innocence.[89] This problem of audience reception also explains why women so frequently addressed their memoirs to future generations: only a later appreciation of the whole woman and her whole life could hope to reestablish the truth. Thus, for example, Roland makes an "Appeal to Impartial Posterity"[90]: she expects no sympathy from a public that enjoys execution spectacles. Roland was executed during the Terror, the last and most grotesque paroxysm of uniform sentencing. She was not surprised at receiving the death penalty—in later times rarely given to women—but rather was enraged that the jurors could have ignored her individuality. In her memoirs Roland sought to correct this historical insensitivity by constantly affirming her own perceptual su-

---

[89] Raymond de Ryckère, *La Femme en prison et devant la mort* (Paris: Masson, 1898), 126–27.
[90] In some editions Roland's memoirs are called "Appel à l'impartiale postérité," e.g., the Louvet edition of 1795.

periority. The future's answer to such insensitivity will be to understand the usefulness of Roland's personal drama:

> Perhaps one day my simple stories will beguile the time of some unfortunate captive who will forget the fate that awaits her by being moved to tears over mine; perhaps the philosophers, who wish to paint the heart through the course of a novel or the action of a play, will find cause to study it in my story.[91]

In the prison texts of eighteenth-century women there is remarkable consistency of textual chronology: the unification of past, present, and future. Cappelle-Lafarge, however, placed little hope in future generations. Her status as civilly "dead" enabled her to believe only in a personal Christian afterlife. With the general evolution of private chronicles toward less linear and more complex structures—in this century they approach the novel in organization and texture—women's journals grew less preoccupied with chronology.[92] For example, Sarrazin's *Journal de prison 1959* makes virtually no reference to dates or times: it is an impressionistic record of the author's inner voice.

Memoirs also allowed the imprisoned woman, in a severely limited way, to engage in the analysis/synthesis that was so dear to positivism—that is, to show her "imagination" in the weakest sense of arranging the images of her life. The diary, an unreworked confessional form, likewise allows the woman to deny having pretensions to authorship. Instead, she can document herself by recording her state of mind, both authentically and impressionistically. Women's "documents of the self" have great value beyond the individual projections they provide: they also are rich analogues to women's lives in general. Like the confessional writing of all women, prison diaries can reflect an existence that is "emotional, fragmented, interrupted, modest, not to be taken seriously, private, restricted, daily, trivial,

---

[91] Roland, *Mémoires*, 238.
[92] See Fothergill for the development of the diary as "literary composition" by the nineteenth century and for the importance of the "psychic life" for twentieth-century diaries.

formless, concerned with self, as endless as their tasks."[93] Women's lives in prison intensified this dissatisfaction. And, since women's position in society generally precluded "the assertion of the individual ego,"[94] their texts, especially through the nineteenth century, project a self-image that is supportive rather than dramatic, egotistical, or singular. The private genres to which women have historically turned have plots, suspense, complications, and patterns as do traditional genres, but with differences that force us to ask new questions about the line between art and life and about the values that have, until now, been considered "human" and vital.

The male and female prison traditions diverge, finally, in the questions the authors ask—questions stemming from different motivations and giving rise to different thematic concerns. What questions have female outcasts asked? Centrally, "Who am I?" "Who was I?" and "Who will I be?" These constitute the prime topoi of female prison literature. Women's texts, whether autobiographical or fictional, are self-contained in their intimate search for identity. Because women have operated under codes imposed from without, they have not achieved heroic ascension or extended their personal codes. Women turn to themes in the realm of the verifiable, not the speculative: veracity lies in what has been, not in what ought to be. Even the potential for transcendence and for the "unawareness of self"[95] that religion provides—and that Genet used in his mythification of criminals—has not served women. Paradoxically, though women have historically been closer than men to religion and mysticism, these influences have been too real and concrete to permit liberation and have, in fact, impeded women's spiritual escape. Thus, for example, while Cappelle-Lafarge's text *Heures de prison* speaks increasingly of her devotion, it also portrays her increasing passivity: "What will happen to me now?" is the leitmotiv of her

---

[93]*Revelations: Diaries of Women*, ed. Mary Jane Moffat and Charlotte Painter (New York: Random House, 1974), 5.
[94]Fothergill, *Private Chronicles*, 87.
[95]See Beauvoir's *Le Deuxième Sexe* for her analysis of women's relationship to creativity.

Philosophical and Literary Tradition

martyrdom.[96] Anne Huré's heroine, Noëlle, in a close echo of this uncertainty, thinks at the moment of her liberation: "What would become of her in the months that followed?"[97] Women's attitude is not one of destructive hostility toward others, but is instead diffuse and sometimes self-depriving in proportion to the adversity they have met.

The theme of the self and the problem of identity, as Brombert has shown, are not unique to women—indeed, they are fundamental to Romatic literature. For Romantic figures, however, this existential anxiety enjoyed a dialectical relation to the themes of pride (the Prometheus image), revolt, redemption, beauty, and infinite desire. Imprisoned women feel little ambivalence about their situation: rather than finding prison to be both suffering and protection, oppression and liberation, mental death and beneficial self-concentration, Baudelarian constriction and expansion, women have seen it as a singular experience. Their writing moves only toward the interior and conveys the "association of the prisoner's descent into the self with the quest for a personal truth, the quest for an original identity."[98]

The theme of seeing and being seen reinforces the search for self-knowledge and self-presentation in women's texts. Authenticity and truth should, they maintain, be judged on the basis of what is visible. The importance of the visible for women is also apparent in their numerous portraits and tableaus. The wish to direct the reader's judgmental eye springs from the fact that the imprisoned woman is accustomed to being watched. Unlike the "specular" way of looking that Luce Irigaray has analyzed as vital to the masculine imagination, women's viewpoint has been that of the object observed.[99] The result for all women has been dispossession of the self; for the prisoner routinely stripped of her clothes and searched, that dispossession is far greater.

---

[96]Madame Lafarge (née Marie Cappelle), *Heures de prison* (Paris: Librairie Nouvelle, 1854), 7.
[97]Huré, *En prison*, 256.
[98]Brombert, *Romantic Prison*, 10.
[99]Luce Irigaray, *Speculum de l'autre femme* (Paris: Minuit, 1974).

Newspaper stories invariably describe female criminals in physical terms: Roland's portliness, Staal-Delaunay's engaging face, Cappelle-Lafarge's pockmarks. Cappelle-Lafarge says, "I no longer belong to myself."[100] Sarrazin, at the beginning of *La Cavale*, describes her admission to prison. When she is stripped and examined, she portrays herself as being in the wrong place. In a comparable body-search scene in Boudard's *La Cerise*, the imprisoned man appropriates the space around him; Sarrazin sees herself in relation to objects around her.[101] Imprisoned women's need for visibility to establish their identity also accounts for their exclusively individual, rather than collective, perspective on their experience. While individual destiny is projected to a group tragedy in some masculine texts—Dostoevski's *House of the Dead*, for example—there is little "democratization" in women's works, save those of political prisoners or of preprison feminists such as Nicole Gérard.[102]

The last theme common to women's prison texts is that of self-possession: once they project a truthful self-image, women impose Cornelian control to maintain it. There is an apparent contradiction in needing "courage" to preserve what is sincere and natural. What is really difficult, however, is expressing that self-image. The references to "grasping" and "order" in these texts do not apply to that constraint necessary for the mythification of a heroic persona. It is not Baudelaire's metaphor: "A stretch of sky, glimpsed through a basement window, or between two chimneys . . . gives a deeper sense of infinity than a vast panorama seen from a mountaintop."[103] Women's self-possession is a way to hold the truth in place; it is a force of sustainment, not expansion. As prison shrinks space and deforms time, women push to the limits of "normal" life, maintaining boundaries rather than appropriating or destroying what is beyond them. If for imprisoned men "space is above all

---

[100]Cappelle-Lafarge, *Mémoires*, 3:18.

[101]Alphonse Boudard, *La Cerise* (Paris: Plon, 1963), 328–29.

[102]Nicole Gérard, *Sept ans de pénitence* (Paris: Robert Laffont, 1976). Though not feminist in inspiration, this testimony reveals Gérard's sense of group identity with women.

[103]Baudelaire's *Correspondance générale*, cited in Brombert, *Romantic Prison*, 133.

an image of power,"[104] for imprisoned women the periphery has been left alone, outside their pretensions. Female prison literature in general, through its topos of solipsistic self-justification, evinces a strategy for survival. This literature is, both for the woman and for all of society, a life-sustaining response in the face of external hostility, not a retaliatory destruction and domination of that hostility.

At all times, the female criminal has tended both to reject and to exploit the moral and social stigmas placed on her, since she has had no legitimate connections to society and no positive means of self-presentation. Thus, for example, Roland uses the Rousseauesque notions of "sensitivity" and "utility" for her own purposes. By portraying the other women in prison as archetypal female deviants—that is, as debauched, vulgar, and insensitive—she can point up her own sensitivity and intelligence. Likewise, Cappelle-Lafarge, reflecting her period's simplistic moral lexicon as well as its penchant for empirical positivism, makes use of both discourses: she explains how her conformity to moral norms was turned against her (her suffering was called remorse, her strength hardness, and her courage audacity); and she twists the precision of typologizing in her own portraits, caricatures, and terse judgments. Steinheil subverts the superficial and theatrical labels ("hysteric" and "hallucinator") used against her by developing her own aesthetic and stylistic criteria for judgment: she claims that she appreciates true creativity through the work of her artist friends, whereas her fellow prisoners lack any artistic discrimination whatever. Huré, in a complete rejection of the affective-sexual etiology of modern criminological thought, presents characters who appear to possess neither emotional nor erotic needs and who instead move in the sphere of pure thought. Finally, Sarrazin, reacting to the modern criminological theories of both sexual maladjustment and social conditioning, exploits these focuses: she presents, explicitly, her own understanding of her sexual

---

[104]Herrmann, *Les Voleuses*. This essay, "Les Coordonnées féminines: Espace et temps," is partially reproduced in translation in *New French Feminisms: An Anthology*, ed. Elaine Marks and Isabelle de Courtivron (Amherst: University of Massachusetts Press, 1980), trans. Marilyn R. Schuster, 168–73. Reference here is to p. 168.

maturation to counter gynophobic definitions of her "troubled" development; and, refusing the assigned social causes for her behavior, she offers her own explanations for her crime.

Through this manipulation of the very discourse that had articulated their condemnation, imprisoned women have in effect "coded" their texts. These works, which display neither eccentricity nor conformity, adopt an effective strategy for dealing with hostile conditions. Yet overall few women responded to the hostility of prison by writing, for reasons of education and individual motivation. The women who did write reacted to their specific confinement as well as to an exercise of power—by the judiciary and the prison—that one would normally assume to be free from prejudice. Their acute experience of prejudice and powerlessness, which for most women in society is more diffuse, apparently pushed them to respond. The corpus of women's prison texts shows in an extreme form the convergence of social and individual forces that have affected women in general and that have been determinant for all women writers.

The texts that follow, despite the noble and stirring expectations of domination, power, and transcendence found in critical studies of prison writing, do not reorganize experience in an attempt to shatter or correct the world. Any such "muscle" is self-consciously ironic or offhand. Nor do these texts display a consistent judgment of the world: their anger shows private ambivalence rather than unbridled energy. And they do not offer an alternative vision of society: they wrestle with the primary act of self-expression.

Yet these texts force us to question not the power of their author's vision, but the very literary tenets that have guided judgments of that vision—tenets that are incompatible with women's texts and that have relegated them to critical darkness. Women's prison texts force us to question the monolithic, universalizing, and power-centered criteria that have long named and validated the "literature of revolt."

Part Two

Women's Texts

Madame Roland in prison, 1793. Dessin Bibl. nat. Photo N. D. Roger-Viollet

4

Madame Roland

> I am Galigai, Brinvilliers, Voisin, all that is imaginably monstrous, and the women at the market treat me like Madame de Lamballe—Madame Roland, *Correspondance*

In identifying herself with four notorious female criminals, Madame Roland shows she understood the confusion that marked perceptions of her deviance and the accusations leveled against her. By comparing herself to three civil prisoners (Galigai, the sixteenth-century witch; Brinvilliers, the seventeenth-century poisoner; and Voisin, the seventeenth-century midwife and black magician) and then with the Princesse de Lamballe, Marie Antoinette's confidante, Roland encapsulates the public's blurring of her alleged social, political, and sexual crimes. Roland, like these infamous forerunners, was executed in a context that equated women's activism with moral defectiveness. And because of this confusion of political and sexual assertiveness, the "Egeria" of the Revolution's Girondin faction was the target and the victim of that generation's contradictory views of women.

Roland's trial in 1793, like most during the Terror, was a sham, so it is that much harder to determine the precise charges brought against her. From her own *Notices historiques,* her record of her *Interrogatoire,* and her *Observations rapides sur l'acte d'accusation contre les députés par Amar, Notes sur mon procès,* and *Projet de défense,*[1] one can glean vague political accusations

---
[1] All these texts, plus the "Mémoires particuliers," have at different times been published separately. They have appeared together most recently as

that she "attended secret meetings that took place at night" (p. 58), "[gave] advice or furnished means" for a federalist conspiracy (p. 372), and engaged with the principal Girondin leaders in "correspondence that served to facilitate their freedom-destroying plans."[2] A close reading of Roland's "Interrogation of June 12" reveals that her Commune accusers were in fact more interested in her husband, the former minister of the interior Jean-Marie Roland, than in "Citizen Roland" herself: by positing at the start that Madame Roland, "being only a woman, had no business meddling" in public affairs (p. 95), her interrogator undercuts the importance of his subsequent political charges against her, since Roland is therefore not to be taken seriously *as* a political figure. The interrogator's reproach also immediately makes clear the real issue: her transgression of proper sexual comportment.

Underlying Roland's problematic status as a political criminal is the fundamentally sexual nature of the general perception of her wrongdoings. This gender-specific focus, rooted in the traditional and ongoing confusion of women's biological and social identities, was intensified by the government's crackdown on female activism in general. *Le Moniteur*'s scathing judgment of Roland (see p. 88) as a "monster" whose literary and political pretensions had wrenched her from normal feminine pursuits appeared on the heels of the National Convention's outlawing of women's clubs.[3] The Convention's report contains the same blending of political and sexual matters: in response to the question, "Should women exercise political rights and meddle in the affairs of government?" the report answers no, since women lack the "unlimited attention and devotion," the "strict immovability" necessary to govern. The question, "Do women have the moral and physical strength" required to debate and deliberate over matters of

---

Mémoires de Madame Roland (Paris: Mercure de France, 1966). All future parenthetical references will be to this edition, and all translations are mine.

[2]Françoise Kermina, *Madame Roland, ou La Passion révolutionnaire* (Paris: Librairie Académique Perrin, 1976), 353.

[3]*Women in Revolutionary Paris, 1789–1795: Selected Documents Translated with Notes and Commentary*, ed. Darline Gay Levy, Harriet Branson Applewhite, and Mary Durham Johnson (Urbana: University of Illinois Press, 1979), 215ff.

state draws the answer, "Universal opinion rejects this idea."[4] The ban against women's participation was securely fixed when Madame Roland's case was offered as irrefutable justification: "Remember this haughty wife of a stupid, perfidious husband, *la Roland,* who thought herself fit to govern the republic and who rushed to her downfall."[5]

The most violent and explicitly sexual denunciation of Roland appeared just before her second arrest,[6] in the pro-Convention newspaper *Le Père Duchesne.* Most apparent is the use of physical insults and obscenities: she is called a "toothless bitch," an "old antirevolutionary bag," and an "old hag" or "old she-monkey" who entertained, in her "den of corruption," Girondin "brigands" to whom she played up "as a cat in love [does] with a fat tomcat that is prowling around her.[7] Indirect reference to Roland's writing, in the same piece, uses ambiguous literal and figurative terms to equate literary self-revelation with sexual promiscuity: for example, Roland "unbuttoned herself/spoke frankly to" Father Duchesne, and she "revealed the secret of the affair." If, as Françoise Kermina claims, Roland's enemies, particularly Marat, spread rumors about her promiscuity, "in order more effectively to strike the public imagination,"[8] one can see that such opprobrium had currency in the public mind.

How did Roland respond to such judgments of sexual and political deviance? An examination of her *Mémoires,* written during two months' incarceration in 1793, reveals her multifaceted acknowledgment and manipulation of those judgments as she attempted to establish what she believed was the truth. "Truth," "sincerity," and "authenticity," the leitmotiv not only of Roland's text but also of all women's prison writing, is for her synonymous with justice. She claims, "I wish to do justice

[4]Ibid., 215.
[5]Document cited in *Women in Revolutionary Paris,* 220; original emphasis.
[6]Madame Roland had first been arrested illegally, that is, without an arrest warrant. The authorities, not wishing to lose their star prisoner on such procedural grounds, released her and immediately rearrested her "correctly."
[7]All extracts from *Le Père Duchesne* of June 20, 1793, are reproduced in Roland's *Mémoires,* 375–77.
[8]Kermina, *Madame Roland,* 240.

by presenting truths" (p. 202), particularly since she is accused of "disguising the truth" and of "[forgetting] the duties of an accused person, who especially owes the truth to justice" (p. 388). Like texts by other female criminals, Roland's writing itself becomes a document of truth: "My language had to be pure and moving, it was the language of the heart and of truth" (p. 304). As such it would, by its existence, "destroy the falsehood" that surrounds her case (p. 305). Finally, André Monglond says of the pre-Romantic reading public in general that "they preferred adventures whose authenticity was guaranteed by the sole fact that *they had happened.*"[9]

The authenticity of Roland's *Mémoires* is based on her using as textual material the very judgments that had condemned her. That the accusations were *amalgams* of sexual, moral, and political elements, together with the fact that penal theory and practice also manifested this mixed nature, offered rich possibilities for counterjudgments of her own. In the discussion that follows I shall trace how the *Mémoires* exploit and frequently invert the various paradigms according to which Roland had been evaluated and punished. More precisely, I shall consider certain aspects of genre (narrative structure and movement); stylistic devices (figures of speech); techniques of character depiction (roles, portraits, authenticity of self); and social implications (invalidation of judicial norms and procedures) of the *Mémoires* as they reflect a strategy of subversion.

Roland chose memoirs in part for reasons of vogue and precedent: when prisoners could write freely, before Robespierre clamped down, many, particularly women, had turned to confessional forms; and Roland's idol Rousseau had produced his own *Confessions.* But other reasons compelled her to select a genre that, by its link with the Catholic sacrament, had long attracted social outcasts and that had qualities she could effectively exploit. Since women writers were expected to be prudent in the conflicts they presented, they generally relied on moralizing narrative structures that avoided dramatic and

[9]André Monglond, *Le Préromantisme français: Le maître des âmes sensibles,* vol. 2 (Grenoble: B. Arthaud, 1930), 316; his emphasis.

adventurous peripeteias. And the story of her own social "fall," in which the woman criminal was principal narrator and protagonist, offered the strongest possibilities for moral enlightenment. Roland, who persistently denies committing any crime, twists the terms of error and judgment so that in effect *she* remains constant while the society around her succumbs to corruption: using the dominant Rousseauesque discourse of "honor," "duty," and "virtue"—as so-called justice had used it against her—Roland denounces the powers that "send to the gallows all men whose virtue offends them" (p. 236). Elsewhere her inversion of moral codes is more explicit: "I took my own peaceful, affectionate, generous, and sincere heart for the common measure of all mankind's morality. I made this mistake for a long time, and it was the sole source of my errors" (p. 291). Roland also counters the sexual overtones of her presumed error and fall by defining "perversity" in her own way: "When innocence walks toward the punishment to which error and perversity have condemned it, it arrives at glory" (p. 373). Thus the terms of ascent and fall are effectively switched as one means of countering moral stigma.

This exchange of rises and falls and of those who undergo them is in fact the largest incidence of a stylistic strategy that pervades Roland's works: the extended use of oxymorons, or incompatible opposites. Roland's texts contain alloys and unsuccessful unions of all kinds; in light of her perceived "monstrousness," this reflects, if not aesthetic intention, at least a response to the contradictions that surrounded her. The power structure that had condemned her is compared to a bad marriage in a simile that plays with the fragility of such a precarious union:

> In a marriage in which the parties have been ill-matched, the virtue of one of the two parties can maintain order and peace; but sooner or later the absence of happiness makes itself felt and brings with it problems of greater or lesser gravity. The structure of such unions resembles that of our political system: its foundation is deficient, it is destined to fall one day, in spite of the artistry used in its construction. (p. 306)

Such an unnatural organization as the Terror's government is not just fragile; it is also deviant, dangerous, itself monstrous:

> However beautiful the written principles of a Constitution may be, if I see pain and tears among those who adopted that Constitution, I shall believe it is nothing but a political monstrosity; if those who are not crying rejoice in the suffering of others, I shall say that Constitution is terrible and that its authors are either imbeciles or scoundrels. (p. 306)

This strategy of rejecting and inverting the identity of the monstrous party is introduced when Roland opens her memoirs with the following metaphor: "Our government is a kind of monster whose methods and acts are equally revolting; it destroys everything it touches and at the same time consumes itself: this last excess is the sole consolation of its many victims" (p. 234).

This personified government, the monster that "devours itself," becomes the character destined to fall in the course of Roland's memoirs. Roland as character can then be the heroine she sees herself to be: constant, supportive, truthful, and in control. Once the moral stature of her accusers is debunked, Roland is free to right her historical persona and cast it in terms of her own fatalistic drama. Fatalism, which at the time normally predetermined the female protagonist's demise, becomes for Roland a means to guarantee the opposite course of events: her enemies fall while she remains constant and consistent. Prophetic signs in her earlier life allow Roland to "impose an internal logic and the ineluctable order of a destiny on her existence."[10] Such irrefutable order in her life proves she is "more than a mottled amalgam of incomprehensible adventures."[11] The true monster is identified at the outset, and it is not Roland.

The collective character of the Parisian public is drawn into this process of redefining the drama's villains and heroines. In her partiality for her provincial supporters, Roland decries the

---

[10] Gita May, *De Jean-Jacques Rousseau à Madame Roland: Essai sur la sensibilité préromantique et révolutionnaire* (Geneva: Droz, 1964), 235.
[11] Ibid., 235.

Parisians' "vile cowardice" and blames them for spurring on the Tribune's bloody injustices (p. 36). It becomes apparent, however, that Roland's disdain for the city's populace masks a self-aggrandizement based on taste and class or, ultimately, on her own notion of moral vulgarity. Some sample judgments:

> The common people would not have understood at all that one could prefer to live modestly on the wages and accoutrements of a ministerial position. (p. 91)

> The common man thinks little, believes everything he is told, and acts by instinct. (p. 227)

Roland's need to establish in her story the roles of the morally upright and the corrupt is heightened by the chaotic organization and deplorable material conditions of the prisons in which she was confined. Prisoners of all classes, ages, sexes, and criminal backgrounds were housed together.[12]

> No distinction of any kind is made between an act of heedless youth and a perpetrated crime; I have seen a botany student who had spoken ill of Marat locked in the same room with highwaymen. There is no respect for morals; I have seen a fourteen-year-old girl whose parents were begging to have her back placed in the same cell with the woman who had kidnapped her and who had been arrested for that same crime. (p. 189)

This intermingling, particularly at Sainte-Pélagie prison, becomes especially intolerable for Roland when she sees prostitutes mixed with "honorable" women: "There, under the same roof, in the same row, . . . I live with fallen women and murderers" (p. 181) whose revels are characterized by "brutal pleasure, vulgar talk, and foul acts" (p. 188). Thus not only is Roland free of any presumed moral error, her condemners are blind to the character of truly dangerous corruption, as is seen in their indiscriminate incarceration of the innocent with the

---

[12]For a detailed description of conditions in eighteenth-century prisons (including Sainte-Pélagie and the Conciergerie), see Charles-Aimé Dauban, *Les Prisons sous la Révolution, d'après les relations des contemporains* (Paris: Plon, 1870). See also Kermina, *Madame Roland*.

guilty. Prostitutes, the "common people," all Parisians, and the entire regime itself, by its moral obtuseness, are foils for Roland's own superiority. The material conditions of Roland's captivity also spark her awareness that she is different in caste from other prisoners. The forced contact with other inmates, plus the darkness and the vermin, provide narrative substance for her memoirs. Roland partly meets her need for private space by taking advantage of the class system, which extended to prisons at that time. She rents a semiprivate *pistole* cell, orders restaurant food, and pays for the housekeeping services of other prisoners. She also avoids the faceless collectivity that the other prisoners have become for her. Thus, like her previous "alcoves" and "refuges," Roland's prison cell becomes a corner of security. At one point she decides to transform prison into a structure of her own making: following the principles of stoicism she has long admired, she voluntarily reduces her food intake to that of the poorest prisoners (a pound and a half of bread and some beans) and trades her mattress for a thin layer of straw. Such self-deprivation is echoed in her long evocation of childhood days in a convent. If, however, the parallels between convent and prison are striking, the differences in Roland's affective state could not be stronger: the congregation's "calm" and "delights" and the nuns' favoritism toward Roland (pp. 223–24) made for a contentment unmatched in her later life and certainly in contrast to her misery in prison. Finally, the loss of her sexual identity, which has traditionally been considered the hardest deprivation for imprisoned women, leads Roland to affirm her pleasure in sensuality, as do the physiosexual judgments of her discussed earlier.[13]

Along with the sexual nature of the prevailing definitions of female normality and deviance, punitive theory shaped Roland's presentation of herself and others.[14] Two characteristics

---

[13]For the best presentation of the progressive losses and deprivations experienced by the prisoner, see Erving Goffman, "On the Characteristics of Total Institutions: The Inmate World," in *Perspectives on Correction*, ed. Donal E. J. MacNamara and Edward Sagarin (New York: Thomas Crowell, 1971), 31–61.

[14]See my article "A Response to the Void: Madame Roland's 'Mémoires particuliers' and Her Imprisonment," *Romance Notes* 20, no. 2 (fall 1979): 75–80.

of that period's penal ideology strongly marked the *Mémoires*, and these, as Michel Foucault documents, changed with industrialization in France. First, the purpose of imprisonment was purely punitive, rather than corrective; second, the punisher was clearly identified, not anonymous. These factors shaped the essential qualities of both narrator and interlocutor.

An essentially punitive system exerts control over the criminal's act rather than over her or his life. Thus at Roland's time punishment was generalized, not individualized, and it was most grotesquely uniform during the Terror. Roland was outraged less by the severity of her penalty than by her jurors' ignoring her individuality. To correct this historical insensitivity, she affirms her superiority in the same terms she used to counter charges of "defeminization": her perceptual and intellectual strengths. By asserting the primacy of feelings, Roland not only allies herself with Rousseau's aesthetics, she also joins the courageous minority of women writers who convey sensitivity as other than female weakness. "Feminine" literature was expected to emphasize the heart and senses, but Roland declares, "I thought with my heart" (p. 250), thereby joining mind with senses and elevating perception.

It is a revealing contradiction that elsewhere in her text Roland expresses the prevailing view that women courted danger by writing: "I have never had the slightest temptation to become an author one day; I saw very early on that a woman who earned this title for herself lost much more than she gained" (p. 304). But once moved by her condemnation and punishment to correct the injustice done to her personal identity, Roland does write in prison and takes up the authorship she had earlier refused. She is now aware of the double standard at the core of conventional judgments of men's and women's writing and realizes "that the men who ridiculed women authors were perhaps guilty of nothing other than ascribing to women only that which they themselves shared as well" (p. 278). Thus, though she claims to keep to her woman's role and subscribes to the supposed superiority of men, Roland reveals the forceful egoism that is the core of her self-justification.

Roland's self-image is further elevated in her *Mémoires* as she clearly establishes her place in relation to other heroes, literary or real. She opens her "Mémoires particuliers" by declaring her dislike for her given name, "Manon": "I apologize for it to the lovers of novels; this name is not noble, it does not at all befit a heroine of great stature" (p. 205). Because of her salon and her social and political influence, Roland implicitly identifies with the earlier women of the court. Her own value is further enhanced when she makes heroes of all those who were imprisoned for the same cause as she. Roland is therefore not obligated to look for reinforcement to her "vulgar" fellow prisoners, whom she disdains; rather, she can focus on other examples of her own dignified image. But she uses the notion of relative personal worthiness most effectively when she creates a noble interlocutor who carries the other half of the dialogue in her memoirs. Her envisioned listener/reader of necessity belongs to a future generation from whose corrective judgment Roland expects to benefit. This reader/redeemer will, of course, recognize the lies surrounding her present persecution; but she or he will also be one of the "philosophers" of human truths who will recognize in Roland's story the moral history of an entire era.

The relation between punisher and punished in the eighteenth century was one of raw power, with the person in authority well known to the prisoner. Unlike contemporary "rehabilitative" incarceration, where the focus is on modifying the prisoner, Roland's imprisonment served to prove Robespierre's control. The depersonalization of criminals like Roland, in contrast to the highly personalized punishing authority, was compounded by the secrecy that shrouded the judicial process: no precise charges were ever brought against Roland, and the length of her confinement was never announced. This anonymity infuriated her and fueled her need to affirm her individuality. Her insistence on her self-control and her strength of will reflects her resistance to the lopsided power relation between herself and her punisher. Furthermore, Robespierre's identifiability—Roland addressed numerous unanswered messages directly to him—convinced her of his moral deafness. His insensitivity, coupled with the public's hostile complicity, put Roland in a communicative void. It is no wonder she would invent a sensitive interlocutor and would address her memoirs to attentive future generations.

Roland's solipsistic method of using self-presentation to counter external judgments, characteristic of all the women studied here, is shaped by the specific moral/lexical framework of her generation. The ideal woman, as described in medical treatises like Roussel's[15] and further extolled in Rousseau's doctrines, offers the terms of superiority upon which Roland can draw. For Roussel, in accordance with his animist medical principles, physical well-being necessarily brought supreme female happiness and moral uprightness, in their varied manifestations. For the animists, however, "the deviations of an exacerbated sensitivity [from the norm]" were associated with "psychophysiological imbalances."[16] That Roland subscribes to the link between the physiological and the psychological (called "moral" at the time) is obvious when, for example, she describes her "curiosity to see if one's facial features corresponded to one's soul" (p. 129). Rousseau supplied a metaphysical dimension for ideal womanhood: "The ideal, healthy, happy woman is the one who has learned to free herself from the constraints of fashion and of prejudice, but who in her own domain achieves a *proper combination* of feminine and male virtues."[17]

If views like Roussel's provided Roland with material for her authentic physiopsychological self-portrait, Rousseau's ideas informed her mythic persona. The key word in Rousseau's description above is "proper"; if, like Madame Roland, a woman were perceived to have exceeded the appropriate proportion of male virtues, she passed from mythic to monstrous. The fragility of Rousseau's concept is striking. Roland, aware that this "excess" was thought to underlie her deviance, adopted such

---

[15]Pierre Roussel, *Système physique et moral de la femme, suivi du système physique et moral de l'homme*, 6th ed. (Paris: Caille et Ravier, 1813).
[16]May, *De Rousseau à Roland*, 236.
[17]Paul Hoffmann, "L'Héritage des lumières: Mythes et modèles de la féminité au xviiie siècle," *Romantisme: Mythes et représentations de la femme au xixe siècle*, nos. 13–14 (1976), 16; my emphasis. The works of Rousseau that most explicitly present this ideal are book 5 of *Emile*, *La Nouvelle Héloïse*, and the *Lettre à d'Alembert*.

precepts for her own purposes: "She takes the apparently less dangerous road [than that of the radical feminist revolutionary, Olympe de Gouges] of *exceeding* the limits of the traditional feminine role even while she uses a traditional vocabulary to hide from those around her and from herself the fact that she is anything but a traditional woman."[18] Though seeming to conform to models of female normality, Roland in fact undercuts those models by redefining them in her own way. Unlike, for example, her contemporary prison memorialist the Comtesse de la Motte—accused of plotting against the honor of Marie Antoinette in the 1785–86 "affair of the necklace"—who reinforces normative feminine models by evoking herself as "unaccustomed to thinking, swept along by the whirlwind.... corrupted by ever-present bad examples, and used to dealing too lightly with matters of moral duty,"[19] Roland denies that such paradigms are accurate or that they apply to her.

More specifically, the core qualities of Roussel's physio-psychological female paragon that Roland adopts are natural sensitivity, organic harmony, and the resulting social usefulness. All these terms and their equivalents appear frequently in Roland's *Mémoires,* and they are too numerous to cite exhaustively. Most important, however, in her first paragraph Roland designates feeling as her very essence: she is "a solitary individual who is depicting what she possesses naturally and expressing what she feels" (p. 33). Since her "natural sensitivity so dominated [her] other qualities" (p. 202), her soul is "the most loving possible" (p. 240). But Roland's insistence on the delicacy of her organs and the consequent acuteness of her senses is more than a mere rebuttal of accusations that she is "desensitized." Beyond affirming individual identity, Roland's *Mémoires* present a moral lesson that future philosophers will find useful "to paint the human heart" (p. 238). Her story, though seemingly personal, also illuminates, she claims, the criteria for sen-

---

[18]Angela Ljunström, "Rôles féminins dans la révolution française de 1789: Marie-Jeanne Roland et Olympe de Gouges, l'antiféminisme et le féminisme," thesis, University of Stockholm, 1977, 22; my emphasis.
[19]La Comtesse de la Motte (Jeanne de Valois), *Mémoires justificatifs de la Comtesse de Valois de la Motte écrits par elle-même,* 3d ed. (Paris, 1886; first published 1789), 92.

sitivity itself. Her experience "would offer great enlightenment for those wishing to know the human heart and a great lesson for those who are sensitive" (p. 333). She, who has never been desensitized—and therefore never "defeminized"—implicitly criticizes society's definitions of female normality by showing that they do not apply to her. Indirectly questioning women's circumscribed role as rooted in their tyrannous senses, she joins those well-known writers of her time who place feelings and thoughts in the broader context of the general society.

The animists' "harmony" and "organic unity" are concepts Roland exploits not only lexically, by tirelessly describing her own "natural order," "equilibrium," "regularity," and "unity of private self," but also structurally. The genre of memoirs best allows for a chronological continuity between past and present and thereby permits the narrator—in this case a condemned woman—to structure the way she depicts her psychological constancy. Roland uses memoirs' potential for proving personal immutability by showing parallel moments in her past and present life and pointing out similar responses to each incident. For example, early in her "Mémoires particuliers" she establishes her resistance to arbitrary authority by recounting how, when she was sick at the age of seven, she had refused to obey her father's order to swallow medicine because he had whipped her (p. 209). Later on, despotism, whether from a severe Jean-Marie Roland or from the Terror's leadership, sets off in Roland the same courageous inflexibility:

> All the details of this scene [her father's beating her] are as present to me now as if it had just occurred; all the sensations I felt then are still as distinct; the same stiffening I felt in me then and have since during solemn moments; and I would not, today, have to do anything more to climb proudly up to the gallows than I had to then to surrender to the barbaric treatment that might have killed me, but not defeated me. (p. 210)

Another set of analogous elements in the *Mémoires* is Roland's series of private refuges. Her childhood reading alcove is mirrored later in her convent room, then in her tiny ministerial office, and finally in her prison cell. Such hidden shelters bespeak her ongoing need for solitude and reflection; they also, by their repetition, show how she "sensitized" the space around her by making such corners "one of the greatest powers of integration for [her] thoughts, memories and dreams."[20] Thus Roland's firmness and self-possession, as well as her strength and self-sufficiency, not only are unchanging traits of her personality, but are the signposts of a life pattern that gives coherence to her personal narrative.

The "harmony" that women were expected to manifest, which was believed to be rooted in their bodily equilibrium, is another area from which Roland drew specific narrative techniques. The physical dysfunction and disharmony considered to cause female deviance have special relevance in light of late-eighteenth-century punishment techniques, which focused on the criminal's body as source and symbol of wrongdoing. The body thus was the object of punishment, not the mind or spirit. This focus on the punished body as proof of justice done was most evident in the torture and beheading spectacles of the time.[21] Most important for understanding Roland's response was the *visibility* of this form of justice, for it not only dissuaded potential criminals but also gave the public an active role in the punishment ritual. Indeed, this participation in part accounts for Roland's mistrust and condemnation of the Parisian masses.

The central importance of the body underlies, of course, the physical and sexual nature of the crude attacks on Roland, such as the insults in *Le Père Duchesne*. But along with her personal use of the standard "error-and-fall" moral structure, Roland manipulates the primacy of corporality in two other principal ways: first, by utilizing the common technique of portraiture to counter negative views of her; and, second, by tracing particu-

[20]Gaston Bachelard, *The Poetics of Space*, trans. Maria Jolas (New York: Orion Press, 1964), 6. Translation of *La Poétique de l'espace* (Paris: Presses Universitaires de France, 1958).

[21]See Michel Foucault, *Surveiller et punir: Naissance de la prison* (Paris: Gallimard, 1975), also published as *Discipline and Punish: The Birth of the Prison*, trans. Alan Sheridan (New York: Pantheon, 1977), for Foucault's analysis of punishment as part of "the history of the body." See also Mireille Vincent-Cassy, "Prison et châtiments à la fin du Moyen Age," in *Les Marginaux et les exclus dans l'histoire*, Cahiers Jussieu no. 5 (Paris: UGE 10/18, 1979), 262–74, for a concise analysis of the medieval origins of the social importance of visible phenomena.

lar sexual experiences in her life so as to establish her authentic, versus an ascribed, sexual identity. Roland's confidence in the truth of her portraits and self-portraits, grounded in her era's belief in the validity of the visible, is strongly expressed in various exhortations throughout her *Mémoires:*

> *Blind* slanderers: *Follow* Roland's tracks, *examine* his life closely, *observe* mine; *consult* the communities where we have lived, the cities we have inhabited, the countryside where you cannot *conceal* who you are, *scrutinize*. . . . The closer you *see* us as we are, the angrier you will be: that is the reason you want to destroy us. (p. 337; my emphasis)

She likewise consistently denies any "dissimulation" or "disguise"—precisely the "hiding" and "concealing" of which she is accused.

Much of Roland's *Mémoires* consists essentially of portraits: the "Portraits et anecdotes" presentations of major and minor Gironde and Montagne figures, the "Brissot," "Danton," and "Anecdotes" descriptions of political leaders, and the "Mémoires particuliers" series of childhood friends and relatives. All the portraits, says Roland, are a consequence of her imagination:

> My rather lively imagination portrays all the people I find striking doing some action that I feel suits their character; I cannot watch an unusual physiognomy for a half hour without clothing it in the costume of some profession or assigning it some role that it has evoked or reminded me of. (pp. 76–77)

The technique of portraits allows Roland to assign roles in the "drama" (or "strange masquerade," p. 138) her memoirs are unfolding. Since her punishers have assigned her a predetermined role—and this is particularly apparent during her interrogation, when Roland rejects the prepared "script" of the "public prosecutor who seems to want [her] to provide in [her] own answers the text of accusations that he has so zealously prepared" (p. 366)—Roland will respond by "imagining people dressed in the costume and performing the action that [she deems] befit their character" (p. 138).

The most explicitly strategic use of portraiture is in Roland's description of herself. Her premise is her "well-organized constitution" (p. 253), and from it arise her excellent moral and sexual qualities. The rather long passage moves from her face to her feet and from her "sweet expression" to her "affectionate soul." It encompasses the key words of the era's feminine lexicon—"sweetness," "tenderness," "affection," "the plumpness of perfect health," "the shyness of modesty," "austerity," "restraint" (pp. 254–55)—and asserts the necessary connection between her physical and moral health. Roland's insistence on her sexual desirability is particularly evident in her description and to some extent contradicts her professed modesty. The passage is revealing in several ways:

> As for my turned-up chin, it has precisely those characteristics the physiognomists describe as indicating sensual pleasure. When I compare them with my personal experience, I doubt that anyone has ever been more suited to pleasure and yet has tasted so little of it. (p. 254)

This self-identification with the desire for sensual pleasure, one instance of Roland's continued insistence that she is irresistible to all the men she meets, reflects her narcissistic tendencies. In the face of external physical deprecation and sexual judgments, she evokes herself favorably as both eminently desirable and at the same time "prudent through sensuality" (p. 253). Far from the depravity her accusers have ascribed to her, Roland's self-attested blend of desirability and modesty corresponds perfectly to prescribed feminine harmony and limitation.

Roland's highlighting of moments in her sexual maturation is another technique that arises from her punishers' insistence on corporality and the visibility of justice. Like Albertine Sarrazin centuries later, she wants her reader to "see" her accusers' misperceptions of her physiosexual and affective identity. If, in contrast to Sarrazin, Roland speaks of these events as traumas, not as joyous memories, it is because of the change between their eras in attitudes and in the explicitness of their criminosexual theories. The codified feminine sexual passivity under which Roland lived gave way in our century to an allowance for female activity, albeit still defined and controlled by androcentric values. The incidents Roland recounts include her being forced, as a child, to feel a boy's genitals, the onset of her menstruation, and her wedding night.[22] Playing with judgments of her, she calls the effect of these traumas important "for its influence on my moral nature/on my morale"(p. 217). Paradoxically, sharing her sexual history with the reader, far from being an avowal of careless morals, is to her an act of great resolution and courage.

Roland's insistence on the rightness of her own moral perspective on her sexual history is so strong that at one point in her memoirs she intervenes to address the reader directly and confidentially. Using the first-person imperative, "Let's stop here a moment" (p. 221), and so including herself in the message that follows, Roland proceeds to preach at length about mothers' responsibility for their daughters' purity: "Let all mothers contemplate with horror the extent of the vigilance that is their prescribed task" (p. 221). As her sensitivity offers, she believes, a general lesson about the human heart, so her particular knowledge of female sexuality represents women's common estate. Roland transforms her perceived abnormality by construing her private experience as the female norm.

By this paradoxical method of turning her own moral and sexual story, considered by others as abnormal and deserving censure, into the female norm, Roland gives her text a social purpose. Rousseau and others proclaimed women's "usefulness"; Roland agress, but she recasts that "usefulness' in her own terms. That her story will provide moral enlightenment, in keeping with the social tenet "We are born to seek happiness and to serve the happiness of others" (p. 341), is but an extension of her individual ability to "please others and do good deeds for them" (p. 202). Roland's condemnation had been founded on her perceived antisocial behavior. To negate that charge and convert its terms to positive ones, Roland must describe her vilification itself as socially useful. Thus her "Notices historiques" present her imprisonment as "a procedure

---

[22]Marie Cappelle-Lafarge likewise describes at length the shock and unpleasantness of her wedding night, with the difference that she presents Charles Lafarge as a raging animal, whereas Roland considers her husband "sexless, as it were" (*Mémoires*, 330). Roland, throughout her memoirs, insists on reason over body to counter charges of her promiscuity.

[she] will make useful to [her] country" (p. 42). Punishment and its accepted social usefulness are subverted to the extreme when Roland at one point contemplates suicide as the ultimate lesson in true responsibility. Rather than acknowledging guilt, as legal theory had it, her suicide would in fact frustrate her punishers by denying them further opportunity to exercise their tyranny. Roland makes all the elements of judicial procedure—interrogation, confession, and punishment—into tools with which she redefines justice and constructs her own model of social responsibility.

These judicial rituals of interrogation, confession, and punishment, combined with certain properties of memoirs as a form of confessional narrative, provided Roland with various devices for showing the erroneous basis of her ascribed "abnormality" and for righting society's views of her. Note that she expected little sympathy from her contemporaries; for that reason she calls her text "An Appeal to Impartial Posterity," the title of the 1795 edition of her *Mémoires*, in the hope that future generations will appreciate her true historical persona. One judicial element Roland uses is confession. The ritual of confession and its literary correlate, confessional writing, were expected at the time to reveal secrets. For Roland this idea of confession was absurd. Her writing was, rather, a means to "live a second time" (p. 201) and to have "some life in the next generation" (p. 277). Her memoirs, like Rousseau's *Confessions*, in no way imply avowal of guilt; on the contrary, they expose the sins of her condemners.

In a similar manner interrogation, which also allowed the accused to participate somewhat in the ritual of justice, gives Roland a framework for correcting history. Two characteristics of the usual interrogation dialogue are particularly important for her: its goal of eliciting detailed factual responses from the accused and its reliance on logical "cause and effect" to determine the truth of the testimony. In her last days, while at the Conciergerie, Roland wrote "Notes sur mon procès et l'interrogatoire qui l'a commencé." In it she describes how her judge and accuser distort the questioning procedure: instead of seeking to uncover the facts of her case, says Roland, "they did not like it when I answered in detail" (p. 366). Her condemners made a travesty of the inquiry and "used all means to reduce [her] to silence" (p. 368). From their perspective, Roland's assertion of the facts of her story is annoying "chatter" and Roland herself "a chatterbox" (p. 368). Far from being an admission of guilt, her responses to questioning prove her innocence, since the interrogation procedure itself is invalid.[23]

The technique Roland most often employs is to undermine the causal logic that was generally prized during the Enlightenment and that specifically underlay "explanations" of crime and deviance. Shaped by her century's insistence on reason, she subscribes fully to the categorization of human faculties—reason, imagination, heart, passion—and to the belief in the superiority of the mind's powers: "I kept my imagination in check and followed lines of reasoning" (p. 303). Like Roussel, who saw imagination in women as dangerous, Roland exalts her intelligence and its ability to combat "the susceptibility of [her] imagination, from which [she] had great need to protect [her]self" (p. 261).

The strength of her reason, however, is used not to reinforce accepted dicta, but to establish an alternate system of explanation. Roland's system, founded on the axiom that she is right and innocent, makes use of irony to expose her accusers' illogic. The very first sentence of her *Mémoires* stands their reasoning on its head: "It [her situation] is virtue's fate in times of revolution" (p. 33). "Virtue" immediately sets the tone for Roland's designations of true guilt and innocence, and "fate" evokes the ineluctable tragedy that results when these terms are perverted. This ironic use of logic is also another instance of Roland's use of oxymorons, in this case one that collapses her personal definition of terms into the preexisting structure of cause and effect.

The causal arguments underlying her censure are more explicitly challenged in the first sentence of "Portraits et anec-

---

[23] A similar condemnation of women's speaking out appears in a 1790s document denouncing the poltical activist Claire Lacombe: she is "very dangerous in that she is very eloquent" (text of 1793 meeting of the Jacobin Society, reproduced in *Women in Revolutionary Paris*, 183).

dotes": "I have been imprisoned for over two months *because* I belong to a good, upright man who decided to be virtuous during a revolution" (p. 99; my emphasis). Here Roland is condemned not only in spite of her innocence, but "because" she and her husband are blameless—an "explanation" clearly empty of any sense. What is more, that Monsieur Roland performs nobly during a revolution suggests that this comportment is unusual in such circumstances—a claim that implies a moral judgment of his adversaries' dishonorable behavior. Once again Roland adopts her opponents' weapons for her own counterattack. The perceived logical connection between woman's physiosexual being and her "abnormal" acts, with its textual concomitant in women's narratives of a fatal downfall, supplied Roland with eminently exploitable materials that shaped both the content and the form of her memoirs.

More recent critics of Madame Roland have hardly been kinder or less gynophobic than their predecessors. In the 1930s, Pierre Trahard once again voiced Roussel's concepts of female normality. Calling Roland a victim of her "imagination," which for him is "the source of our misfortunes," Trahard says: "Madame Roland was to sin . . . by *excess* of imagination and by pride, by ambition and by rancor. Her changeable nature, her theoretical exigencies, her tactical errors, her awkward maneuvers were to ruin her Girondin friends and herself as well."[24] One of his contemporaries, Albert Mathiez, focuses squarely on Roland's "dominating her old husband" and on the "depth" of her hate for her political enemies,[25] implying that all her acts sprang from this unwomanly sentiment. That both critics see as primary her "woman's rancor" poignantly belies Roland's faith in the comprehension of future generations. Equally ironic are such literary judgments of her text as Monglond's—he calls it "perfectly useless"[26]—which contradict the

[24]Pierre Trahard, *La Sensibilité révolutionnaire: 1789–1794* (Paris: Bouvin, 1936), 215; my emphasis.
[25]Albert Mathiez, *La Révolution française: La Gironde et la Montagne*, Vol. 2, 2d ed. (Paris: Armand Colin, 1951), 45–46.
[26]Monglond, *Préromantisme français*, 320.

central purpose of her writing. And though Roland might well have enjoyed nineteenth-century dithyrambic appreciations of her and her writing, such as those of Lamartine, Michelet, and to some extent Stendhal and Goethe, it is also true that these idealizations did not fulfill her hopes for historical accuracy.[27] Alone among critics in understanding both the general and the specific conditions from which the *Mémoires* arose, Gita May rightly identifies Roland's use of themes and clichés of her time, which she "adapted to the new and so very dramatic circumstances of the Revolutionary era."[28] I would add that Roland, apart from the circumstances of France's exceptional Revolutionary period, represents a woman condemned and punished more for reasons of gender than for her political loyalties. It is not coincidental that Roland's contemporary, André Chénier, used the demanding genre of poetry to establish his immortal literary identity. Free from externally imposed definitions of his character and motivations, Chénier could challenge his punishers from the heights of his poetic glory. Roland, however, had to expend imaginative energy countering society's view of her, in the basic task of affirming her personality and principles. Her authority as writer rests on the force of her "imagination in remembering,"[29] that is, her success in reinterpreting the past rather than in charting the future.

It is paradoxical that, on the basis of accusations so ambiguous and poorly delineated—I would even say unarticulated, since the true sex-specific charges against her were never expressed—Roland received the most unequivocal of penalties, execution. It is even more revealing that witnesses to her beheading praised her "virile" courage and her "manly" stoicism in the face of death. For to exalt as fundamentally sexual such unexpected female behavior in defeat, and yet to have con-

---

[27]Lamartine called Roland "a creature who lived solely according to her heart" (cited in May, *De Rousseau à Roland* 19), and Stendhal called her "the living incarnation of all public and private virtues" (ibid., 19). The relation of women to individualism had clearly been transformed.
[28]May, *De Rousseau à Roland*, 215.
[29]Ibid., 230.

demned exceptional female comportment when it enjoyed a measure of glory is at best paternalistic and at worst (for Roland) fatal. Produced by an extreme example of women's victimization by cultural contradictions, Roland's *Mémoires* are a compelling private plea for understanding that ultimately brings into question an era's misperceptions about women in general.

5
Marie Cappelle-Lafarge

> Nature has assigned to each sex its mode of life and its station. The woman who is unfortunate enough to depart from that life and station is, in moral terms, a monster—Odilon Barrot, public prosecutor, 1840

The legacy of eighteenth-century moral/sexual judgments of criminal women is evident in Odilon Barrot's summation against the accused murderess Marie Capelle-Lefarge.[1] Barrot's explicit equating of sex-role conformity with accepted morality, however, more directly encapsulates the nineteenth-century codification of the concepts of morality and deviance. In fact, no modern period in Western culture has manifested such ambivalence toward criminality as the 1800s: even while criminological and penal theories grew more punitive and prescriptive, notions of prisoner rehabilitation and redemption encouraged reforms that softened conditions. Foucault has exposed this deceptive "humanitarian" current as a mere shift in punishment techniques—toward the mind, not the body—rather than the commonly perceived concern for the individual criminal's well-being.[2] Calls for "improved" prison conditions, rather than ending cruelty, thus simply extended the field of punishment.

---

[1] The spellings of "Cappelle"/"Capelle" vary, as do the forms of the author's name that appear on the different editions of her works (sometimes "Marie Cappelle," sometimes "Veuve Lafarge"). I shall use the compound name "Cappelle-Lafarge" in this discussion. Barrot is quoted in Léon Abensour, *Le Féminisme sous le règne de Louis Philippe et en 1848* (Paris: Plon-Nourrit, 1913), 208.

[2] See Michel Foucault, *Surveiller et punir: Naissance de la prison* (Paris: Gallimard, 1975), esp. chap. 1. Also published as *Discipline and Punish: The Birth of the Prison*, trans. Alan Sheridan (New York: Pantheon, 1977).

Cappelle-Lafarge by Chapon, 1836. Photo Harlingue-Viollet

This apparent contradiction between harsh sanction and humanitarian reform is only one of the many inconsistencies that mark this complicated era. Along with France's political wavering between empires and republics went jockeying between individual and societal priorites, as reflected in literature and philosophy. More specifically, the antagonistic currents of Romanticism and positivism coexisted, though the latter increased its hegemony through the century. From the pre-Romanticism of Rousseau, whose insistence on private feelings and public welfare had marked Madame Roland's writing, emerged the exaggerated individualism of Chateaubriand's spiritual struggle that in part informed Cappelle-Lafarge's works. At the same time, the Romantics' personalizing and internalizing of experience was progressively devalued by the postivists' faith in external, verifiable reality. And so Cappelle-Lafarge had also to honor this new definition of the authenticity of experience. Finally, increasingly powerful norms for female modesty made even more rigid the themes and forms women writers were expected to use. Pressured to conform to confessional modes just as individual and sentimental priorities were losing ground, women like Cappelle-Lafarge found themselves "discredited both as women and as Romantics."[3] Springing from these various opposing forces are two major prison works of the 1840s and 1850s, Cappelle-Lafarge's remarkable *Mémoires* and her journal, *Heures de prison*,[4] both of which are in essence responses to the conflic-

---

[3] Maïté Albistur and Daniel Armogathe, *Histoire du féminisme français du Moyen Age à nos jours* (Paris: des femmes, 1977), 263.
[4] Several editions of Cappelle-Lafarge's works have been used because dates, content, and subdivisions within them vary. Editions used are as follows:
  Marie Cappelle (veuve Lafarge), *Mémoires écrits par elle-même*, 4 vols., 3d ed. (Brussels: Hauman, 1842–43). Contains the memoirs, correspondence, notes, and trial documents. All quotations will be from this edition unless otherwise indicated, and volume and page numbers will be given parenthetically in the text. All translations are mine.
  Mémoires de Marie Cappelle (veuve Lafarge) écrits par elle-même, 4 vols. (Paris: A. René, 1841–42).
  Madame Lafarge (née Marie Cappelle), *Mémoires* (Paris: Michel Lévy Frères, 1867).
  Madame Lafarge, *Correspondance*, 2 vols., 2d ed. (Paris: Mercure de France, 1913). Will be referred to as *Correspondance*.

tual climates—criminological, moral, and literary—in which the author lived.[5]

Cappelle-Lafarge's story itself is full of contradictions and reversals; the only constant is judicial and penal severity. After twenty-four years of a life that bore striking parallels with that of Madame Roland—bourgeois family upbringing and education, the moral "perfection" of convent reclusion, and a late, loveless, and disappointing marriage—Cappelle-Lafarge became the center of one of the century's most infamous trials, the twenty-two-month-long "affaire Lafarge." She was accused simultaneously of poisoning her husband, the Correzian forge owner Charles Lafarge, and of stealing a friend's diamonds.[6] She also endured two "stacked" trials and two sequential sentences amounting to twelve years of hard labor, the harshest punishment then given to women. Even the public response was contradictory, since her contemporaries were divided over her guilt or innocence. The first autopsy performed on Charles Lafarge had revealed no arsenic in the body, but subsequent medical testimony reversed that opinion: "Science abruptly overturned the verdict of science. Science determined there was crime where, two days before, it had found innocence, and found poison where before it had not seen any poison."[7] Cappelle-Lafarge, the victim of positivism's enthusiasm for scientific "evidence," however slim,[8] also underwent a host of legal (and illegal) procedures that give her trial the formal hollow-

Madame Lafarge (née Marie Cappelle), *Heures de prison*, 3 vols. (Paris: Librairie Nouvelle, 1854).
Madame Lafarge, *Heures de prison* 2d ed. (Paris: Librairie Nouvelle, 1856). All references will be to this edition unless otherwise indicated. All translations are mine.
[5]For a detailed presentation of the events in Cappelle-Lafarge's life as well as a historical analysis of connections between her behavior and her social context, see Mary S. Hartman, *Victorian Murderesses: A True History of Thirteen Respectable French and English Women Accused of Unspeakable Crimes* (New York: Schocken Books, 1977), chap. 1.
[6]Cappelle-Lafarge's friendship and split with Marie de Nicolai, who accused her of theft, is recounted at length in the *Mémoires*. This lesser infraction, while important, is of less concern here than the crime of poisoning.
[7]Comment of A. René, editor of the 1841–42 edition of the *Mémoires*, 1:5.
[8]Cappelle-Lafarge was only recently exonerated, in 1979, when typhoid was declared the real cause of Lafarge's death.

ness of much of positivistic analysis. For example, the bill of indictment was published before Cappelle-Lafarge was notified of its contents. Also, only prosecuting evidence could be presented during the preliminary hearing; the presiding judge labeled Cappelle-Lafarge "a thief and a poisoner"; the prosecution's key witness, found guilty of perjury, was then exonerated; and all poisoning charges were deliberated in a single jury vote.[9] For these reasons the *Mémoires* are themselves principally the document for the defense that was not allowed during Cappelle-Lafarge's trial. Like Madame Roland's text, they are above all restituted "truth," but here the truth must counter the force of "scientific proof" as well as of judicial condemnation: "I don't believe in the judges of this society; it's not from a six-man tribunal that I will ask justice; rather, it's the world that will give me justice, absolution, and honor in exchange for truth" (*Mémoires*, 4:85).

To establish judicial and moral "truth," a criminal such as Cappelle-Lafarge had to work against far more than the improprieties of legal procedures: like Madame Roland, Cappelle-Lafarge faced the hostility of general perceptions about deviant women, which had to be shown not to apply. But, while definitions of female criminality in the nineteenth century remained sexual in that they expressed fear of female assertiveness, they took on the same taxonomic precision as criminological discourse in general. In fact, the models often became so specific that no real individual could conform to them.[10] Whereas Madame Roland was believed to have erred morally in her acts, women like Cappelle-Lafarge were considered innately degenerate, representative of a criminal *type* possessing distinct and verifiable physiopsychological traits. The female criminal was now defined by her sex as well as her criminality. One can speculate that the era's theoretical studies of criminal women were in part spawned by the feminist activism of the time,

---

[9]All these irregularities are outlined in the *Mémoires*.

[10]For example, Lombroso's later "anthropometrics," which supplied precise physical measurements of criminal "types," in fact preceded and predetermined reality rather than vice versa.

which rekindled fear of female "domination" and solidified the fundamental belief in the antagonism between the sexes.

Both of Cappelle-Lafarge's texts, her *Mémoires* and her *Heures de prison*, can be seen as responses to her generation's contradictions, and they use the substance and methods with which those contradictions were articulated. Like Roland's *Mémoires*, Cappelle-Lafarge's works subvert the terms and techniques they adopt. In this case I shall consider the premises, discourse, and methods of nineteenth-century criminological theory as they are used and undercut for Cappelle-Lafarge's purposes. First I shall treat the strict but inconsistent typing of "normal" and "deviant" women, in which empirical methods and a moral lexicon masked the impossibility of reconciling women's corporeal and spiritual "natures." Then I shall discuss the ideology and reality of punishment in terms of the personal losses they engendered and the textual compensations that served Cappelle-Lafarge (silence, religiosity, and insistence on physical over mental acts, as they inform her themes and style). Finally, I shall describe the general philosophical and literary forces Cappelle-Lafarge encountered and discuss how they too shaped her writing.

Criminal typologies abounded in the nineteenth century, and they continued to insist on the monstrous, mixed "nature" of the female criminal: for the prison reformer Joséphine Mallet, the deviant woman was a "mixed creature" in whom the passions dominated;[11] for the head of the Seine Prefecture, H. A. Frégier, she was a "dangerous" creature whose "religious instinct" was overcome by her "desire for pleasure" and her tendency toward prostitution;[12] and for the ultraempirical criminologist Cesare Lombroso, she was only "half woman" by virtue of her "masculine" intelligence coupled with her monstrous "exaggerated sexuality."[13] At the base of all criminological the-

[11] Joséphine Mallet, *Les Femmes en prison: Causes de leurs chutes, moyens de les relever*, 2d ed. (Paris: P. A. Desrosiers, 1845), chap. 2.

[12] H. A. Frégier, *Des classes dangereuses de la population dans les grandes villes et des moyens de les rendre meilleures* (Paris: 1838), 185.

[13] C. Lombroso and G. Ferrero, *La Femme criminelle et la prostituée*, trans. from the Italian by L. Meille (Paris: Félix Alcan, 1896), 429–30. The English translation, *The Female Offender* (London: T. Fisher Unwin, 1895), is incomplete.

ory was the powerful tenet that untrammeled empiricism put in place and that succeeding generations discredited: the belief that "the moral sciences are so tightly linked to the natural sciences."[14] This nineteenth-century notion, an extension of the earlier animist idea of connections between the physiological and the psychological, came to be seen as irrefutable scientific fact. And this perceived inextricable link between morality and science, with its concomitant of empirical documentation, became in turn one of Cappelle-Lafarge's prime weapons against her accusers.

The parallels between natural and moral classifications of behavior, of course, immediately suggest Balzac's fictional universe, with its internal laws and its character types. But if many of Balzac's male protagonists comprehend, embrace, or transcend vice and corruption, their relation to moral codes does not reflect women's experience. For most women, increasingly confined and isolated from social encounters, moral norms were internalized, never challenged. When women were unsuccessful in meeting sexual and family norms, they were subject to "protection," treated legally and judicially as children. Imprisonment, one such form of "protection," reinforced these norms. The prescriptiveness of such views of women, mirrored in the constant lexical blending of criminological and moral discourses, was another tool Cappelle-Lafarge used. In the following description of women by the criminologist Henri Joly, the key words Cappelle-Lafarge redefined are italicized:

> Woman has always been meant to be controlled by, and one could add *respected* for, the very *passion* she inspires in others. That is the price she pays to safeguard her *grace* and the *virtue* of her consoling influence. Furthermore, should her *dignity*, which is made up of *delicacy* and *reserve*, change, its alteration is quicker and more profound than man's, since she has neither [a man's] active life nor the public benefits of patriotic *devotion* to help her *rehabilitate* herself. For that reason, the less her *morals* ensure her

[14]Ibid., p. 1.

the *respect* necessary to maintain her *purity* and her *charming weakness*, the more she needs to be *protected*.[15]

It is no wonder Cappelle-Lafarge meant her memoirs to serve an essentially moral purpose: "The moral effect is the goal and purpose of my efforts."[16]

Another aspect of the rigidly codified view of women was the paradoxical focus on the body in explaining female normality and abnormality. Lombroso contrasted the anatomy, insensitivity/sensitivity, and frigidity/sexual appetites of normal and deviant women. Yet, ideally, women's bodies were to be repressed in the name of spiritual priorities. Many women, including Cappelle-Lafarge, adopted an increasing religiosity, and she explicitly denied the unleashed sensuality presumed to mark the female deviant. Yet she herself invokes the impossibility of reconciling spirit with flesh that underlay contradictory views of women's corporality and criminality when she suggests her own affinities with George Sand's Lélia:

> That great and beautiful Lélia, whom society has put on the Index, whom women, in their virtuous simplicity, repudiate and refuse to understand! . . . That poor woman, who endured all possible pain, doubts, and discouragements, who was riveted to earth by her evil passions, lifted up to the heavens by her sublime instincts; who possessed in equal parts the power of good and the power of evil; who did not want to be a weak woman and who could not become an angel! (*Mémoires*, 4:84)

Lélia, who sprang from and inspired both the fears and the fantasies of her era, is here described, lexically and stylistically, in all her duality—as the monster who, like Pascal's fallen angel in the last sentence, was irreversibly exiled. But such exile of the condemned individual coexisted with the belief that the sinner could be redeemed. Though society wished to have such fictional and real women as Lélia and Cappelle-Lafarge spiritually rehabilitated and purified, the author, on the contrary, implies that domesticity, convents, and prisons cannot achieve that

---

[15] Henri Joly, *La France criminelle* (Paris: L. Cerf, 1889), 392; my emphasis.
[16] *Mémoires*, René ed., 4:310.

conversion.[17] In an earlier passage, much as Madame Roland did, she describes her childhood stay in a convent, thus prefiguring her subsequent prison encounter with attempts to reconcile body and soul. And in this same passage she, again like Madame Roland, uses oxymorons mixing the spiritual with the material to mock the hypocrisy underlying bourgeois morality: "Our dress was the guarantee of our moral perfection just as our purses and hats were the guarantee of our virtues" (*Mémoires*, René ed., 1:40). As Foucault claims in *Surveiller et punir*, tracing the link from convents to prisons, the same society that sought to modify the individual's soul through punishment also exploited the individual's body for economic production, thereby creating an unresolvable dualism in penal priorities and techniques.

With most criminologists subscribing to the belief in the inmate's criminal degeneracy and Lombroso and his followers attributing "masculine" traits to criminal women, the resulting "virilized" monster was also endowed with sadistic motivations.[18] Only sadism could explain the disguised and domestic nature of most women's crimes, in particular the "feminine" murder weapon of poison. Literary examples of such scheming heroines flourished—Dumas's Milady de Winter, D'Ennery's Dame de Saint-Tropez, and even Cappelle-Lafarge's own "ruined woman" of her lost drama "La Femme perdue"—and were extensions of popular notions of women's general "crafty, dissimulating," and lying nature.[19] It was generally assumed that there was no masculine equivalent of the "born woman poisoner," since this type was specifically a woman who was "hypnotized . . . by the thought that a man's life was in her

---

[17]It is an interesting corollary that prisons of the time stressed physical over mental work, out of mistrust for the prisoner's intellectual development. Far from promoting spiritual liberation, such physical labor, says Cappelle-Lafarge, means that "she is no longer allowed to grow" and that she will become "a pariah in the land of intelligences" (*Heures de prison*).

[18]Lombroso in fact cites Marie Lafarge as an example of the criminal woman of "exceptional intelligence"—a "virile" quality. The proof is her committing a "premeditated" crime and then writing about her life (*Femme criminelle*, 449).

[19]Michelle Perrot, "Sur la femme délinquante et criminelle au xixe siècle," unofficial copy (from course on "Delinquency and Repression," Jussieu-Paris VII, 1978–79), 38.

hands."[20] Slow poisoning, it was believed, was more than an occasion for vengeful power: it gave a woman the chance to profit fully from her expected domestic devotion, to "play the role of the devoted woman even while she continued to increase her evildoing in order to hasten its conclusion."[21] The stress on appearance, disguise, and roles that marked Roland's writing continues in Cappelle-Lafarge's works, with the difference that Roland's external political "spectacle" is now moved indoors to become the domestic "tragedy" that Cappelle-Lafarge describes. There could be no more persuasive proof that "passion" perverts women's natural affective strengths, it was thought, than a family crime requiring her to use her "unbalanced imagination."[22]

Her contemporaries' insistence on women's irreconcilable physical and spiritual roles is seen in the indictment brought against Cappelle-Lafarge. Essentially moral in content, it damns her for refusing her sexual obligations even while it decries her perceived sexual assertiveness. The charges point first to a letter she wrote to her husband on their wedding night, a letter falsely "admitting" adultery as a desperate means to end the marriage. The accusation condemns her for refusing her "conjugal duties" and then for being "suspiciously friendly" toward her husband afterward; it goes on to deplore Cappelle-Lafarge's "desire for independence," which it says motivated her crime.[23] Very much like the sensational Madame David, accused in the same period of shooting her husband and called a "monster" with "the dreadful morals that liberated women are preaching,"[24] as woman Cappelle-Lafarge was deemed at once responsible and not responsible for her situation. The belief in the criminal woman's insupportable physical and spiritual androgyny allowed moral tenets and empirical "findings" to reunite and was a forerunner of the idea of "hysteria"—the organic internal split that by century's end was

---

[20]Camille Granier, *La Femme criminelle* (Paris: Octave Doin, 1906), 159.
[21]Ibid., 208.
[22]See especially coverage of the Weiss affair in the "Dossier-criminalité" at the Bibliothèque Féministe Marguerite Durand, Paris 5ᶜ.
[23]Charges reproduced in *Mémoires*, 3:119ff.
[24]Abensour, *Féminisme*, 220.

thought to account for all female deviance. And, as if to predict the later association between women's hysteria and psychological disorders as well as to counter belief in her own criminogenic mental impairment, Cappelle-Lafarge described her situation not as stemming from madness but, on the contrary, as sure to cause it.

Certain elements of penal theory and practice also informed Cappelle-Lafarge's texts. Changes in the concept of prison, combined with the increasing categorization of inmates by age, sex, and type of crime, made for more and more precise rules and conditions of confinement. Her status as a twice-condemned criminal made Cappelle-Lafarge an "exceptional" prisoner, subject to extra security measures and deprivation. Unlike political prisoners, who were allowed to read and write, Cappelle-Lafarge was a civil prisoner and therefore ineligible for "equality before suffering."[25] Although class distinctions still functioned in incarceration—and Cappelle-Lafarge's privileged status was denounced in the judge's calling for "equality before the law" (*Mémoires*, 3:312) as well as in subsequent press reports objecting to her "lenient" treatment—Cappelle-Lafarge's situation can hardly be called "soft." She first describes the Brives jail, with its small depressing cell, but where she at least had her servant Clémentine (*Mémoires*, 3:13), then goes on to evoke Tulles prison not in physical terms, but as an emotional horror that aroused "an agony a thousand times worse than the agony of the dying" (*Correspondance*, 1:303). Finally, in Montpellier prison she successively loses her books, visits, furniture, companionship, and clothing. Thereafter she virtually ceases to mention her material conditions and instead pushes inward to describe her state of mind. Like Roland, she barely evokes quotidian events or objects, but because of her spiritual conversion rather than a concern with political theorizing. Cappelle-Lafarge, as a criminal considered "civilly, a dead woman," experiences a rupture with the material life that surrounds her.

The rule of silence imposed in prisons was particularly harsh because it forbade writing as well as speech. Letters were censored and frequently impounded, making prisoners "mute wit-

[25]*Heures de prison*, 1854 ed., 2:64.

nesses" (*Heures de prison*, 1854 ed., 2:49). But the loss of speech, the result of official adoption of the Auburn prison isolation system and the influence of religious practices, hurt women the most. For Cappelle-Lafarge it recalled the childhood restrictions on speaking imposed under her mother's severe code of behavior (*Mémoires*, 1:124). The onset of madness in her fellow prisoner Madame Grouvelle, preceded by a long period of aphasia, sparks great fear in Cappelle-Lafarge and leads her to connect destruction of the mind with legal and expressive death: "They are mutilating my intelligence; they are subjecting it to the pressures of some compressive rule that creates a void around it and that will drive me mad after it has driven me stupid" (*Heures de prison*, p. 134). The absence of mental "air" or life, an apt image for the "death" of madness, also reveals Cappelle-Lafarge's adoption of the scientific penchant of the positivists. Here and elsewhere she is obsessed with madness—"No, I am not mad, no, my fear is lying to me" (*Correspondance*, 1:303). One can see her acceptance of the postivistic belief in the connection between physical organs and mental faculties. The link between the physical and the mental is not, however, evoked to explain the cause of criminal behavior, but instead is identified as the *result* of the oppressive punitive system. Her comment that the loss of reading in prison "stunts her growth" encapsulates her reversal of the accepted body/mind connection, for she claims that mental damage effects physical change, not vice versa. As we will see, Cappelle-Lafarge also makes use of the prevalent theory of discrete intellectual faculties, but she ties that theory to mental chaos rather than exalting its organizational usefulness and strength.

Within Cappelle-Lafarge's two texts themselves there is an evolution, over her ten years of writing, in her response to prison's effects. The genre change from memoirs to journal implies a change in structure from the *Mémoires*' expanded descriptions of past events to the laconic noting of present ideas and feelings in the *Heures de prison*. This shift in focus from external scenes to momentary thoughts reflects Cappelle-Lafarge's increasing separation from the images of this world (*Heures de prison*, p. 310) and is accompanied by a movement from description to aphorism, toward shorter and shorter paragraphs and sentences, and, finally, to the silence of her interrupted text. An analogue to sex-specific aphasia in women, the "death" of Cappelle-Lafarge's narrative voice is one of several signs of her weakening. The assertive and often humorous tone of the *Mémoires* gives way to passivity and resignation in the *Heures de prison*. Such strong statements as her views on women's education reflect her earlier declamatory, even judgmental style:

> Everything in education must, I believe, have a moral purpose, and it is not by overloading the brain with a thousand superficial things that one can achieve intelligence of the soul. . . . They say women can be frivolous and superficial; I don't agree; but it should be the case that, along with the mere outer trappings, women be given solid basics as well. (*Mémoires*, 1:48–49)

Her wit, anger, and irony dwindle as she begins to ask questions whose form and substance indicate growing passivity. The opening sentence of *Heures de prison*, repeated, insists on her loss of control over her life and her work: "What else is going to happen to me? What else is going to happen to me?" (p. 7).[26] Likewise the query, "What would have become of me?" (p. 11) and the indirect questions that end the *Mémoires* ("I don't know when I'll be leaving Tulle prison, I don't know where I'll go"; 4:62) show Cappelle-Lafarge placing her fate in higher hands. And the increasing religiousness that accompanies this abdication of responsibility for herself is lexically mirrored in her borrowing the language of Christianity. If the earlier Cappelle-Lafarge had evoked herself in purely positive character terms, the aging author blatantly compares herself to the suffering Christ: "My battered feet stain with blood the stones of the path, and I bend under the weight of my cross" (*Heures de prison*, p. 70).

Cappelle-Lafarge's extreme self-abnegation measures her loss of self-image during her long confinement. The internal sources of this loss of identity are complex, but it is likely that

---

[26] Anne Huré's protagonist, Noëlle, who also opts for spirit rather than flesh in *En prison* (1963), asks a similar question a century later: "What would become of her in the months that followed?" (256).

her twelve years of oblivion were largely responsible. For, as the public forgot her, Cappelle-Lafarge lost even its opprobrium, from which her energetic response had arisen. Her dialogue with the normative models that had once described and condemned her faded. Yet, paradoxically, her silence ultimately best serves her stated desire to offer a true picture of herself as the martyr she believed she had become.

If, however, Cappelle-Lafarge conforms to the search for the illusory "liberation" of religious devotion that many women chose, she does so, at least initially, as a means to "reappropriate" herself. Madame Roland had sought in her writing to "reacquire" the sexual identity her accusers had stripped from her; Cappelle-Lafarge, accused of innate moral degeneracy, sought rather to regain the spiritual identity of which common ideology deprived her. Thus the leitmotiv of loss and repossession of self traverses all Cappelle-Lafarge's works:

> I no longer *belong* to my self; ... I *belong* to justice. (*Mémoires*, 3:18; my emphasis)
>
> I feel myself suffering without being able to analyze my suffering. I am living *outside myself*. (*Mémoires*, 3:22–23; my emphasis)
>
> I *have no more* country! I *have no more* home! (*Heures de prison*, p. 8; my emphasis)
>
> How sad it is, dear God, *not to belong to yourself* anymore! (*Heures de prison*, p. 100; my emphasis)

Both her writing and her faith, removed from her material existence, offer the possibility of wholeness and integrity: "It seemed to me that by refusing life I had *regained possession of myself* and that my chains, if borne freely, would no longer weigh on my heart" (*Heures de prison*, p. 52; my emphasis). In this way Cappelle-Lafarge turns the resignation expected of her as woman and criminal into her own tool for reestablishing self-identification.

A further element of Cappelle-Lafarge's imprisonment gave concrete form to the general mind/body dichotomy she faced, which exalted external, physical experience even while it relegated women to the inferior regions of internal knowledge.

MARIE CAPPELLE-LAFARGE

Prison rules, by promoting physical over mental activity, added to Cappelle-Lafarge's difficulty in reclaiming her identity through spiritual quest. What is more, the then newly developed procedures of the spontaneous body search and uniform clothing (the penal *bure*, or sackcloth robe) accentuated the women's sense of being corporal objects. A surprise body search becomes Cappelle-Lafarge's worst horror (*Heures de prison*, p. 52); and the dreaded uniform, a humiliating mark of crime, is the only punishment she staunchly refuses (*Heures de prison*, p. 94). There is, to be sure, a strong element of class snobbery in her objection to being made a "spectacle for the eyes of the common people" (*Mémoires*, 3:15), the vain and foolish lower-class women who share her prison. But Cappelle-Lafarge's general sympathy for her sister prisoners, if condescending, is nonetheless grounded in some sense of a "shared fraternity of misfortune" (*Heures de prison*, p. 84). In subverting the hostile views surrounding her, she makes prison rules—meant to encourage Christian humility, repentance, and reform—into just the opposite: gratuitous and degrading punishment.

The objectification of the body in prison, in which the prisoner becomes a sort of spectacle for the ruling authorities,[27] served Cappelle-Lafarge in ways beyond sparking her denunciation of the punishment techniques used. Like Madame Roland, she makes the "seen" and the "visible" the very basis of her story's authenticity. Roland's generation had focused on visible acts as signs of guilt, and Roland replied with her own portraits and tableaus from her verifiable past. Cappelle-Lafarge also uses descriptions to establish truth, but with the greater formal precision demanded by her contemporaries' growing attraction to science. She in effect takes the paradigms of their empirical discourse and empties them of their already lifeless content. For example, the cold and—more important—false analysis of the official "facts" of Charles Lafarge's death are countered in her memoirs by a detailed, sincere, and moving account of the events. At stake here is the credibility of

[27] The shift from the eighteenth century is critical: if the act of punishment was the "show" during the Terror, the criminal herself or himself was now the thing observed.

judicial "truth," for Cappelle-Lafarge was consistently accused of struggling against evidence and appearance in maintaining her innocence.[28] What society keeps insisting is "right", however, is precisely what Cappelle-Lafarge rejects. To the society that had condemned her, in the name of positivism's "universal" scientific tendencies and against Romanticism's individualistic ideals, such unverifiable sources of knowledge as dreams, illusions, and feelings were severed from reality. But to Cappelle-Lafarge it is exactly these "unreal" elements that constitute the truth of her story, since accepted "reality" means for her being "buried alive" and "dying after a life that has not been lived" (*Correspondance*, 1:10). In other words, practicality and reality not only deny the validity of dream, they also squelch truth and nobility of purpose:

> It is the world, society, and reality that you must blame for the initial heartbreak that marks the transition from your beautiful life of dreams and illusions to your present life of disappointments and obligations. (*Mémoires*, René ed., 2:262)

> How denatured man's most noble purpose, duty, can be by society, habit, and convention. (*Mémoires*, René ed., 1:171–72)

By accepting as truth not observable "evidence" but internal knowledge, and by insisting on individual rather than collective experience, Cappelle-Lafarge undermines her accusers' case against her.

For Cappelle-Lafarge, the facts and actions surrounding her alleged crime took place on the stage of her inner reality: "A person's real life is *within himself;* events are only its setting."[29] In this internal drama, other elements dear to positivisitic methods are redefined to suit her own needs. Thus, for example, investigation and inquiry become a "descent into her heart" (*Mémoires*, 3:23), not an examination of visible corpses or

---

[28]Jules de Gaultier, *Madame Lafarge et la lutte contre les évidences* (Paris: Mercure de France, 1934), 467.

[29]*Mémoires*, 3:71; my emphasis. A closely similar thought appears in Albertine Sarrazin's *Journal de prison 1959:* "Events themselves are not important. . . . *Events take on the color we give them*" (her emphasis).

old letters. Further, in her special use of theatrical portraiture, people are no longer the highly individualized beings they were in Madame Roland's historical parade of rogues. Instead, Cappelle-Lafarge, exploiting to the full her era's mania for typing and categorizing, draws portraits more in the vein of La Bruyère's moral types. But here again her types are not recognized by the measurable external features that anthropological criminologists of the time were at pains to enumerate. Rather, she calls such superficial and strident classifications "lowly panegyrics" (*Mémoires,* René ed., 4:313) and identifies types by "character"—a purely subjective criterion discernible only through the observer's internal knowledge. Her justification for viewing the world as composed of character types also shows her personal use of the prevalent moral lexicon of her time:

> Society, which is nothing but an exchange of superficial sentiments and to which one goes not to express one's intimate thoughts but instead to forget them, should judge us only on *that part of ourselves that we reveal to it*. . . . Why not be satisfied with the vast *display* of ridiculousness, vanity, and pettiness *spread out before us*? Why not laugh at the fake expert when he begs for praise, the old coquette when she calls on us to discern the graces and past conquests beneath her folds and wrinkles? Why not laugh forever at the prudes, hypocrites, and misunderstood lovers who implore you to sound their depths? Laugh, for these embodiments of faults are born among you and for you, they belong to you; and the tribunal that they deem fit to lavish them with praise is also fit to *unmask* and ridicule them. (*Mémoires,* René ed., 2:244–45; my emphasis)

Cappelle-Lafarge, calling attention in this long exhortation to the inadequate caricature that is the "truth" produced by purely empirical explanations of human motivations, deflates the criminological models used against her.

In her use of portraits, Cappelle-Lafarge chooses favored stylistic practices of her time in order to comment on the cultural priorities they transmit. The following portrait of Cappelle-Lafarge's servant Clémentine is typical of the many that appear in the *Mémoires* and *Heures de prison*:

IMAGINATION IN CONFINEMENT

> Clémentine is a typical spritely young "Parisienne." Her thoughts speak for themselves and the extent of her education is easily discernible. She knows a little about everything without having learned anything. She falls in love with everything in an hour without becoming passionately fond of anything. She is frivolous from inclination and sensible from instinct.... In order to cry herself, she has to see someone else cry. In order to get bored she has to get bored along with someone else.... Her heart is excellent; her head is a little crazy.[30]

This portrait is composed of dualisms, with an equilibrium that reflects scientific objectiveness and also characterizes Cappelle-Lafarge's style in general. But there are also frequent reversals of pairs, much as in Madame Rolands's *Mémoires*. In Cappelle-Lafarge's case the consistent doubling of words specifically mirrors Clémentine's instability when she is alone, her need for another presence to authenticate her acts. Thus Cappelle-Lafarge introduces uncertainty into a structure of balanced sureness. And the verbs in the passage are essentially those of feeling or being, indicating Cappelle-Lafarge's insistence on categorizing the intangible, not the measurable, and thereby criticizing her era's empirical preferences.

The antithetical word pairs that Cappelle-Lafarge uses in all her works symbolize the contradictoriness, the uneasy coexistence of opposites that marked her century. Oppositions such as life/death, nature/heaven, head/heart, reality/imagination traverse the texts. One consistently finds the vocabulary of Romanticism encased in the rigidly simplified forms of scientific discourse. Thus, for example, her detailed description of scenes and objects at the Lafarge family home, le Glandier, in the end produces the effect of a gothic novel. But her most effective juggling of Romantic and anti-Romantic priorities is her personalized use of the then-popular division of the human faculties. Treatises on the differences and interrelations between intellect, heart, will, memory, senses, and passions

---

[30]Portrait reproduced in Fernande Lhérisson, *Madame Lafarge, écrivain romantique: Pages choisies précédées d'une étude sur sa vie et sur son oeuvre* (Bordeaux: Delmas, 1934), 36–37.

abounded in France and elsewhere.[31] The mind and heart were generally considered antagonistic, a Pascalian idea that Cappelle-Lafarge plays with: "My head is the madwoman in my attic . . . and perhaps my heart is her virtue" (*Correspondance*, 1:67). Whereas cold scientific organization of the human faculties sprang from a mistrust of the imaginary and the irrational,[32] Cappelle-Lafarge uses these categories to extol the heart at the expense of the intellect. For her, her contemporaries are "fanatic sectarians of reason" (*Heures de prison*, p. 28). "Imagination" is for her "that which creates the opposite of the realities of existence" (*Mémoires*, 1:138). And, given the intolerability of her existence, the unreal is decidedly preferable. Elsewhere in her memoirs she claims: "My mind is stubborn, willful, proud; only my heart can control it, and it is by following my heart that I can direct myself" (*Mémoires*, René ed., 1:145). This twist of the ultrarationalists' notion of uncontrollable sentiment versus disciplined thought is Cappelle-Lafarge's answer to the charge that, as a criminal, she was at once the "feminine" victim of her passions and the "virile" possessor of intelligence.

Judgments of Cappelle-Lafarge's writing reveal the same inconsistencies between sentimental and intellectual values. These judgments are further complicated by their associating women's writing and affect even while sentiment was losing currency. Raymond de Ryckère called her writing cold, unnatural, and insincere, saying it displayed "none of those bursts of true and sincere passion that move and arouse pity, none of those cries from the heart that are so strangely and painfully resonant."[33] For Ryckère, whose premise about prison

[31]See, for example, Henri Joly, *L'Imagination: Etude psychologique* (Paris: Hachette, 1883); Jules Guillemin, *Les Oeuvres d'imagination: Essai d'esthétique littéraire* (Warsaw: J. Sikorski, 1882); Gabriel Tarde, *La Criminalité comparée* (Paris: Félix Alcan, 1886); D. Hack Tuke, *Le Corps et l'esprit: Action du moral et de l'imagination sur le physique*, trans. from the English (Paris: J. B. Baillière, 1886); and Th. Ribot, *Essai sur l'imagination créatrice* (Paris: Félix Alcan, 1900).

[32]See Sartre, *L'Imagination* (Paris: Presses Universitaires de France, 1936), also published as *Imagination: A Psychological Critique*, trans. Forrest Williams (Ann Arbor: University of Michigan Press, 1962), part 1, chap. 1, for the ways the positivists nearly destroyed imaginative freedom.

[33]Raymond de Ryckère, *La Femme en prison et devant la mort* (Paris: Masson, 1898), 126–27.

writers was that "men confess, women deny" (p. 84), Cappelle-Lafarge's rejection of her stigma was tantamount to false content and precious style. Others judged her, like Madame Roland, a "bluestocking," a "scribbler" capable only of writing "pastiches."[34] Still others saw her as "sentimental," careful to translate exactly her "moods" and sensations.[35] And another critic compared her works to Silvio Pellico's *My Prisons*, by their "grace of wit and the clarity of their intelligence."[36]

No one foresaw better than Cappelle-Lafarge herself the ambiguities surrounding the condition of the woman writer. In a letter to Alexandre Dumas, accompanying pieces she hoped would be published, she opposes writing to women's real "work":

> How can I choose between the woman of the night and the woman of the day, between the noon worker and the midnight dreamer, between the lazy woman you love and the courageous woman you have been good enough to praise and admire from time to time? Ah, my dear Dumas, this self-doubt is the cruelest of all doubts. I need encouragement and criticism; I need someone to choose for me between the needle and the pen (*Correspondance*, 2:121)

Cappelle-Lafarge, oscillating between weakness and strength, between the "woman" and the "man" in her, goes on to opt for authorship ("I already think of myself as an author, I already think of myself as a poet"; p. 122), hoping eventually to "live respectably by her pen one day" (p. 123). Yet she denies such literary aspirations elsewhere in her *Mémoires:* "I am just a poor woman ... who knows how to suffer better than she knows how to write and who does not hold pretensions of being an author" (4:268). Judging from the fragments that Cappelle-Lafarge sent to Dumas—all oversentimental passages much in-

---

[34]See two articles in the "Dossier–Marie Lafarge" at the Bibliothèque Féministe Marguerite Durand: Pierre Bouchardon, "Une Cause célèbre: Madame Lafarge," *La Revue catholique des idées et des faits* (December 5, 1930), 4–12; and Jean-Jacques Brousson, "La Bibliothèque de Madame Lafarge," *Nouvelles littéraires* (October 13, 1934).

[35]André Gayot, "La Littérature de Madame Lafarge," *La Nouvelle revue* 17 (January 1, 1913): 25.

[36]Lhérisson, *Madame Lafarge*, 19.

ferior to the memoirs, which she herself excluded from the *Mémoires*[37]—she understood the prudent, nonheroic, nostalgic, and moralizing structures expected in women's writing. In her *Mémoires*, however, those same structures give rise to strong affirmations about her identity and sincerity. Robert Fothergill's assertion that, during the nineteenth century, memoirs and journals became increasingly self-conscious literary compositions applies to the works of Cappelle-Lafarge.[38] She consistently calls attention to her text—to her writing—and turns her memoirs into more than Madame Roland's scrupulously chronological account. Besides reversing pairs of words to counter prevailing moral judgments, Cappelle-Lafarge uses the visual devices of underlining and italics. When she quotes other speakers these ensure that the reader will recognize both the falseness of the words themselves and the irony of their being the grounds for Cappelle-Lafarge's condemnation. Such visual devices in the text signify a reversal of accuracy and meaning. Italics occasionally point out omens of disaster that the author implies she should have recognized. In particular, scenes of her arrival at le Glandier, in which she quotes gratuitous comments by Lafarge's family, force the reader to perceive the hypocrisy the words betray. For example, in an early conversation Lafarge's aunt makes the following comment about George Sand: Sand "wrote like a *cook* and thought like a *fishwife*" (*Mémoires*, 2:96; emphasis in original). Such vulgar characterizations, Cappelle-Lafarge is telling us, more aptly describe the speaker herself. In calling attention both to her writing and to the audience's reading of her text as she reconstructs the events of her life, Cappelle-Lafarge has purposes beyond historical fidelity. She engages in her own version of the analysis-synthesis that her scientific contemporaries extolled—she separates and recombines her life's elements, but in keeping with her own internal sense of truth.

Cappelle-Lafarge also manipulates the chronological aspects

---

[37]The pieces Cappelle-Lafarge sent to Dumas include fragments of travel memoirs and of prayer essays on "affliction," "friendship," and "evening visions."

[38]Robert A. Fothergill, *Private Chronicles: A Study of English Diaries* (London: Oxford University Press, 1974), 32–33.

of her chosen genres more self-consciously than her literary predecessors. For Roland, memoirs primarily show continuity between past and present; that is, they establish the constancy of the author's identity. Cappelle-Lafarge likewise joins time with character as a method of self-presentation, but she is less concerned with presenting her own resistance to change than with showing how she is victimized by events and people around her. Roland is confident of her unshakable internal harmony and contentment; Cappelle-Lafarge admits her happiness is a construct that she has built (*Mémoires*, 2:193) and circumstances have destroyed. In one sense, then, the time frame of memoirs allows Cappelle-Lafarge to insist on her preference for imagination and illusion in the face of reality's harmful encroachment: "If the future is too narrow for all the illusions that are competing for space there, the past is wide enough to provide a grave for all our disappointments and regrets" (*Heures de prison*, 1854 ed., 1:192). Rousseau's belief in woman's "natural" access to happiness gives way to the Romantic assumption that contentment is impossible in a hostile world.

Cappelle-Lafarge and Roland share the feeling that the present is a void, and both therefore seek refuge in past and future. But their different ideas about the nature of happiness, coupled with the acute differences in the punishments they endured, make for diverging views on the promise of the future. Roland, who knows she will die soon, projects to a completely new generation that will redeem her; Cappelle-Lafarge, condemned to age and "waste away" in prison, sees the future in her *Mémoires* as oblivion—mental and civil "death." Her contemporaries expect her criminal intelligence to turn to madness; Cappelle-Lafarge too sees insanity as her fate, but because of her punishment, not her own temperament: "A madwoman! I would like to know what happens to the soul of a madman . . . madness! What is madness? It's a duel between the soul and matter" (*Heures de prison*, p. 115). The schism between her corporeal and spiritual needs, which she had already encountered in the convent's imposed morality, is most strongly induced by her confinement. And yet in *Heures de prison* Cappelle-Lafarge subverts even madness by altering the consequences of the mind/body split it signifies: refusing mental "death," she opts for Christian epiphany and its promise of an afterlife. The future is for her not the earthly rehabilitation of succeeding generations, but the promise of heavenly redemption. Thus the "death" of Cappelle-Lafarge's narrative voice at the end of her journal coincides with an affirmation in the future tense: "God's scales have measured out the time of my existence. I will never again waste a single one of my days" (*Heures de prison*, 1854 ed., 3: 288). It is not surprising that, very soon after being pardoned and released by Louis Napoleon in 1852, Cappelle-Lafarge died.

Marie Cappelle-Lafarge was a victim of her era's particularly hostile expression of traditional views about deviant women. Like women before and after her, she was caught between the contradictory fears that have always shaped those views. But the peculiar nineteenth-century theoretical tendency toward sharpened focus and organizational uniformity, coupled with a crystallization of social and economic priorities, made for unusual rigor in conceptions of normality and deviance. Cappelle-Lafarge was the only female criminal of her time who spoke out; and the power of her writing is a direct response to the severity she endured.

The contrast in methods of punishment over the fifty years between Roland's incarceration and that of Cappelle-Lafarge is striking. That criminal women should at one time be summarily beheaded and not long after be exempt from execution on the grounds of their sex is more a commentary on social hypocrisy than on the relativity of punishment. Both women were thought to have transgressed sexual norms. In punishing Roland's body, her generation acknowledged its physiosexual target. Cappelle-Lafarge's peers, on the contrary, hid her woman's body behind prison walls for years of neglect, thereby denying her physical being in the name of sexual "modesty." Roland's execution can even be said to mark a point of "equality" in punishment for men and women that was never again matched, for the physical exclusion and concealment of women like Cappelle-Lafarge paved the road to Victorian repression and denial of female sexuality in general.

6

Marguerite Steinheil

> Most of the crimes committed by women are "beautiful crimes"
> —Georges Clarétie, 1901

When Marguerite Steinheil's husband, Adolphe Steinheil, and her mother, Madame Japy, were found strangled in May 1908, the "affair of the impasse Ronsin," as the murders were called, became the focus of attention in Paris. It resembled two other celebrated trials of the time, that of the accused extortionist Thérèse Humbert and that of the accused murderer Henriette Caillaux. In each, a woman who traveled in powerful social circles found herself at the center of a "ballet of amatory pleasure and of political intrigue" against a "backdrop of vaudeville."[1] Yet Steinheil's case was deadly serious, and it is precisely this confrontation of lightness, comedy, and superficiality with gravity, tragedy, and peril that marks the *belle époque* in general.[2]

Male criminals of the era were usually seen as Verlainian *poètes maudits*, and, concomitantly, the most dangerous were condemned to the real marginality of deportation (the *bagne*, or overseas penal servitude in French Guiana or New Caledonia).

---

[1] René Tavernier, *Madame Steinheil, ange ou démon: Favorite de la République* (Paris: Presses de la Cité, 1976), 18 and 178, respectively.

[2] For an excellent discussion of the importance of theatricality, real and metaphorical, during the *belle époque*, see Roger Shattuck, *The Banquet Years: The Origins of the Avant-Garde in France, 1885 to World War I*, rev. ed. (New York: Vintage Books, 1968).

Madame Steinheil, 1908. Photo Harlingue-Viollet

Those who were kept in the country were sent to correctional institutions in which their cheap and plentiful industrial labor masqueraded as "rehabilitative" treatment. Female criminals, for whom deportation was outlawed, remained corporally fixed both by Paris's Saint-Lazare prison and by public scrutiny. They did stereotypically feminine work for industry, such as sewing or knitting. For both women and men, prisons of the *belle époque* were undergoing change as secular and religious groups fought for jurisdiction. For women in particular, the dismantling of the congregations' role in prisons by anticlerical government policies led to a profusion of "new and more elaborate" penal theories.[3] Most of these "reeducative" models for prisons shared a fundamentally optimistic philosophy[4] that typified the apparent spirit of their era.

Women criminals like Steinheil were observed, judged, and essentially "pretried" according to the prevalent values of visible respectability and invisible sexuality. Steinheil was also subject to the newborn, tentative ideas about the intangible psyche. These early ideas about psychological motivation were more descriptive than scientific and focused on "personality" explanations. Steinheil's *Mémoires,* written about 1911–12, are a loose, uneven, yet complex text that uses and rejects the public's vague, often crude explanations of and reactions to her behavior; it also represents a woman criminal's first conscious search for literary effect in her writing.[5]

Although neo-Lombrosian notions of female deviance persisted, they were overshadowed by two new, diverging currents: "psychologizing" theory, a reflection of the recently acknowledged and still exploratory area of psychiatric phenomena, and sociological theory, which recognized exogenous antisocial influences on behavior. Yet both currents prolonged belief in criminal women's sexual and moral maladjustment, and both, by shifting from Lombrosian "perversion" to expla-

---

[3] Henri Gaillac, *Les Maisons de correction, 1830–1945* (Paris: Cujas, 1971), 250.
[4] Ibid., 197.
[5] Marguerite Steinheil, *Mes mémoires* (Paris: Edmond Ramlot, n.d., approx. 1911–12). Steinheil wrote her memoirs after her incarceration, based on journal notes she had kept in prison. The date of the French edition is uncertain; the English edition, *My Memoirs,* was published in 1912. Page references to the French edition will appear parenthetically; all translations are mine.

nations based on women's lack of responsibility, in fact intensified hostility against them.[6] For both women and men, designated "degrees of perversity" underlay the correctional categories established, and the general classifications of "intelligent," "vicious," "indifferent," and "retarded" existed in all prisons.[7] The character distinctions applied to women, however, were more highly refined. Euphemistic categorizations of female abnormality by "temperament types"—hypersuggestible, hallucinating, fantasizing, somnambulistic, lying, hyperesthetic, hysterical—permitted fear of female sexuality and assertiveness to masquerade as theories about "antisocial" "personality" disorders. Criminology focused on interpreting an individual's manifest symptoms rather than on understanding their origins, rendering its models essentially descriptive and aesthetic.

The perfect metaphor for such visible "character types" was the theater, and theatrical terminology dominated both specialized and popular discourses on crime. In the way that psychogenic and sociogenic theories linked abnormal and normal comportment, the image of the theater made criminals into roleplayers. Because of the confusion between personality and morality, however, the criminal woman was perceived as visibly dangerous: her "roles," even if not innate, proved harmful when acted out in society. Thus, for example, the notorious prostitute and murderer Gabrielle Bompard was classified as a "hysteric" and "hypersuggestive" who was easily influenced by others. Her unstable character was given form when she killed a sheriff's officer.[8] Steinheil was described in similar terms, as

[6]The increased hostility against women at this time was doubtless also linked to the extraordinary feminist activity taking place among bourgeois and working-class women. It was also a time of numerous and varied feminist publications and newspapers in France. The Bibliothèque Féministe Marguerite Durand, Paris 5e, is rich in documents of the period.
[7]Gaillac, *Maisons de correction*, 197.
[8]In 1889 Bompard, along with Michel Eyraud, killed a sheriff's officer while stealing money to repay their creditors. After a short-lived period of public favor following her denunciation of Eyraud, she was sentenced to twenty years of hard labor; Eyraud was guillotined. Before their trials, Bompard, but not Eyraud, was subjected to a "psychiatric examination" that found her completely lacking in moral sense, morally blind, and, physically, a "hysteric" (see E. Locard, *La Malle sanglante de Millery: L'Affaire Gabrielle Bompard-Eyraud*, Paris: Gallimard, 1934).

at once the pathetic victim of her sexuality and a potentially dangerous performer of her will: in her indictment she was accused of being a "denatured daughter," an "immoral actress" with a "guileful and perfidious personality."[9] Women like Steinheil were viewed as villains in the popular social melodramas of the time: she was the "tragic widow," the "mythomaniac," the "romantic and sentimental woman," the "whimsical actress," and her trial was a "Shakespearean drama" with "clowns" and "traitors," a "theater the night of a grand opening."[10]

The overwhelming prevalence of aesthetic concepts in French bourgeois social and cultural life is complexly rooted in the economic and political conditions just before World War I as well as in those inherited from the previous century. The positivists' mistrust of the imagination and their mania for ordering verifiable experience left a legacy of insistence on the purely visible. The faculties believed to underlie human behavior, which had been rigidly codified in the 1880s as heart, mind, senses, memory, will, and imagination, were now defined by their external, concrete expression. For such thinkers as Ribot and Dugas, the imagination was suspect when left "pure" and "subjective" rather than given concrete form: unrealized, it became "fantasy" or "the oversentimental"; that is, "what the imagination begets if it is not applied to real objects."[11] Freud also linked any turning from reality toward "imaginary constructions" with one's "phantasmic life" and, eventually, with neurosis.[12] And the most influential philosopher of the era, Bergson, is invoked by Sartre in similar terms: for Bergson "the thing *is* the image," thus making the universe into a world of material images.[13]

[9]Accusations reproduced in the *Mémoires*, chaps. 22 and 26.
[10]These expressions are taken from the *Mémoires* and from studies of Steinheil: Tavernier, *Madame Steinheil*, and Marcel Nadaud and André Fage, *Les Grands Drames passionnels de Casque d'Or à Mata-Hari* (Paris: Georges-Anquetil, 1926).
[11]L. Dugas, *L'Imagination* (Paris: Octave Doin, 1903), 172. See also Th. Ribot, *Essai sur l'imagination créatrice* (Paris: Félix Alcan, 1900).
[12]Freud's "Introduction to Psychoanalysis," cited in Gabriel and Brigitte Veraldi, *Psychologie de la création* (Paris: Marabout, 1972), 30–31.
[13]Jean-Paul Sartre, *Imagination: A Psychological Critique*, trans. Forrest Williams (Ann Arbor: University of Michgan Press, 1962), 39; my emphasis. Translation of *L'Imagination* (Paris: Presses Universitaires de France, 1936).

MARGUERITE STEINHEIL

The consequences for French society of this insistence on the visible were multiple: first, a reassuring optimism—things *were* what they seemed—at the expense of a psychic repression that was not yet fully understood or acknowledged;[14] second, a heightened penchant for a newly articulated faculty, "taste," or the ability to discern "the appropriateness of *form* and *style* to a [particular] object, in terms of the correctness of proportion, the accuracy of measurement, and the harmony between the conception and the execution [of that object]";[15] and, third, the most important for criminological theory, an association between the suspect "pure" imagination and illness, easily translated into a link between illness and dangerousness. Since illness generally could be cured, criminal dangerousness too could be modified or reversed. As a result, psychiatric and penal discourses showed marked resemblances even as penal policy optimistically sought personality modification rather than mere repentance. The categories used to divide prisoners now mirrored contemporary descriptions of psychosexual temperaments.

An example of this blending of psychological and moral vocabularies occurs in one of the press judgments of Henriette Caillaux's crime. *L'Echo de Paris* of March 17, 1914, condemns the murder she committed as an act representative of the more widespread "immoral anarchy and social disorganization" for which all the French, as an "unbalanced, crazed, and amoral" people, are responsible.[16] The perceived link between normality and abnormality, which tightened through the twentieth century, is already visible in this judgment.

Marguerite Steinheil, held for one year in preventive detention and ultimately acquitted,[17] functioned completely within

---

[14]The psychic "release" vaunted by the surrealists was, of course, one later response to this imaginative repression.

[15]Jules Guillemin, *Les Oeuvres d'imagination: Essai d'esthétique littéraire* (Warsaw: Joseph Sikorski, 1882), 42; my emphasis.

[16]See "Dossier–Henriette Caillaux" at the Bibliothèque Féministe Marguerite Durand.

[17]The judicial system of the time made for frequent acquittals. After a guilty verdict, the judge passed sentence, and the jury could not know in advance the severity of the punishment. Also, condemnation for parricide would have meant an automatic death penalty. See René Floriot, *Deux femmes en Cour d'Assises: Madame Steinheil et Madame Caillaux* (Paris: Hachette, 1966).

this aesthetic universe, both as woman and as author. The facts of her life themselves reflect the interplay of sexual diversion and political intrigue, of the superficial and the serious. Her childhood, described in the *Mémoires* as a period of complete happiness, contrasts with the tragedy that befalls her. Steinheil's passion for her father and his jealousy and protectiveness toward his daughter are cast by her as mutual affection. She presents her parents as having an "ideal marriage" (p. 7) and thus sets up a contrast with her own loveless union.

After a "girl's" education at home that taught her to "recognize beautiful things" (p. 9), she married the little-known painter Adolphe Steinheil, who was twenty years older and for whom she felt little affection. The end of her "dream of love and happiness" (p. 30) with the phlegmatic Steinheil led her to set up an artistic and literary salon. Having joined the social whirl of *tout Paris,* she became President Félix Faure's mistress, in a relationship she calls "collaboration" between "confidants" (chaps. 6–10). This is only one example of Steinheil's use of euphemism in an effort to assert her true identity in the face of slander. Denying that she was in any way an *éminence grise* for Faure, she does insist she played an important role in some "serious" and potentially "disastrous decisions" (pp. 62–63). Steinheil's presence at Faure's mysterious death in 1899 led various newspapers to accuse her of poisoning him, but the charges were never pursued. Even today the suggestion remains of a cover-up of Faure's death and Steinheil's role in it. Likewise, the odd political overtones surrounding the subsequent 1908 murders and Steinheil's acquittal—mysteries that are still unclear—added further to the mixture of tragic and superficial elements in her life. Steinheil added to the confusion surrounding the murders by accusing three different men who were acquaintances of her family. And her *Mémoires,* a mélange of tones and subgenres that change with each turn of events, read like a script for a bourgeois melodrama. Steinheil mixes dramatic forms and calls her text "a strange *story,* . . . a *song* of happiness, . . . a poignant *drama,* . . . a frightful *tragedy*" (p. 6; my emphasis).

To be sure, Steinheil chose memoirs for some of the same reasons as Roland and Cappelle-Lafarge before her: to right

MARGUERITE STEINHEIL

misperceptions of her identity by presenting a "rigorously accurate account of [her] life" (p. 6). As was true for other women prison writers, her text is to fulfill her need to establish "the truth, the whole truth" (p. 6). Showing the continuity of her life, which had engrossed her predecessors, took on even greater importance for Steinheil, since psychological and sociological theories of criminality now sought information from the suspect's antecedents. The court's "personality examination," officially required by law as of 1912, was concerned specifically with "the character and the past history" of the accused.[18] Steinheil, believing her past life had been thoroughly deformed during her trial—"they ransacked my past, damaged it, shredded it" (p. 17)—set about to realign her perceived identity with her articulated self-image. In comparison with her forerunners, however, she evokes the past less for nostalgia than to achieve a highly self-conscious personal reconstruction. Roland and Cappelle-Lafarge had been satisfied to describe their childhood happiness and rediscover unwaveringly loving, supportive personas; Steinheil, bouncing around among time periods, moods, and styles, seeks to *re-create*—not simply justify—her positive, essentially dramatic persona.

Steinheil's "re-creation" of self draws on certain concepts and leanings of her era. In view of the dominant characterological understanding of human motivation, she casts herself as the protagonist in a sequence of scenes and encounters, each of which she calls a "new life." The different parts she plays support Tavernier's description of her life as a "protean existence."[19] Thus, for example, the salon portion of the *Mémoires* consists of vignettes starring Steinheil and well-known figures. Later, shady details about a pearl necklace and secret documents that Faure confided to Steinheil just before his death conjure up a spy novel, complete with a mysterious "German visitor" and Steinheil's own hypothesis about the motive for the intrigue—blackmail (pp. 102–5). Events preceding the 1908 murders read like a mystery story in which Steinheil herself is the detective. The segment on her arrest and trial resembles a

---

[18]Gaillac, *Maisons de correction*, 255.
[19]Tavernier, *Madame Steinheil*, 23.

persecution nightmare, with a Kafkaesque Steinheil watching herself "gripping the railing" of the witness box and "dropping her head in her hands" (p. 365). And the closing chapters on her rediscovered tranquility and intimacy with her daughter are in fact the monologue of a private diary.

By presenting herself as a dramatic personage, Steinheil not only conforms to the preferred lexicon of her contemporaries, she also avoids the disturbing search for the self and the pure subjectivity that were suspect at the time. Instead of reconfirming the pathology of her supposed "perverted imagination" by dwelling on her innermost feelings,[20] she looks at herself from without. In this sense she is at the opposite pole from Marie Cappelle-Lafarge, whose explorations remained internal. Nowhere is the topos of seeing/being seen, which unites all women's prison writing, more strongly emphasized than in Steinheil's text. Subscribing to the belief that appearance is reality, she in essence exploits this fundamentally optimistic tenet of her era's "reassuring literature":[21] her memoirs are certain to prove her innocence, since the reader, guided directly and explicitly by the author's vision, will assuredly believe what he or she "sees" described.

What is more, in a twist of the criminological notions that infantilized accused women by viewing them as not responsible for their acts,[22] Steinheil infantilizes and reassures her readers as she guides them through her story. She gives little credit to her interlocutors and at one point summarizes the course of events preceding the murder: "And now that my description of the robes and hats worn by the assassins [who she claimed tied her up and gagged her on the night of the murders] is firmly anchored in the reader's mind, let us follow the inspector as he visits Guilbert, the costume dealer" (p. 168). Elsewhere Steinheil helps the reader discern patterns in the mysterious events she has recounted: "The reader will decide with time if there is

[20]Camille Granier, *La Femme criminelle* (Paris: Octave Doin, 1906), 208.
[21]Tavernier, *Madame Steinheil*, 15.
[22]See, specifically, the theories of Dupré and Cabanis, presented in M. P. Caignart de Mailly, *L'Evolution de l'idée criminaliste au XIXe siècle et ses conséquences* (Paris: Secrétariat de la Société d'Economie Sociale, 1898), and Georges Heuyer, *Les Troubles mentaux: Etude criminologique* (Paris: Presses Universitaires de France, 1968).

a connection between these three mysteries [those of the necklace, the German visitor, and the 1908 murders]" (p. 108). She later reproduces questions and answers in a kind of Socratic exchange with her audience (chap. 13), so that they may judge "if it were really possible and permissible" to find her "not only a criminal, but a criminal who had premeditated her monstrous deed" (p. 117).

What was visible not only was thought real in Steinheil's time, it was considered the basis of reason itself: "Reason is that which recognizes truth and *verisimilitude*."[23] The suggestively theatrical word "verisimilitude," once the very core of the aesthetics of French classical drama, was now the criterion for judging individual rationality. Thus, when Steinheil found herself accused of lacking "method" (by the presiding judge of her preliminary hearing) and of displaying the "distracted reason" ascribed to "hysterics,"[24] she responded in a variety of ways that made use of and subverted those very judgments.

First of all, much like Cappelle-Lafarge, Steinheil recounts in minute detail the events surrounding the crime. In doing so she not only engages her reader, but also proves the equilibrium of her mind. Her ability to discriminate between suspicion and fact as she pieces together disparate shreds of empirical evidence shows that *she*, not events, has remained on a steady course. To further demonstrate her unswerving attention to observed fact and to chronological order, she goes beyond her own story to invoke important political events of the early 1900s. The Dreyfus affair appears in descriptions of her "Dreyfusard" and "anti-Dreyfusard" friends and acquaintances; the political turmoil within the Republican party before Faure's election is described; and the explosive Fashoda incident in Egypt involving England and France becomes interwoven in the record of her "collaboration" with Faure. Including the larger social and political embroilments around her allows Steinheil to exhibit her political astuteness and thus confirm her awareness and judgment.

Steinheil also makes rich use of the vague psychosexual lexi-

[23]Guillemin, *Oeuvres d'imagination*, 25; my emphasis.
[24]D. Hack Tuke, *Le Corps et l'esprit: Action du moral et de l'imagination sur le physique*, trans. from the English (Paris: J.-B. Ballière, 1886), 83.

con of her era. She and Caillaux were, for example, condemned in the press for their "atrocious and egoistic psychology,"[25] and Steinheil's accusers pointed to her "crafty and perfidious temperament" (*Mémoires*, p. 370). At no other time have aesthetic and psychiatric discourse mingled so completely, for the latter has become increasingly specialized through this century; thus Steinheil was able at once to reject and reuse the codes under which she was judged even while she constructed a text replete with aesthetic concerns. Redefining her true, innocent persona in the light of moral accusations coincided precisely with her asserting her artistic and literary sensitivity. Steinheil reappropriates her identity by insisting throughout that she is a "woman of taste" (p. 311), thereby making this valued "faculty" the core of her personality. Roland's "reason" and Cappelle-Lafarge's "heart" have here been supplanted by a sense of style and quality. To support her claim, Steinheil cites her appreciation of the nuns' choir and organ music she hears in prison. She likewise contrasts her felicitous way of speaking to the "rough language" of her fellow prisoners, which aroused in her an "insurmountable distaste for all that was vulgar or coarse" (pp. 259–60). There is, to be sure, a good deal of class snobbery in Steinheil's judgments, and in that sense she represents the last in a line of privileged inmates of Saint-Lazare.[26] Steinheil admits the effects of class differences on the women's ability to adjust to prison: "If it was possible for a woman like Firmin [her cellmate], raised in the most humble fashion, to live in a cell, how much more horrible it was for me, who had always lived in relative luxury and had always been very spoiled" (p. 259). Steinheil's self-presentation as a "woman of taste," however, rests more explicitly on visible respectability than on money or education, as she draws her fellow prisoners into the process of righting her identity: "[The other women] stopped screaming 'Murderer!' and 'To the guillotine!' when they *saw* me.... They *saw* that I never answered their

[25]*Télégramme de Toulouse*, 1914, in "Dossier–Henriette Caillaux."
[26]The existence of *pistoles*, or private cells, ended in 1914. Roland and Cappelle-Lafarge had also enjoyed the privileges accorded prisoners of means. Steinheil had only one cellmate, a heated cell, and her own fine linens and clothes.

insults. . . . They began to *respect* me" (pp. 318–19; my emphasis). Like Roland and Cappelle-Lafarge, Steinheil uses other accused women solipsistically in order to distinguish herself from them. Steinheil further utilizes the aesthetic preoccupations of her generation, in particular the vague, theatrical judgments of her, to counter accusations that, as a "hysteric" and "mythomaniac," she indulged in vain and unproductive fantasy. If her accusers thought she "lived on illusions" (p. 30), she knew her intelligence had found real expression. Her long, enumerative description of her salon is her means of proving she understands authentic creativity. That she possesses discrimination is proved by the appearance at her salon of well-known artists, poets, and writers: Bartholdi, Bonnat, Coppée, Gounod, Loti, Massenet, Zola. These prominent figures, aside from validating her claim to taste, also provide substance for a textual strategy employed by all imprisoned women: portraiture. Like Cappelle-Lafarge and Roland, for whom portraits had shown the importance of the visible, Steinheil draws individuals for her own purposes. She responds to "psychologizing" notions of personality types with portraits glorifying her guests' character and thereby reconstitutes vague categories of her own. Artists are evoked for their "liveliness," "wit," or "taste" and are described in such superficial terms as "charming," "seductive," "handsome," "superior," "cracked," "vain," and "brilliant." Zola is called "ungainly and aggressive," though he is also "talented, energetic, and good-hearted" (p. 40). The scandalous painter of female nudes, Henner, comes across as colorful, down-to-earth, and unabashed. Finally, the belief that she, like all deviant women, was "hyperesthetic"[27]—that is, possessing deformed and exaggerated sensitivity—is countered by Steinheil's claim that she discerns harmonies and subtleties in the works of her salon guests. This discernment allows her to reproduce for her own needs an aesthetic hierachy parallel to the one operating in her social milieu.

Many of the descriptive psychiatric terms then current appear in Steinheil's memoirs but are either interpreted literally

[27]Locard, *La Malle sanglante*, 117.

or infused with new meaning. For example, the view that criminal women were "not responsible" and "weak" is made concrete by Steinheil's tendency to faint under pressure. The "illness" from which she presumably suffered is translated as the "nerve problems" that plague her. In a slight twist, the perverse "lying" that supposedly characterized women like Steinheil is interpreted instead as the "normal stories" of any imaginative child (p. 8). The idea that abnormal women are easily "influenced" is more fully exploited. It is presented early in the *Mémoires* as a positive quality, the one responsible for Steinheil's agreeing to marry Adolphe Steinheil: "He seemed so anxious to hear me say yes to him that I did not have the heart to say no" (p. 20). Later on this trait becomes the center of her counterattack against the press for its sensational coverage of the case. She blames the press for "feeding" her false information, "ripping" a confession from her, and then writing about her as weakened and broken (chap. 19). At the end of the text, suggestibility becomes a guarantee for the veracity of Steinheil's version of the crime's events, as she describes the plasticity of one of the real killers, a "red-haired woman" whom she calls "the mistress of one of the criminals, who insisted on accompanying her 'man' " (p. 406). Thus Steinheil distinguishes herself from other women, who are easily swayed. This attribution of weakness to others, like her renaming of "lying" and "fantasy," serves Steinheil's claims to appreciate subtle nuances of character.

The concept Steinheil most thoroughly subverts is the most powerful and frightening one used against her: madness. Accused unceasingly of mental and physical instability resulting from "hysteria,"[28] she sets about to correct the misapplication of that concept to her case. Madness, far from being an affective impairment or a "constitutional anomaly" within her (as seen by Dupré), is the *result* of external events. For example, Steinheil repeats that, upon learning from a neighbor of her husband's and mother's deaths, she "became mad" (p. 145). The ensuing events, she says, sapped her health and her sanity:

[28]"Hysteria" represented the juncture of physical and psychological diagnosis, since it was believed to be organic in origin (a lesion on the uterus) and psychological in expression (speaking out, uncontrolled sexuality, and lasciviousness).

"Am I still in possession of my reason or am I mad?" (p. 201). Her entire judicial and penal experience, which she recounts as a persecution horror story not unlike Marie Cappelle-Lafarge's, is offered as the source of her ongoing sense of alienation, of her feeling that "[she] was no longer a human being" (p. 236). In fact, she claims that all the character disorders ascribed to her from the start have been imposed from without. Steinheil, echoing Cappelle-Lafarge's plaint that all her defenses were turned against her by her enemies, ends her memoirs with a similar denunciation of the deforming circumstances she has endured:

> Others will suffer as I have as long as certain French prisons remain the way they are; as long as examining magistrates can treat prisoners the way I was treated; as long as certain parts of the trial procedure are not changed; as long as there is no law that forbids newspapers to judge and condemn suspects. (p. 409)

Whereas Roland and Cappelle-Lafarge had addressed themselves to a receptive future audience—either a succeeding generation or the God of an afterlife—Steinheil takes her own contemporaries to task. Her text is to be useful now: she wants it to "open certain eyes, awaken certain consciences, change the state of certain things" (p. 412). Thus raging against judicial and penal institutions as the cause of the very disorders they purport to correct, Steinheil prefigures modern critiques of "rehabilitative" punishment techniques.

The new sociologically based views of criminality that looked to an individual's milieu for the origins of behavior provided more material for Steinheil's responses. Since her social and moral activities were perceived as abnormal adaptations, she was careful to present proof of her sociability. Her desire to live "intensely, ardently, feverishly" explains her interest in "everything and everyone" she encounters (p. 30). Her salon itself, the perfect image for social interaction, is further evidence of Steinheil's profoundly social personality. Recording large chunks of her conversations with guests, and at times straining the credibility of her memory, she emphasizes her ability to make others speak. In conveying to her guests that she has understood their work, yet effacing herself during the exchange, Steinheil sees herself as meeting the needs of others. Much like the self-aggrandizement that Anaïs Nin accomplishes in the guise of self-abnegation, she states, "I live only for others" (p. 49), thus rendering herself secondary yet indispensable to them. The very social whirl whose demands, she claims, wore down her faculties ("my brain, my nerves, my heart," p. 48) and inundated her privacy is also the "ship" she "captained" while constantly saving "a shipwrecked sister or brother who was drowning" (p. 50).

Some accusers had used the comfortable conditions of Steinheil's imprisonment as evidence of her separation from society—and, indeed, her relative privacy, coupled with her condescension toward the other prisoners, supports that argument. The press reinforced the notion of Steinheil's social nonconformity with charges that she, not her husband, "wore the pants." Some newspapers even spread the rumor that Steinheil had poisoned her husband and mother before strangling them, showing the persistence of the myth of the "woman poisoner." It is not surprising that Steinheil viewed the public as "the masses," a collective violent character in her story. In an unfortunately ironic and damaging twist of the image of the sadistic female criminal, she makes the crowd itself into a vengeful feminized personage: imagining the scene of her trial, she says, "I really felt that if I saw myself surrounded by ladies who sneered at my misery, smiled, and stared at me, . . . my pain would become more bitter, my ordeal more painful, and my victory more difficult to achieve" (pp. 344–45).

Steinheil was much concerned with describing her own kindness and generosity, and her lay charity, because of what she felt were misperceptions of her character. Although the spiritual content of Capelle-Lafarge's prison conversion is absent, the shell of Christian morality and devotion remains in Steinheil's words. She says of the world,

> It forgets my very deep *love* for my mother, the *assistance* I had given my husband in his work . . . the long weeks I had spent *taking care* of him, the innumerable *favors* I had done not only for my own and my husband's family, but for friends and for

friends of friends, my complete *discreetness* regarding secrets I held, the difficulties I overcame by force of *will* and *courage*, and my *devotion* to so many unfortunate people. (pp. 157–58; my emphasis)

Like marriage and her salon, prison was an arena in which Steinheil could express her concern for others. She likewise insists that she is a devoted mother and in fact "explains" the various inconsistencies in her story as stemming from her desire to protect her daughter Marthe. If Marthe knew nothing about her mother, she could blame her for nothing. The *Mémoires* frequently reveal such heavy-handed reorganization of the past, based on the notion that what is said is what really happened. In this sense Steinheil, more than her predecessors, is aware of the creative power of her text.

It would be innacurate to think that the conditions of Steinheil's trial and incarceration were so soft that she was merely offering empty sympathy to less fortunate prisoners. Although she enjoyed privacy, her own clothes, and restaurant food and was permitted to decorate her cell and to sew, she was nonetheless subject to many of the discomforts that gave Saint-Lazare its appalling reputation. She frequently mentions the filthy, damp, verminous, and unhygienic conditions, documented by Boucard as late as 1930,[29] describing the prison as "a hotbed of infection and filth, of ignominy and material and moral decay" (p. 261). What is more, Steinheil was one of the last prisoners to be locked up in medieval *souricières*—tiny, freezing cages— during her hearings.[30] The persistence of such harsh corporal punishments indicates the unsettled state of psychiatric diagnosis and of penal policy as the old notion of prison as "prophylaxis" was slowly replaced by the idea of confinement as "cure" through temperament modification.

While Steinheil by no means evinces the authentic compassion for other women that, for example, brought Cappelle-

---

[29]Robert Boucard, *Les Dessous des prisons de femmes* (Paris: Editions Documentaires, 1930). This misogynistic and essentially uninformative book does provide a few useful facts about women's prisons.
[30]The use of chains on prisoners was not in fact outlawed until 1922; ibid., 182.

Lafarge to understand Madame Grouvelle's decline into aphasia and then madness (Steinheil's charitable self-image is less than convincing), she does criticize the systems that led to her own alienation. By frequently using the term "rehabilitate" in order to undermine its application to her case, she implicitly attacks the "psychiatric examination" that women, but not men, had to take and that determined their cell assignment. The nature of this "examination" is revealed in *Le Matin*'s coverage of a contemporaneous event, Henriette Caillaux's arrival at prison in 1914: Caillaux is described as receiving lenient treatment in that she was exempted from the normal "anthropometric examination."[31] This carryover of a Lombrosian concept indicates how confused physiological and psychological traits still were in Steinheil's time. That prison classifications were based on visible symptoms—with such "treatments" as silence and bromides designed to squelch the manifestation of hysteria, spoken self-assertiveness—makes Steinheil's self-affirmation through writing an act of expressive survival. The "character" categories of the early 1900s foreshadowed the "personality dossiers" of midcentury, and Steinheil, and later Sylvie Paul, sensed the danger of such a permanent stigma.[32]

A substantial portion of Steinheil's memoirs deals with the injustice of the trial procedures and the psychological and physical harshness of her preventive detention. At one point she admits her text is purely functional in recording her preliminary hearing sessions. During such hearings in the 1900s, the accused's words rarely were transcribed fully in the record of court proceedings (p. 300). The investigating judge exercised a good deal of discretion, recording what he deemed essential in the suspect's answers.[33] Steinheil is shocked by the incompleteness, the lack of nuance, and the disturbing similarity among all the recorded testimonies—since the judge's unimpeded selectiveness has diluted and homogenized them—and undertakes to supply an alternative to the court docu-

---

[31] "Dossier–Henriette Caillaux."

[32] See Sylvie Paul, *Ne me jugez pas!* (Paris: Gallimard, 1962).

[33] It was also legal procedure at the time that the accused *buy* the judicial records of his or her own inquest. Steinheil claims she had to "bargain" for the dossier her lawyer obviously needed to prepare her defense (chap. 24).

ments. The hostility of the presiding magistrate is particularly apparent in the tone of Steinheil's transcription and is reminiscent of Cappelle-Lafarge's own record of her hearing. Judge André treats Steinheil as guilty and tries to make her contradict herself, turning the eight-hour interrogation into a duel. The reasons for André's hostility are not clear, though Steinheil attributes his need to "win" and to be pereived as a "saver of society" to his desire for promotion (p. 302).

Although we cannot be certain Steinheil's selective memory is any more accurate than the judge's, we can see in his comments the then-common perceptions about "dangerous" women: he presumes that the murder of Adolphe Steinheil was only a "domestic crime" motivated by a bad marriage (p. 272), thus negating the possibility that Marguerite Steinheil was involved in larger political affairs. He goes on to say that Steinheil's account "retains all the *romantic improbability,* the whole unacceptable quality that characteristically pervades the *fantasies* of criminals" (p. 294; my emphasis) and once again demonstrates the overlap of aesthetic and legal vocabularies; finally, he assumes that "the crime was most likely not committed by only one person" (p. 293), subscribing to the belief in women's suggestibility and their necessarily secondary role in criminal acts. As her own response during the hearings Steinheil records the refrain, "I hold firm to what I said before." Since during the sessions she was able only to stand her ground passively and maintain the truth, she later writes her memoirs to expose and counter the hostile arguments aimed at her.

When she describes her subsequent public trial at the assizes, Steinheil returns to her familiar theatrical imagery. All the defense witnesses portray her as a sympathetic character, as "considerate," "kind," "obliging" (p. 373). Steinheil and her daughter Marthe stage a scene of pathos on the witness stand, with the child "reaching its arms out toward you [the public] as if to defend its mother" (p. 380). And, in terms similar to those Albertine Sarrazin was to use fifty years later, Steinheil speaks of the "dizziness" that overcame her in court, making the scene around her into a distant drama (chap. 26) and herself into an observed character.

Imagination in Confinement

The frequent separation in Steinheil's memoirs between herself and her "theatrical" persona prefigures the perspective of modern women prison authors on their experience. Unlike Roland and Cappelle-Lafarge, for whom the confessional genre had minimized the gap between author and narrator, Steinheil manipulates memoirs with the clear purpose of "creating" her true persona. Gide's autobiographical protagonists come to mind as she paints herself in various situations that exemplify the connection between aesthetic and moral issues. And like Gide, Steinheil focuses on the beauty of art and form as her principal moral value and as the supreme justification for self and text. Steinheil was the last female prison author to write within a highly codified moral and lexical framework; but by her imaginative exploitation of those codes she points the way toward women's subsequent naming of their own experience.

Steinheil's text is neither a descendent of the nineteenth-century male *poète maudit* tradition—it does not seek to shock or to disrupt prevailing literary and moral tenets—nor a true representative of the early-twentieth-century "reassuring literature," Christian and secular, which expressed collective optimism or faith in individual redemption.[34] Her *Mémoires*, falling between the poles of negativism and hope, are primarily a tool of maintenance: they are the written expression of a woman's struggle not to destroy or transcend, but to remain visibly and verifiably intact. And Steinheil's presentation of herself in terms at once moral and aesthetic symbolizes the beginning of the rapprochement between views of abnormal and normal behavior. For in her work deviance and conformity, no longer separate spheres of activity but points on the same continuum of comportment, began to assume their modern definitions. As criminals and as authors, women began leaving the ignominious margins of society, and women prison writers moved toward affirming their identity as authors rather than denying the criminal labels imposed on them.

[34]Some critics compared Steinheil to Mauriac's Thérèse Desqueyroux, whom Steinheil does resemble slightly in class and marital history. But there is little basis for further parallels between Mauriac's intensely cerebral redeemed sinner and the unreflective, appearance-centered Steinheil.

7
Anne Huré

> The reason for the downfall of a rational culture does not lie in the essence of rationalism itself but only in its exteriorization, its absorption in "naturalism" and "objectivism"—Edmund Husserl, *Phenomenology and the Crisis of Philosophy*

When feminist inquiry in both France and America began, in the 1960s, to ask fundamentally radical questions about women's lives and work, new directions were opened for women writers. Some experimented with unexplored languages that would more closely translate their female experience; others examined, with varying degrees of criticism, the transcendent social and intellectual issues from which women had traditionally been dissociated. The second avenue, theoretical analysis, lent itself more easily to conservative responses, as a few women aligned themselves with masculine traditions in philosophy and literature. Anne Huré is one such author—a conventional intellectual steeped in French modes of thought who uses those modes for her own purposes.

One of her purposes was to respond to her repeated imprisonments, from 1962 to 1971, for a series of minor financial infractions: fraud, bad checks, theft, and nonpayment of bills. Her novel *En prison* (1963) sprang from her seven years of confinement at la Roquette and Haguenau—severe punishment for relatively small crimes.[1] While there is nothing sex specific about harsh sentencing for what Huré calls the "dis-

---

[1] Anne Huré, *En prison* (Paris: René Julliard, 1963). Page references will appear in parentheses in the text. All translations are mine.

honorable" and antisocial act of theft,[2] the press focused on Huré's unorthodox personal and sexual history. Like the earlier authors studied here, she had been raised in an upper-bourgeois milieu. She spent four and one-half years in a Benedictine convent—another parallel with Roland and Cappelle-Lafarge, though in Huré's case it was a voluntary retreat—and left at age twenty-four for "strictly intellectual reasons."[3] After a rich classical education, she obtained a doctorate in theology, making her as well educated for her generation as her predecessors had been for theirs. She then became involved in complicated, unsuccessful, and scandalous personal and commercial affairs with a number of men, just before her first infractions of the law.

En prison shares with earlier women's prison texts the principal topos of self-presentation, as Huré depicts herself through her protagonist Noëlle. The solipsistic use of fellow prisoners for self-identification also appears, as do techniques for self-maintenance and survival in a hostile environment. But *En prison* breaks more strongly with the past in two ways: first, along with Albertine Sarrazin's *La Cavale*, it is one of the first novels about the prison experience and thus a move away from confessional genres;[4] second, it shows a woman exalting the traditionally male domain of the mind and the "universality" from which women have been excluded. These departures from previous female prison writing in part flow from general literary and social currents—for example, the increase in women novelists since the 1960s. But they also result from specific facts of Huré's life, including her background in philosophy, the prevalent criminological theories about women and the conditions of her

---

[2] From an interview with Alexandra Kalda, "Anne Huré raconte ses prisons," *Arts* (September 25, 1963), 3. Huré calls crimes for money the most "dishonorable" because they are a direct attack against the principal "social symbol."

[3] From an interview with Henriette Charasson, "Une Romancière: Anne Huré," *Ecrits de Paris: Revue des questions actuelles* (December 1963), 87.

[4] Other women have written from prison since the 1960s—including Gabrielle Russier's posthumous *Lettres de prison* (1970), Nicole Gérard's documentary journal *Sept ans de pénitence* (1976), Nicole Valery's Catholic tract *Bénie sois-tu prison* (1976), and Paulette Veiber's journal *Mes dix-huit mois* (1975)—but none has transformed the experience into a novel.

particular imprisonment. I will examine these influences as they inform Huré's text.

Huré wrote before and after her incarceration, as did Madame Roland and Albertine Sarrazin.[5] Huré's scholarly bent marks all her works with a gravity and a discursiveness, and her convent experience is reflected in their spiritual preoccupations, which in *En prison* contrast sharply with the banal temporality of Huré's crimes. All her works are set in closed, suffocating places in which idealized characters, always on the margins of society, and prison imagery point up the similarity between monastic and prison life. The use of nuns as guards in la Roquette is a vestigial symbol of the long-standing parallels between convents and prisons.[6] The extraordinary spiritual discipline and purely intellectual passions of Huré's heroines transform their reclusion into a disembodied, highly personal form of asceticism.

This same urge for intellectual recognition and the claim to universal truth unfortunately give rise to the central weakness in *En prison*, signaling the problems inherent in pretensions to universality: *En prison*'s static, discursive quality, with the protagonist's intelligence claimed, not dramatized, makes the quest for intellectual distinction unpersuasive; and the book's treatment of transcendent philosophical issues totally cut off from any connection with imprisonment and yet arising from unusually repressive prison constraints renders such general assertions specious at best. *En prison* is much closer to a journal than a novel, to a meditation than a realization, putting Huré somewhere between Steinheil and Sarrazin in terms of literary effect. Conscious use of literary conventions was beginning to be visible with Steinheil and finds its strongest expression and transformation in Sarrazin; Huré's novel as pretext for analytical exposition falls between the two.

En prison follows, in the French simple past tense, Noëlle's

---

[5]Huré's other important works include *Les Deux Moniales* (1962), *Le Péché sans merci* (1964), and *Descente en enfer* (1966).
[6]In her earlier confession, *Ne me jugez pas!* (1962), Sylvie Paul had described Huré's second prison, Haguenau, as "highly religious" and as "teaching the women shame."

judicial progress but has almost no action or narrative clash. The third-person point of view and the time separation between author and narrator that is effected by the verb tense reflect Huré's wish to "present her character as if the latter were outside herself"[7] and thereby keep the prison (and the reader) at arm's length. This "unemotional treatment," with its "utter remoteness,"[8] mirrors Noëlle's own aloofness from prison life and allows her to deal only with lofty issues. Literary and philosophical references abound in dialogues thus rendered noble, if wooden. Noëlle's private hierarchy is clear: "It is not my tendency to sentimentalize. I confine myself to reason" (p. 30). Another example, at the point of Noëlle's transfer from la Roquette (for accused prisoners) to the prison at Haguenau (for the condemned):

—[The prison's chief doctor to the head nun] I think . . . that at the Haguenau penitentiary, someone like her [Noëlle] will enjoy many advantages.
—[Noëlle] I think so too, sir . . . What interests me above all is that I not lose time for essential things, that is, for intellectual work and for artistic and literary culture in general. (p. 163)

Such "aching pseudo-intellectual profundities,"[9] if ineffectual in creating narrative movement, nonetheless make the novel's priorities abundantly clear. For, in spite of the coldness and distance in Huré's presentation, it is evident that she admires her heroine and, inevitably, herself. By surrounding Noëlle with the respect and attentiveness of all administrative officials and fellow prisoners, she makes her prisoner seem the ruler of her little universe rather than the lawbreaker whom others control.

Noëlle's intellectual superiority is based on a strict separation between intelligence and morality. This separation underlies the demarcation between Noëlle's private domain (the library) and the rest of the prison and, more critically, underlies Huré's

---

[7]Charasson, "Romancière," 94.
[8]Irving Wardle, "Closed Society," *The Observer*, no. 9100 (November 28, 1965), 28. A review of *En prison*.
[9]Robert Nye, "Left Ear, Right Nose," *The Guardian* (November 24, 1967), 11. A review of Huré's *Le Péché sans merci*.

response to external views of herself. Huré believes that the ordinary conditions of incarceration reflect and reinforce a moral judgment that determines decisions about the inmate's life. The prisoner's intelligence is often a detriment, or is at best unimportant to administrators: "The [prisoner's] intellectual and social level was not necessarily taken into account. It was her moral level that determined everything" (p. 213). The determinant moral judgments imply that the prisoner has no course but contrition and regret if she wishes to be approved and rewarded. But Noëlle resolutely rejects the expected humility that would violate her self-esteem:

[To her friend Hélène] Would you be my friend if I feigned a contrition that I do not feel? I have been dishonest, but I have never been contemptible. (p. 16)

[The director to Noëlle] You lack humility and flexibility. (p. 55)

[Noëlle] What I do regret is that at one time I found myself in a situation from which there was no way out except the one I had to choose. (p. 208)

Thus Huré emphatically reappropriates the moral identity that prison would quash. She challenges the perceptions of expected female behavior and, with them, the premises about "rehabilitation" that promote that behavior. But Huré does not confront the psychosexual roots of normative views of women; instead, she deflects those views by insisting on taking up spiritual/intellectual, not sexual, issues.

Although theories of female criminality have varied greatly in recent decades, almost all have assumed a precision, a "scientificness," of which Heuyer's "genital-phase" notions are only one extreme example. Virtually all models through the 1960s still saw women's crime as sexual in nature and thus perpetuated the morphological extension of the endocrine functions that underlay "explanations" of women's deviance. And as the unconscious gained credibility as a site for conflict and maladjustment, the link between criminal acts and ordinary neurotic behavior tightened. Already visible in Steinheil's time in the association of "perversion" with "illness," this connection between crime and neurosis has had particular implications for criminal women. On the new grounds that they merely differ in degree of "abnormal" sexual adaptation, "deviant" and "normal" women have been viewed in similar ways, and criminal women have been moved inward from the margins of society. The concomitant goal shift in penal policy from personality modification to social rehabilitation and reintegration mirrors such criminological thought. But the apparent softening and greater understanding toward female behavior masks the ongoing myth of women's "nature" and, paradoxically, furthers it by couching it in specialized terms. The emphasis on women's sexual adaptation made it necessary, for example, to explore their personal affective histories during judicial inquests; and the insistence on prisoners' social "amendment" hardened the definition of "healthy," "rehabilitated" female comportment.[10]

These psychocriminological views about female sexual identity elicit denial from Huré. She virtually dismisses her sexual identity from the novel and makes Noëlle, her transposed self, thoroughly cerebral and desexualized. Rather than subverting theories about female sexuality, Huré either ignores them or attempts to "transcend" them with her heroine's "superior" philosophical generalizing. The opening scene of *En prison*, for example, establishes Noëlle's distrust of the ineffective psychiatric theory that presumes to explain her criminality. It also makes explicit the connection theorists draw between criminal behavior and neurosis, a connection Huré treats as suspect. Noëlle is being examined by a prison psychiatrist as she tries to obtain a medical furlough. The doctor says, "A neurosis is nothing more than the exaggeration of a character trait, madam." Noëlle answers, "In short, doctor, I am neurotic, but not to the point" (p. 9). The psychiatrist determines that Noëlle is not ill enough, and her request for a leave is denied. As the scene ends, she defines two other key psychiatric terms: "Anxiety is the anticipation of a future danger.... Anguish is the experience of that danger—as it is being lived" (p. 9). These two feelings, anxiety and anguish, exist strongly in

[10]For an excellent analysis of the definitions of female sexual normality promoted in prison, see Catherine Erhel and Catherine Leguay, *Prisonnières* (Paris: Stock, 1977).

Noëlle, yet they are not fully detected by the doctor. The psychiatrist, hardly a physician in Huré's view, resembles Foucault's "adviser on punishment."[11] In her second prison, Haguenau, known at the time as a "test house" or "experimental penitentiary" for "scientific observation," Noëlle undergoes a similar clinical "examination" that also proves more punitive than curative. Thus the opening chapter's "anxiety" and "anguish," which Noëlle lives out in the course of the novel, are not accessible to the clinician because they constitute not psychological disorder, but profound spiritual malaise. The novel's spiritual register is thereby set, and Noëlle's imperviousness to "rehabilitative" measures is established. Like each succeeding scene in the book, the first is part of prison chronology but comments on a broader issue—in this case the insufficiency of scientific concepts to explain human motivations.

The concern with spiritual and philosophical issues that pervades *En prison* suggests that the effect of imprisonment that Huré most strongly fears is mental paralysis. She knows that the absence of a challenging environment "reduces the brain's power of alertness."[12] She redoubles her insistence on intellectual distinction by recessions of philosophical reference: Noëlle, the prison philosopher, librarian, and scribe, in her cerebral mode discusses well-known authors and thinkers—her intellectual impulse is somewhat derivative. Abstraction dominates the dialogue of this already abstract, actionless book. Noëlle quotes Pascal, Descartes, La Bruyère, Spinoza, Barrès, Alain, Valéry, and Gide, among others who also represent for her purity and clarity of thought. She says: "The first necessary condition of a philosophy is precision of thought and clarity. Feeling comes after" (p. 29). This primacy of reason over sentiment is the basis for Noëlle's sense of superiority and infuses the identity she reappropriates in prison.

With the focus in prison on physical rather than mental activity, it is not surprising that Huré draws such a disembodied, intangible character. It is also evident that, along with

---

[11]Alain Schifres, "Foucault: L'Archipel carcéral," *Réalités* (July–August 1975), 64.
[12]Jacqueline Renaud, "La Prison modifie pour toujours l'organisme," *Science et vie*, no. 685 (October 1974), 50.

intellectual death, the prison's objectification of the body as spectacle gives rise to Huré's disincarnation of her heroine. The constant observation of the female prisoners' bodies, most directly during surveillance and examination, renders them transparent: "The inmate must at all times be ready to be observed and inspected, in every corner of her domain—that is, her cell and her body."[13] The women are in a sense "violated" and dispossessed of their selves, in a highly focused extension of their situation in society. But Huré pushes Noëlle's "transparency" to the limit: her body is totally absent from the story. Noëlle is in this way the fictional translation of Huré's philosopher idol Edmund Husserl. Huré, a self-proclaimed proponent of Husserlian phenomenology and "elucidation," makes Noëlle the symbol of the intellectual distinction and clarity Husserl promulgates. Noëlle "sees" and is not seen; and her unimpeded "vision" lets her constitute her own intellectual space. As in Husserlian phenomenology, "thought appears to itself without intermediary, thinking and to know that one is thinking are all one,"[14] thus making Noëlle's center her psychic state of pure thought. Huré even borrows Husserl's idea of "intuition," a privileged experience of "pure consciousness": Noëlle's chosen form of knowledge and truth is her "intuition," "which she knew from secret knowledge" (p. 108).

Husserlian concepts and their insistence on transcendent, contentless, intuitive experience buttress Huré's reduction of objects and description in her novel. "Psychology," which she rejects from the outset as the inferior "residue" of philosophy that has "[had] amputated from it the best parts—logic and metaphysics" (p. 166), is omitted altogether as the concrete, explicative, and content-filled domain Husserl mistrusted.

---

[13]Erhel and Leguay, *Prisonnières*, 101. This book, the only feminist theoretical analysis of the imprisonment of women and one of the few studies written by former prisoners, discusses at length the issue of female desire in its relation to confinement.

[14]Jean-Paul Sartre, *Imagination: A Psychological Critique*, trans. Forrest Williams (Ann Arbor: University of Michigan Press, 1962), 67. A translation of *L'Imagination* (Paris: Presses Universitaires de France, 1936). See also Edmund Husserl, *Phenomenology and the Crisis of Philosophy* (New York: Harper and Row, 1965).

Noëlle's body is one such "object" that is removed: it is referred to only metonymically, as Noëlle's "piercing blue eyes." This dichotomizing of the material and the immaterial is the basis for Noëlle's affective preoccupations: her passions, centered on her lawyer, remain within her mind. Furthermore, *En prison* offers minimal description of physical surroundings, with a purity and stasis that reflect Noëlle herself and a stylistic rigidity "in which each word has only one possible meaning."[15] Huré's attachment to spiritual concerns means that Noëlle's "internal dispositions," her internal world, are what really count, not things external and physical. But the author seems to suspect the consequences of opting for pure thought with no action when another prisoner says to Noëlle, "You see things well and clearly, but you act quickly and badly" (p. 257). Noëlle refuses "mediocrity" by choosing sincerity in conformance with "that inner predisposition that makes us *contingent*, that allows us anything, that makes everything *possible* for us—the worst, but also the best" (p. 48; Huré's emphasis). But in choosing inaction and resignation from the outset—"There is nothing to which I object" (p. 182)—Noëlle contributes to her own victimization. Huré thus follows the traditional path of women's flight from struggle.

It would, however, be incorrect to focus only on Noëlle's self-imposed martyrdom, though she does, for example, refuse to appeal her remarkably severe sentence ("four years' imprisonment, nonreducible, plus ten years prohibition of travel [in certain locations]"; pp. 157–58) and herself requests an early transfer from la Roquette to the harsh penitentiary at Haguenau. It is in fact more important that Huré takes the impoverished and impoverishing conditions of her punishment and transforms them, in *En prison*, into a chosen asceticism. This process, which would not be possible were Noëlle placed in the prison's communal dormitories and workshops instead of isolated with a few friends in her library, is evoked frequently in the novel. One feels that Huré is transforming her own "exclu-

---

[15]Lia Lacombe, "Victime de la passion," *Les Lettres françaises*, no. 1127 (April 21–27, 1966), 5. A review of *Descente en enfer*.

sion from human society"[16] into Noëlle's positive marginality within prison, making possible her internal search:

> [A fellow prisoner to Noëlle] I'm afraid you are confusing asceticism and purification undertaken in the best possible, most morally uplifting conditions with something that is just the slow unfolding of gestures that have only the most distant relationship to man in his individuality... Later on, if we are found guilty, we will probably find the solitude and the leisure to recreate our authentic individuality, with all the preliminary destruction that re-creation presupposes. (p. 14)

> [Noëlle] Silence, a normal everyday life that is begun again and assumed in spite of the pain we know nothing about—these are the criteria of nobility. (p. 48)

> [Quoting Gide's *Les Nourritures terrestres*] "Nathanaël, you will look at all things as you pass by, and you will stop at none." (p. 70)

> [After Noëlle's refusal to appeal her sentence] And so, once again, the certainty that suffering is more soothing than joy was proved. (p. 159)

Elsewhere Noëlle refers directly to well-known martyrs: Pascal, Archimedes, and Christ. And in the opening scene of her psychiatric visit, she refuses the chance to help herself, by rejecting psychological games of contrition and guilt.

Huré, who had been called "hard" and "dry," like other women before her, makes these labels into positive character traits. Noëlle withstands an extraordinary series of judicial and personal disappointments: she is denied bail; she is prejudged and precondemned by the investigating magistrate, who says during her hearing, "You could have managed to find money some other way" (p. 72); the sympathetic local prison director is replaced by a hostile, insecure one; her lawyer is nearly discredited in a scandal that postpones Noëlle's trial; her sentence is shockingly harsh, and she is twice denied presidential pardon; her mother dies and her father is dying; and her lawyer rebuffs her love. Noëlle is the victim of unexplained circum-

---

[16]From an interview with Marcel Mithois, "On m'a refusé le Goncourt parce que je sortais de prison," *Réalités* (August 1963), 79.

stances; we never learn why justice continually denies her any leniency.

Huré does not hesitate to suggest parallels between Noëlle's experiences and the life of Christ, thereby ennobling her suffering. Both endure harsh and unjust punishment. Noëlle emits an aura that others immediately detect. She develops strong friendships with kindred spirits, but one by one they are withdrawn, leaving her with "the persecution of silence" (p. 85). Her solitude is intensified by her lack of affective ties outside the prison: she says to her friend Hélène, "You know that my family has abandoned me" (p. 13), so we learn nothing of Noëlle's family background. She performs generous deeds for her sister prisoners—though out of what she calls "passive cohesion" (p. 33), not sisterly affection—such as writing official letters for them and comforting a suicidal younger woman during her trial. And Noëlle maintains a stubborn "hopefulness," "one of those remedies that don't cure anything but that let you suffer for a longer time" (p. 55). Though her vague but persistent hope hardly amounts to faith in an afterlife, it is a sustaining force for her. As a secular martyr no longer possessing "faith either in the immortality of the soul or in any kind of providential act" (pp. 103–4), Noëlle echoes Huré's own religious crisis, which only spiritual, not Christian, priorities survived.

The term by which Noëlle designates her ascetic quest—"classicism"—aptly suggests Huré's aesthetic preferences. Noëlle opposes her own penchants to those of "Romanticism," signaling the previously mentioned dichotomy of thought/feeling or classical/Romantic: "One would have to know how to go from Romanticism to a form of classicism" (p. 245). Noëlle applies the term "classicism" specifically to her personal code, which runs counter to the psychosexual judgments against her ("this criminal notion that weighs on me"; p. 205). If those judgments, and the "personality dossiers" to which they gave rise, were the basis for the "character modification" that penal policy still sought to some degree, Huré denies the possibility of such "modification" by subscribing to the classical notion of fixed character. Not surprisingly, she quotes the seventeenth-century portraitist and moralist La Bruyère and also frequently turns to maxims. Noëlle's steadfast pride reflects this fatalistic belief in the fixity of personality, and her pride causes her downfall: were she less firm in her "aristocratic fatalism" (p. 245), she would act to help herself. This constancy of character is also represented in Noëlle's one physical gesture: her smile. After each exchange with a comprehending interlocutor or with herself, she smiles, signifying she has once again verified her self-image (i.e., her unfailing superiority). Every character, without exception, from the prison wardens to the nuns, the judges, and the chaplain, remarks on her uniqueness.

Like all the women studied here, Noëlle makes her sense of her own worth the measure for others—the criterion for solipsistic comparisons. She is aware of her tendency to pride: "How strong one's soul must be not to measure one's superiority in terms of the advantages one has over the common man" (p. 138). Huré, of all these authors, is most explicit in delineating the requirements for superiority; she directly and repeatedly names Noëlle's desirable qualities: "nobility of soul," "honor," "charm," "dignity," "refinement," "loftiness," and "courage." All the women in *En prison* save Noëlle and her select friends—the few "princesses" who subscribe to "a mode of internal life similar to [her] own" (p. 151)—are described as "promiscuous," "vulgar," "so much drab wallpaper" against which Noëlle shines.[17] Huré not only echoes Steinheil with superficial labels bespeaking her "caste spirit" (p. 65) and her "royal attitude" (p. 165), she attempts to elevate her judgments to the "universal" truths of a Cornelian tragedy. Noëlle's lexicon suggests affinities with the classical dramatist, and her tragic vision of the entire prison "spectacle" makes for further similarities. Like all the women before her, Huré reproduces the familiar topos of the visible, of prison as theater: "La Roquette is a village, a kind of theater set" (p. 14). But since, as in classical drama, little of the setting and properties is described, it becomes clear that, for Huré, prison's tragedy operates not in the realm of its external reality, but in the "violence" and "ugliness" of its soul (p. 21). Fre-

---

[17]Robert Baldick, "A Modern Goya in Prose," *The Daily Telegraph*, no. 34, 222 (December 23, 1965), 13. A review of *En prison*.

quent references to Dante—"I now find myself in a place where light itself is mute" (p. 46)—underscore prison's resemblance to a Sartrian, and therefore theatrical, internal hell. Noëlle's definition of prison evokes a universe of inescapable "rules of unity" and hostile forces: "Being in prison for me is simply being in a place you would not be in were you not forced to be there" (p. 82). And, like a tragic heroine, Noëlle is given a flaw, though hardly one that accounts for her fate: she "weakens" by falling in love with her lawyer—scarcely the self-ascribed and determinant character failing of Roland or others. It is instead unremitting external forces that really determine Noëlle's life. In the strongest instance, the terse announcement of her four-year sentence is the sharpest of dramatic turns.

"Theater" most aptly conveys confinement for Huré not in the sense of Steinheil's bourgeois comedy, Cappelle-Lafarge's Romantic drama, or Sarrazin's farce, but through what Huré calls "melodrama" and "bad theater" (p. 28). Whereas these other authors focus on prison's immobile decor, interchangeable actors, and unanchored time, Huré insists on the unreal quality of this special place. She calls prison "a world outside reality" (p. 230), "this break with reality" (p. 205), thus rejecting any of the traditionally accepted connections or echoes between the "outside" and the "inside." Elsewhere Huré expresses her feelings about the loss of reality: "Captivity leads to the creation of myths. Our world [inside] not only is forbidden, it has an unreal, purely imaginary quality" (p. 153). The prisoner's tendency to emphasize his or her "imaginary life" has been associated with loss of psychic oneirism, or dreamlike vision of sexual experiences.[18] According to Renaud, "Contact with reality, and more specifically the ability to give concrete form to what one has imagined, is a vital necessity [in prison]" (p. 53). The resulting "unfolding of one's private movie" (p. 154) will contain various proportions of fact and fiction. The fiction, exaggerated by Steinheil's critics as her "mythomania," was later exalted by Sarrazin as a creative force. Huré channels libidinal energy into the mind: she in effect exploits the "unreality" of prison by writing an "unreal," highly abstract novel. By render-

---

[18]Renaud, "Prison," 53.

ing everything—characters, settings, discourse—insubstantial, Huré (and Noëlle) can seek protection from the harsh but faceless external forces that control their lives. One critic theorized that this stilted "atmosphere of intellectuality" is in fact "the mark of truth," since it is Noëlle's means "to protect herself from realities in herself and her surroundings which might otherwise to be too much to bear."[19]

En prison contains several internal self-representations of the aesthetic credo that corresponds to this rupture between the real and the unreal. At one point Noëlle criticizes Camus on the grounds that his writing "lacks a sense of the eternal" (p. 166) by remaining too attached to human detail, to "the culture of the solitary and impassioned man" (p. 166). Echoing an interview in which she had said, "Everything that is not eternal is worthless,"[20] Huré here not only subscribes to conventional literary standards of "universality" but also, ironically, misreads Camus's own stance on the question, as developed in *L'Homme révolté*. Camus argues that, by choosing to exalt "reality in its crudest state," a "realist" novelist avoids the search for unity and transcendence necessary for any revolt.[21] The two authors therefore appear to agree on this point. In attempting to set up an opposition between herself and Camus on such shaky grounds as the "eternal" and the "temporal," Huré ignores the necessarily referential relation of metaphysics to the physical world.

The same aesthetic credo of pure spirituality is suggested by the painting Noëlle does in Haguenau: her work is impressionistic, luminous, and completely nonrepresentational, an emblem of Husserlian intuitive experience. But Noëlle realizes that this focus on immaterial shapes and colors depends on keeping reality at bay: "Reality fled in front of her eyes" (p. 239), yet it remained a dialectical referent for her work. The character Noëlle herself is perhaps the best textual repre-

---

[19] Richard Mayne, "Kilroy Wasn't Here," *New Statesman* (December 24, 1965), 1006. A review of *En prison*.
[20] Charasson, "Romancière," 89.
[21] Albert Camus, *The Rebel: An Essay on Man in Revolt*, trans. Anthony Bower (New York: Knopf, 1967), 269. A translation of *L'Homme révolté* (Paris: Gallimard, 1951).

sentation, albeit unintentional, of the sterility of separating "reality" from "unreality," the mundane from the transcendent. For Noëlle's tragic fate can be seen as a result of her splitting action from thought, *praxis* from intellectual apprehension, and thus rendering herself inactive. At stake in this traditional debate over the nature and hierarchy of experience is the credibility of Huré's novel as prison writing: by focusing centrally on "transcendent" issues that do not spring from prison and ignoring the prison itself, Huré fails to transcend or transform anything. *En prison* is thus neither the critique and correction of reality that the masculine literary tradition has attempted nor the quest for full identity and sincerity that women's writing has espoused. It is, explicitly, an attempt to achieve the sublimation Gide and other "classical" authors exalted: "Constraint is a marvelous springboard that redoubles the pleasures of the heart as it does the strengths of the mind."[22] *En prison* also seeks to be a transcription of "life," in Gide's terms, from which "one could make a work of art" (p. 86). But the novel declines to present the constraints from which Huré's mind drew its imaginative pleasure and its material for realization. Furthermore, Huré denies Noëlle a chance to grow through a real search for self by establishing her fixed character at the outset: "[Noëlle] would let her character follow its usual inclination" (p. 190). The reader is not brought by some empirical or logical countermethod to understand the "true" Huré/Noëlle, but is given a whole, static character from the start. Finally, the novel's stylistic fixity, its recourse to maxims, its frequent recondite allusions, and its lack of narrative conflict make it dramatically and affectively stagnant as well. One senses that the real story will begin upon Noëlle's release, after the "birth trauma" her

[22]The words of Thérèse, the heroine of Huré's *Descente en enfer* (Paris: Plon, 1966), 22. Thérèse Etiévant, who resembles Mauriac's Thérèse Desqueyroux, is in an unhappy, stifling, upper-class marriage. Her husband Pierre tries to persuade everyone that Thérèse is mad and suicidal, when in fact it is he who kills himself, presumably for fear of losing his reputation in a gambling scandal. Pierre holds Thérèse "prisoner" in their house and in their marriage.

freedom will engender.[23] *En prison* amounts to a slice of sometimes graceful but completely decontextualized salon conversation that, as Sartre was to discover for his own "fiction," does not "come down into the streets" or effect change.

Huré does take one important step toward rejecting externally imposed explanations of women's behavior. Though she does not go so far as to assert her own free will, she does question the presumed connection between the facts of a crime and the criminal's "human worth" (p. 143), between the act and the individual who committed it. She does so by firmly refusing to judge the crimes of her sister prisoners, a judgment that "implies one has a *right* over that individual that another individual should not have" (p. 29; her emphasis). Because for Huré "a crime depends on the circumstances, and no one else can know anything about those circumstances" (p. 171), she can justify separating Noëlle as heroine from the circumstances of her life in the world outside. In this way Huré also renders irrelevant prison's goal of "rehabilitation": not only is human character fixed, it is not even commensurable with the outside forces that would change it.

While rejecting external influences by omitting them from her novel, Huré also removes prison's substitute economic and affective networks and so denies their validity for herself. Noëlle is never touched by the other women's relationships. Huré appears to be subverting the contention that the female prisoner "needs" to establish emotional ties or acquire certain material amenities. And she goes beyond taking Noëlle out of the prison universe: she has her form friendships in her own universe with no thought for practicality. Far from providing for her creature comforts, Hélène, Claude, Martine, and Claire are "more like nuns" (Wardle), serving as perfect spiritual interlocutors. If there is any loss in prison that Huré clearly is taking into account, it is that of speech: Noëlle and her friends engage in endless elegant dialogue in her library cum salon.

Huré's critique of prison organization as inadequate for, and

---

[23]George Mikes, *Prison* (New York: Horizon Press, 1964), xvi–xvii. Mikes compares release from prison to Otto Rank's idea of the trauma of leaving the womb.

essentially irrelevant to, women's needs is strongest and most poignant when she evokes Noëlle's anxiety about her future. The social worker at Haguenau states outright that she cannot help Noëlle find any but manual jobs—a clear indication of the small importance penal authorities granted to women's professional and intellectual identities. No one, not even the highly sympathetic penal magistrate, can help Noëlle. Her fear of the future—or, rather, her fear that she has no future—accelerates and intensifies into obsession:

> I must make my whole life over again. I think about it constantly.... The future is rather bleak. (p. 117)

> My life clings to the present moment. (p. 167)

> Unhappiness does not lie in the material conditions they give us here; it is elsewhere, in the prospect of the future, in solitude.... I don't even dare think about what release from prison will be like. (p. 219)

> [Noëlle] could not take her mind off that fear of the future that harassed her. (p. 239)

> What would become of her in the months that followed? ... It was now that all was really beginning. (pp. 256–59)

The last question regarding Noëlle's future is reminiscent of Cappelle-Lafarge's *Heures de prison* and its author's growing passivity toward controlling her life. Huré suggests at the book's end that the real punishment is not imprisonment, but freedom. It seems that in anticipating Noëlle's future suffering Huré justifies her portrayal of Noëlle's prison experience as a privileged, secular monasticism—scarcely the "hell" she declares it to be. And yet, ironically, it is this privileged, rarefied experience that keeps Noëlle from facing and preparing for her future. If prison cuts her off from reality, and if there is no "afterlife" (Christian or otherwise) beyond the prison, then Noëlle is nowhere. In this way *En prison* presents more effectively than any other text the void that surrounds the imprisoned woman. Roland had addressed herself to an audience beyond that void; Cappelle-Lafarge had turned to God for solace; Steinheil had transformed the void into a positive emphasis on pure form; and Sarrazin reinfuses it with the substance of her own invention. But Huré makes absence—pure subjectivism or abstraction—central: it underlies the thematic, dramatic, and formal concerns of the novel itself.

At the time Huré's fiction appeared, one critic, curiously enough, associated Huré with Violette Leduc, in that both were writers of "teratological literature" whom the public viewed as "carnival monsters."[24] The commonality between the two, however, is more biographical than literary. Both drew public scrutiny for their unorthodox lives, and both were, without doubt, outsiders judged by conventional feminine models. But their autobiographical fictions could hardly be more different: Huré's static, meditative, and metaphysical narratives have little in common with Leduc's tortured and immediate transcriptions of pain and failure. Leduc reflects contemporary feminist concerns with women's authentic language, whereas Huré harks back to an age that believed in the adequacy and precision of discourse.

Huré's literary nostalgia for self-controlled protagonists and self-contained texts, while an admirable attempt to confer nobility on the aftermath of her banal acts of theft, unfortunately also brings with it other "nostalgias." Huré said in a 1963 interview, "I am a conservative. In a word, I am a fierce and extreme right-wing monarchist.... I respect the laws."[25] *En prison*'s royalist vocabulary ("princess," "nobility," "aristocratic"), its hierarchical division of prisoners by caste, and its subscription to individual superiority by birthright mirror this view. And so does Huré's (and Noëlle's) morality, which, like that of most imprisoned women, is highly conventional. Noëlle, despite her claim not to judge others, speaks of her fellow prisoners' "dreadful promiscuity" and of lesbians who, before prison, had been "perfectly normal" (p. 147). In a curious, fleeting attempt to give flesh to Noëlle's otherwise disincarnate attractiveness, Huré has her say to herself, "Soon I will find my womanly curves once again.... I will rediscover coquettish-

---

[24] Gilbert Ganne, "Le Féminin singulier," *La Revue de Paris* (December 1964), 105.
[25] Charasson, "Romancière," 86.

ness, with its makeup, its dusting powder, its perfumed essences" (p. 254). Such a longing for the feminine appearance she had before prison "defaced" her restates traditional conceptions of appropriate sex-specific responses. The same is true for Noëlle's association of her working hard and enduring with "the virile part of herself" (p. 161). Huré most clearly reveals her acceptance of stereotypes through her characterizations of women political prisoners who, far from acting on their own impulses and initiative, "had done nothing but follow the men they loved" (p. 98) and through her description of women judges as "most often unmarried and ugly" (p. 66).

In Huré's universe, divisions among imprisoned women prevail. While all the authors studied here elevate themselves by comparison with other women, nowhere is the consequence of that self-isolation more harmful than in *En prison*. Noëlle's solitude, as she knows full well, affects the court's verdict and, more important, her life after release, but asceticism is given priority over enrichment and reconstruction of self and surroundings. The novel is thus a modern vestige of traditional representations of female martyrdom and of women's passive acceptance of imposed beliefs. Happily, Albertine Sarrazin was writing from prison at the same time as Huré, and with her the "new feminism" of the political arena found its literary voice.

8

Albertine Sarrazin

> With her [Sarrazin], everything begins with prison and, through a lasting apotheosis, ends as literature—Jacqueline Piatier, *Le Monde*

Albertine Sarrazin's prison writings of the late 1950s and the 1960s mirror a more general trend in feminist intellectual activity of recent decades: energetic critique and subversion of social and literary conventions. Sarrazin's departure from previous modes of female prisoner response—in particular, indirect expression of anger and inventive restraint—parallels the larger "new feminist" break of several years later, a break from its original moorings in traditional leftist critiques of society. For Sarrazin too rejects implicit or abstract theoretical expressions of the need for change and opts in her writing for vigorous and concrete defiance. Unlike the works of her contemporary Anne Huré, which follow a more conservative route, employing long-standing forms of analytical inquiry, Sarrazin's works have a subversive significance that has only recently been explored, and they point to vital new directions both in women's prison writing and in women's writing in general.

It would be inaccurate to ascribe a feminist consciousness or intentions to Sarrazin, since she—unlike the contemporary "free" authors Rochefort, Duras, Etcherelli, and Beauvoir—puts forth no such political views. She is, ostensibly, highly traditional in her ideas about women and in her search for legitimization—and this conventionality was emphasized when

Albertine Sarrazin, 1967. Photo Harlingue-Viollet

her works appeared.¹ It would be more exact and useful to isolate two threads within her writing, one tied to the heritage of her imprisoned forerunners, the other leading to originality and freshness. If, like the women before her, she was acted upon and responded to opprobrium and punishment, she also in turn acted upon those same hostile forces and shaped them for her own purposes. Two of Sarrazin's works in particular, the *Journal de prison 1959* and her novel *La Cavale* (1965), reflect these two tendencies—the first, her recognizable connection to the female prison tradition and the second her sharp turn toward a new literary orientation in prison writing.²

Sarrazin's confinement began with her education at a "Bon Pasteur," or reform-school, where she was sent in the early 1950s by her adoptive parents, and it continued barely interrupted until 1964. Jailed initially as an accomplice to armed robbery, then for theft and prostitution, she spent nearly one-third of her brief life incarcerated, dying in 1967 at age twenty-nine. Her most notable period of "freedom," recorded in her novel *L'Astragale* (1964), was her 1957 escape from Amiens prison, when her fellow prisoner and future husband, Julien Sarrazin, rescued her. All her texts, from the earliest Rimbaldian *Journal de Fresnes* (1953–54), to her poems (1953–60), to her last novel, *La Traversière* (1966), written after novelistic success, sprang directly from prison. She bears full witness to that part of herself and her life. And yet though Sarrazin, of all the women studied here, had most fully assimilated her prisons, she was also the one most able to reject them. For her confinement is the core of invention itself and thus the object of her writings' profound critique.

---

¹See, for example, Pierre Daix, "La Taule et 'La Cavale,'" *Les Lettres françaises* (November 4, 1965), 5; Robert Kanters, "Albertine, ou L'Art de la fugue," *Le Figaro littéraire* (November 11, 1965), 5; and, more recently, R. M. Albérès, "Des relations pas mondaines," *Nouvelles littéraires*, no. 2446 (August 1974), 4.

²Editions of Sarrazin's works to be used are the following: the *Journal de prison 1959*, subtitled *Le Times*, is taken from Albertine Sarrazin, *Le Passe-peine: 1949–1967* (Paris: Julliard, 1976), 102–68. Page references to this edition will appear parenthetically, and translations are mine. Also, Albertine Sarrazin, *La Cavale* (Paris: J.-J. Pauvert, 1965), also published as *The Runaway*, trans. Charles Lam Markmann (New York: Grove Press, 1967). Page references to this translation will appear parenthetically.

ALBERTINE SARRAZIN

The *Journal de prison 1959* and the novel *La Cavale* together sum up Sarrazin's responses to imprisonment. They provide a remarkable contrast in organization and effect.[3] The *Journal*, continuing with the confessional genre women had traditionally used in prison, presents a personal quest for authenticity and individual truth. Its purpose is to establish Sarrazin's affective and sexual identity, reflecting the prime focus of all women's prison texts. While the journal's form departs radically from the strictly chronological narrative structure of the earlier personal texts—and its telegraphic form is itself an astonishing landmark in prison literature—its thematic concerns with love and nostalgia are quite familiar. The novel, on the other hand, while anchored thematically in the popular topos of self-presentation, is scarcely defensive or self-justifying. Though absorbed with identity, it is resolutely affirmative: Sarrazin refuses to remain known as a criminal and claims her identity as author. *La Cavale*, a full-fledged novel by an imprisoned woman, exhibits narrative drive and character development and also reflects many of the genre's traditional formal concerns, such as control, fullness of detail, precise chronology, and spatial order. But its thoroughly unorthodox protagonist, its defiant narrator, signals a new perspective on women's prison experience. Before discussing these two texts in detail, I shall outline the general criminological views and penal conditions to which they most strongly respond.

Compared with previous writers, Sarrazin is the most clearly aware of external judgments. The explicitness with which she emphatically reappropriates her identity contrasts with Marguerite Steinheil's euphemistic indirection in the same way 1960s criminological theory contrasts with earlier tentative "psychologizing" notions. Whereas Steinheil's memoirs are stimulated by vague, even metaphorical explanations of her behavior (the "character" flaws of "hysteria" and "hallucination"), Sarrazin's texts challenge the strident, unimaginative

---

[3]For a fuller analysis of these two works as representative of "feminine" and "masculine" tendencies within Sarrazin's work, see my article "Albertine Sarrazin: A Control Case for Femininity in Form," *The French Review* 51, no. 2 (December 1977): 245–51.

ideas generated by such theorists as Thomas, Heuyer, Pollak, and the would-be "new" specialists, Cowie, Cowie, and Slater.[4] Earlier theorists had described women's genital and erotic development in general terms; modern psychocriminologists focused squarely on menarche, childbirth, and menopause. Sarrazin directly rejects the sexual premises of these normative views of women by responding with explicit sexual preoccupations of her own. And she distills the hostility underlying those views and the assurance with which they were put forth into the energy and power of her writing.

The other current in criminological theory that has traversed the twentieth century is the sociological focus on external influences. Both this and the idea of psychosexual disturbance presumably "grew" in certainty with increased specialization and reinforced one another. As the influence of both Freudian and sociological ideas about deviant motivation became entrenched, exogenous forces such as affective-familial background, education, and social conditioning gained prominence in criminological theory. Women criminals in particular, the maladapted but corrigible victims of defective drives, were even further stripped of their autonomy as deviance was attributed to external causes. This ascribed loss of individual responsibility—and with it the loss of will and the power of choice—sparked a strong answer in Sarrazin. Along with righting her perceived sexual identity, her texts seek to prove and exalt her self-determination. She inverts belief in exogenous forces to assert her own free will. Recent feminist studies have exposed the way silence in women's prisons was used to deter autonomy and rebellion, thereby perpetuating myths of female passivity.[5]

---

[4] In *Delinquency in Girls* (1968), their so-called liberal study, Cowie, Cowie, and Slater state, "Common sense suggests that the main factors [in predisposing girls to delinquency] are somatic ones, especially hormonal ones" (cited in Carol Smart, *Women, Crime and Criminology: A Feminist Critique* [London: Routledge and Kegan Paul, 1976], 60).

[5] Catherine Erhel and Catherine Leguay, in *Prisonnières* (Paris: Stock, 1977), note the absence of revolts in women's prisons in the 1970s and the inaccurate explanations offered. The authors, both former prisoners, also cite the nineteenth-century women's prison revolt at Rennes that began, not coincidentally, in the "cellblock for hyperactive women"—the women who spoke out against silence.

Sarrazin's speaking out in her texts, while apparently personal in its goals, thus helps correct misperceptions about women prisoners in general. Sarrazin, more than previous authors, evokes in detail the conditions of her confinement, particularly in *La Cavale*, her vivid fresco of prison life. Whereas Roland, Cappelle-Lafarge, Steinheil, and Huré occasionally remark on the setting around them, they most often turn away from the painful present of captivity. Huré goes so far as to reduce the prison environment to a rarefied projection of her own mind. Sarrazin, on the other hand, as part of her resolution to assimilate her prisons, paints in full the conditions of her imprisonment so she can explore her own reactions. Her characters are flesh and blood and live in the world of objects and desires. Sarrazin supplies ample descriptions and anecdotes as well as rich metaphors that express her heroine's agility and energy.

La Cavale traces the author's experience at Amiens, Soissons, and Compiègne prisons from 1961 to 1962. The novel, grounded firmly in the lived present, dramatizes the findings of case studies of women's prisons.[6] All the conditions that try to effect "rehabilitation" so as to implement paternalistic assumptions about women's proper sexual and affective behavior appear in the course of the text. For example, the women "work" at making nets and doing laundry—tasks that not only are based on traditional domestic activities but also offer them no career training. A 1967 study of Rennes prison states explicitly what Sarrazin shows in her story: "Professional training is no longer of primary importance and is becoming secondary. On the other hand, the female inmate, if necessary, receives the training in housework she may not have gotten."[7] Sarrazin also speaks of the censoring of the inmates' mail, which must deal only with family concerns: "They [the letters] must deal

---

[6]The important case studies of women's prisons, except for Erhel and Leguay's *Prisonnières*, tend to be American and include the following: Kathryn Watterson Burkhart, *Women in Prison* (New York: Doubleday, 1973); Rose Giallombardo, *Society of Women: A Study of a Women's Prison* (New York: John Wiley, 1966); and Esther Heffernan, *Making It in Prison: The Square, the Cool, and the Life* (New York: John Wiley, 1972).

[7]Mariette Bregeon, "Approche criminologique et traitement de la criminalité féminine," doctoral thesis, University of Rennes Law School, 1967, 260.

exclusively with family matters or private concerns; they must not contain any kind of political reference, any scurrilous or insulting allegation, or any threat or accusation whatever and must contain nothing that is contrary to morality or to proper manners."[8] The arbitrariness of what constitutes proper morality leads Sarrazin and other prisoners to write coded letters that appear to conform to regulations while in fact sending subversive messages; it also accounts for the existence of a complicated subsystem of interprisoner communication (*biftons* or "kites") that, in *La Cavale,* forms the novel's subtext of Sarrazin's relationship with her lover, Julien Sarrazin. It becomes clear in the novel that conditions in women's prisons reinforce the most traditional of gender identities: "Prison's and justice's definition of what a woman must be seemed to us a caricature of the social definition of femininity."[9]

The administrative insistence on prisoner hygiene, such as showering and cleaning, is equally prominent in Sarrazin's story and becomes a focus of attention and discipline for the guards. The emphasis on cleanliness, besides reinforcing stereotype, intensifies the observation of the prisoners' bodies, the single most destructive aspect of women's imprisonment. Sarrazin confronts this appropriation and violation of her self by showing her heroine, Anick, squarely in humiliating situations. Sarrazin, as her transposed narrator Anick, undergoes frequent strip-searches, especially during admission to each new prison. This objectification of her body—Anick watches herself being searched—is one element of Sarrazin's overall technique in *La Cavale*—her use of objectification for her own fictional purposes. Twisting the traditional belief in women's "need" for self-display, Anick/Sarrazin is both the observed prisoner and the observing author. This technique is also Sarrazin's particular application of the "seeing/being seen" theme common to all women's prison texts.

A related aspect of punishment for women stems from what Erhel and Leguay describe as the administration's exaggerated concern with sex among prisoners. The myth of uncontrolled

[8]Ibid., 212.
[9]Erhel and Leguay, *Prisonnières,* 15.

and promiscuous lesbianism in prisons, an outgrowth of criminological notions about abnormal female sexual adaptation, pervaded popular perceptions as well.[10] Aside from the obvious moral judgment at the heart of this obsession, there is an assumption about the nature of female desire. Instead of acknowledging that prison destroys desire by numbing libidinal mechanisms, this misperception of rampant female sexual activity denies any possibility of a woman's individual choice. Based on traditional heterosexist beliefs in women's sexual passivity, this idea is also expressed in the prison administration's suspicion of close inmate relationships, making it difficult for women to establish solidarity. All this material influences Sarrazin's conceptions of her characters and her presentation of her own sexual identity. Anick expresses her own uninhibited desire and also describes other women's homoerotic experiences with tranquil understanding.

Another of the prison mechanisms that, at Sarrazin's time, worked against the development of intimacy among the women was the "progressive regime," a vertical structure of punishment and reward in effect until the 1970s. This system was a ladder of phases based on the degree of trust the prisoner had earned. Anick's movement among prisons and among cellblocks within them shows her changing position in this hierarchy of confidence. Most critical for understanding Sarrazin's response to this is that administrative confidence rested on "[the administration's] knowledge of the inmate's personality."[11] "Personality"—the vague but all-important cornerstone of earlier criminological and penal theory—gained respectability through this century as it acquired a veneer of scientific precision.[12] "Personality dossiers," only recently terminated in France, constituted the material codification of this powerful, though intangible, criterion. Women like Sarrazin, who were

[10]See, for example, Robert Boucard, *Les Dessous des prisons de femmes* (Paris: Editions Documentaires, 1930), and Francis Carco, *Prisons de femmes* (1930).
[11]Bregeon, "Approche criminologique," 218.
[12]Cf. Foucault's claim that psychiatrists, specialists in the science of character models, have become the indispensable experts in prisoner evaluation. See Michel Foucault, *Surveiller et punir: Naissance de la prison* (Paris: Gallimard, 1975). Also published as *Discipline and Punish: The Birth of the Prison*, trans. Alan Sheridan (New York: Pantheon, 1977).

subjected to a "personality test" upon entering prison,[13] found themselves saddled with character labels that determined the course of their experience. Both *La Cavale* and the *Journal de prison 1959*, in different ways, rail against this intolerable categorization, this "generalization" of the individual. Case studies of women's prisons document, along with the conditions imposed by penal regulations, the adaptive systems the prisoners themselves create to deal with confinement—the informal networks designed to compensate for their losses. Almost all these losses and substitute networks appear directly in *La Cavale*, indirectly in the *Journal*. Economic restrictions, and the barter in cigarettes and food that they engender, stimulate most of Anick's interaction with her fellow prisoners in *La Cavale*. The loss of affective ties and the compensating "kinship groups" are the backdrop for Anick's, and Sarrazin's, highly individual self-image in the novel. The loss of initiative, "true atrophy of the inmate's ability to choose, to the point where even in those instances that allow [her] to choose, [she] prefers to let [her]self be guided by others,"[14] underlies Sarrazin's affirmation in her journal of the strength of her "Cornelian" will. The loss of the autonomy of speech triggers self-expression through writing in both works. Lack of personal space underlies the escape plot in *La Cavale*, a physical escape that is extended metaphorically to include imaginative movement through writing. And the exercise of her imagination, a response to the loss of a rich environment and the corresponding diminution of "the brain's power of alertness,"[15] is at the core of Sarrazin's conception of both *La Cavale's* protagonist Anick and the idealized interlocutor of the *Journal*. In both cases Sarrazin translates her imaginative impulse into her character's or interlocutor's intellectual concerns. In these two works Sarrazin in essence achieves the ironic manipulation of a purely functionalist prison ideology and organization, converting them into the perfect functional elements she needs for her own fictive universe.

[13]Bregeon, "Approche criminologique," 224.
[14]Jacqueline Renaud, "La Prison modifie pour toujours l'organisme," *Science et vie*, no. 685 (October 1974), 50.
[15]Ibid., 50.

The *Journal de prison 1959*, ironically subtitled *Le Times*, is hardly a documentary of daily life in prison, nor is it a moralizing narrative like previous confessional texts. It is, rather, a fragmented analogue to Sarrazin's life, and she opposes its authentic discontinuity to "the delightful and illusory pleasure of having given order to the World" (*Journal*, p. 139; her emphasis). She departs from the strict logic and chronology that were so important a tool for earlier imprisoned women, making the reappropriation of her identity rely more on content than on formal elements. The journal's emphatic soliloquy, the sole, unmediated voice of Sarrazin the prisoner, answers directly the judgments that had engendered her censure. And it is clear from the power and naturalness of that voice that the deprivation the journal responds to most strongly is the loss of speech. One feels that Sarrazin wishes to fill the silence with the energy and texture of her words; nothing is censored, nothing reworked—it is only in later works that Sarrazin will reorganize speech through her first-person narrators. In the *Journal* Sarrazin is "speaking herself" in a thoroughly natural discourse; in *La Cavale* and other fictional texts, to control her experience she must control language as well.

Sarrazin's angry self-presentation in her journal mirrors the focused hostility she felt in judgments of her and as such is highly reactive. The *Journal*'s leitmotiv is an enraged refusal to be generalized, as she was when her "personality dossier" labeled her "incorrigible." She claims: "So I'm pigeonholed—they decreed it was possible to classify me—'child-adult' (Oh, come on, you psychiatrists!)" (p. 107). Also, since all women were called by their maiden names in prison regardless of their marital status, Sarrazin assumes a twofold individuality: not only does she personalize Julien Sarrazin's name and call herself "la Sarrazine," she does so even before she is married. Soon after, the prison priest refuses to marry Albertine and Julien in a religious ceremony on the grounds that they, like all prisoners, would inevitably be unfaithful. She rails, "This cowardice astonishes me, grieves me—so very much!—and, above all, vexes me. It means we are being judged and generalized, two things I cannot stand" (p. 122). Finally Sarrazin states unequivocally: "One can never, never judge or label others"

(p. 130). Thus in "speaking herself" Sarrazin rejects in her true voice the moral stigma that is imposed by the evaluative words in her judicial file and perpetuated by her silence.

In this desire to establish her authentic self-image in the face of false views of her, Sarrazin joins Roland, Cappelle-Lafarge, Steinheil, and to some extent Huré in their insistence on truth: her journal will "transform what is painful into TRUTH" (p. 120; her emphasis). And, more strongly than her predecessors, Sarrazin considers the written word itself the guarantee of truth. She is intent upon protecting her clandestine manuscript—"It's with full knowledge of the situation that, whenever possible, I take the risk of starting a journal over again, in the hope of preserving a few pieces from disaster" (p. 110)—and she attests its authenticating value by including pieces of it in her subsequent novels. Up to 1959 most of her writing had been confiscated or lost by prison authorities. This and her near-Proustian conception of the limitations of voluntary memory are the principal reasons Sarrazin kept writing her journal.

The *Journal*, and with it truth, must also survive because, like all her forerunners, Sarrazin feels herself to be in a communicative void. As Roland addressed herself to posterity, Cappelle-Lafarge to illusory friends, Steinheil to absent persons of taste, and Huré to a few philosophers, Sarrazin too invents an idealized reader. For, as she says in a letter to Julien, "In my view, it is in relation to others that one occasionally comes close to defining oneself . . . and it is clear that here in prison, there ARE no others."[16] Surrounded by what she calls "a confederation of nitwits" (p. 125), Sarrazin turns to her ennobled reader, the one who will value her true self, her inner "diamond."

Because Sarrazin wrote in the context both of explicit, sexual-affective explanations of her behavior and of stridently retrogressive ideas about women's "defeminization" through crime,[17] her foremost response is to affirm, directly and em-

---

[16]Letter of September 8, 1960, cited in Josane Duranteau's "Preface" to an earlier edition of Sarrazin's *Journal de prison 1959* (Paris: Editions Sarrazin, 1972), 24; Sarrazin's emphasis.

[17]Recent feminist thought has investigated the "defeminization" argument that associates women's criminal activity with an aspiration to "virility," an argument grounded in the Freudian concept of women's "masculinity complex" and perpetuated by such criminologists as Burt (1940s), Lausel (1960s), and, to

phatically, her erotic identity as she knows it. One can see right away a doubly defensive response to ideas about female sexuality in prison: first, in light of the misperceptions about prisoner homosexuality, Sarrazin presents herself as resolutely "straight." Although she had an affair with a young fellow prisoner at Fresnes, she suggests that, far from falling further into homoeroticism, she, from her position of knowledge, has evolved toward resplendent heterosexuality. Second, agreeing with the premise that desire is killed by imprisonment, Sarrazin fights "desexualization" by constantly evoking her desire for Julien. In the *Journal* Sarrazin traces her own sexual maturation to counter general perceptions that centered on her troubled past; she in effect adopts her judges' gynophobic focus on her "perturbed" sexual development in order to exploit it for her own ends.

The *Journal*'s principal theme is heterosexual love, the symbol of which is the mythified protagonist, "we." This "we," Albertine and Julien, the pronoun that opens the journal, share a love that is elevated to moral truth. Such statements as "Love exists in a hyperbolic relationship to us" (p. 114), with their maximlike flavor, ascribe heroic qualities to the couple and embellish love with the "honor" and "election" of Corneille's morally embattled characters. Likewise, the *Journal*'s frequent use of the infinitive rather than conjugated verb forms, coupled with the absence of subject pronouns, has the effect of rendering Sarrazin's experiences more generally applicable. Her mythification of her relationship with Julien seems in part to be her personal version of "the imaginary life" that Renaud claims is the prisoner's "oneirical" blending of reality with "pure invention." In the absence of a sexual life—and Sarrazin calls her union with Julien "a marriage of absence"—she combines memory's lived scenes with her "blueprint" for the future and with pure creation in the development of her own "little

---

some extent, Adler (1970s). Such virilization "explanations" reappeared after autonomous women's movements broke from other radical efforts and engendered such fine feminist analyses as Smart, *Women, Crime and Criminology*; Rita James Simon, *Women and Crime* (Lexington, Mass.: D. C. Heath, 1975); Ann Jones, *Women Who Kill* (New York: Holt, Rinehart and Winston, 1980); and Marie-Jo Dhavernas, "La Délinquance des femmes," *Questions féministes* (November 1978), 55–84.

private movie,"[18] the very cinematic metaphor she repeats to describe her imaginative substitute for real sensory experience. But by elevating her psychic invention into undeniable truth about love, Sarrazin not only reappropriates her affective identity, she also uses the same generalization that she had rejected when it was applied to her.

Belief in the formative importance of criminal women's sexual history often led to examinations of their past, so Sarrazin traces her erotic maturation as she herself understands it. She evokes Julien as central to that evolution, saying to him, "After making my body a woman's body, you made my heart a woman's heart" (p. 126). There is little question here that Sarrazin is restating conventional ideas of female passivity to counter accusations of her sexual precocity. But she goes on to describe the active choice, the "vote" that determined her erotic development with Julien:

> We have to analyze this. Of course we have to start with our litany: our similarities, our tenderness, our sexual desire.... My desire grew even stronger as I made you its object.... There's eroticism in all adventures. (p. 106)

And as the boldest reclaiming of her known self-image, Sarrazin explicitly evokes her experience of sexual pleasure:

> I think I'll always love making love ... that first step. That plunge without a name that still sometimes bubbles up in me now. Basically vertical images. The climb: feeling thirsty and fingers bleeding, you come up onto the glorious platform of the sun.... To blend together and completely up there, one of you has to be climbing while the other is still pulling ... that sudden loss of balance ... blinders fading in front of details invading the image until the scream, the void. (p. 125)

If the public, theorists, and jurists are going to speak uninhibitedly of her promiscuity, infidelity, and desire for purification, she will answer with an equally unashamed revelation of the intensity of orgasm.

[18]Renaud, "Prison," 53, 154.

Sarrazin's surfacing desire is also powerfully expressed in the journal's form, a remarkably suggestive "pulsing" style used well before its significance was ever explored.[19] "Pulses," what Henri Laborit calls "the principle of pleasure" and "the search for biological equilibrium," have a palpable effect on the reader and suggest the physical pleasure the effort of writing brings to Sarrazin.[20] The *Journal*'s wellsprings are sexual in nature and transmit the "white spaces" that, as in Duras's works, are part of women's unresolved desire. "The white spaces that separate textual sequences are an integral part of a whole in which they have their own function," says Josane Duranteau about the *Journal*'s unmediated mode of expression.[21] Sarrazin herself is aware of this most natural of nonrepressed discourses:

> I prefer rough sketches and paradoxes: they allow me to say what I want to say and what I'm thinking. If I claim to be proving something, I lose sincerity and freedom in doing it. Artifice... no! But yes to the incoherent magic of words in disarray. (p. 118)

Sarrazin is understandably ambivalent about her free-flowing discourse in light of society's logocentric preferences, and she wishes throughout for the self-possession to keep herself in check. But authenticity prevails in the *Journal*. "Joyous at feeling [herself] to be varied and unexpected" (p. 111), Sarrazin writes her "long juxtaposition of rages," "phrases that are badly turned, short, then abruptly tortuous and breathless" (p. 111). The journal's rhythmic, unanchored effect—the recurring image of music translates the internal source of that effect—expresses directly and impressionistically a desire for pleasure and freedom.

If one also thinks of the objectification and repression of

---

[19]See, for example, Hélène Cixous, "Le Rire de la Méduse," *L'Arc* 61 (1975): 39–54, translated as "The Laugh of the Medusa," *Signs* 1, no. 4 (summer 1976): 875–93; Hélène Cixous, Madeleine Gagnon, and Annie Leclerc, *La Venue à l'écriture* (Paris: UGE 10/18, 1977); and Luce Irigaray, *Ce sexe qui n'en est pas un* (Paris: Minuit, 1977), for discussions of the libidinal, preconscious, and unconscious elements that are visible and palpable in "feminine" texts, which the *Journal* resembles.
[20]Henri Laborit, *Eloge de la fuite* (Paris: Laffont, 1976), 13.
[21]Duranteau, "Preface," *Journal de prison 1959*, 46.

the prisoner's body that occur in confinement, both of which result from the disruption of natural cycles and from prison's emphasis on the joyless physicality of sleeping, working, and eating, the *Journal*'s response is all the more impressive. Sarrazin here maintains a positive intimacy with her body. Her words inscribe images of interiority—"body," "muscle," "meat," "blood," "flesh," "fiber"—and she calls writing itself the at once painful and joyous process of "birth." The journal transcribes Sarrazin's internal "music," her own rhythm, voice, and movement, as she "sounds" the only instrument available, her body. In all, though the *Journal* is unreworked and unmediated by any authorial attempt to control experience, its evocativeness is unmatched in women's prison literature. Its thematic exposition is bold but fundamentally tied to women's traditional concern with love, dependence, and intimacy. Yet its form, while it has affinities with the unprocessed confessions of earlier condemned women, is much closer to what Michel Thévoz calls "raw written works" and, as such, is essentially "insubordinatable to the institution of literature."[22]

The *Journal* also uses and subverts sociological theories that consider exogenous cultural conditioning the source of criminal behavior. In her quest for self-knowledge, Sarrazin denies the assigned causes for her criminal acts and offers her true reasons. Her affective history as an Algerian orphan adopted by an elderly couple and given a repressive "Bon Pasteur" education invited sociological explanations of her conduct, but Sarrazin maintains, "*We're* the ones who should judge what happens to us. . . . Events themselves are not important; they're colorless. . . . *Events take on the color we give them*" (p. 140; Sarrazin's and my emphasis). As when she repossesses her erotic identity, Sarrazin exalts the power of self-determination.

Further denying analyses of her childhood conditioning, Sarrazin separates herself from coordinates of age and sex: "I'm not comfortable in my role as a girl" (p. 109). In redefining herself and her motivations, Sarrazin ensures that the link between sex and crime, as conceived by Heuyer and others, no

---

[22] Michel Thévoz, *Le Languageḍ de la rupture* (Paris: Presses Universitaires de France, 1978), 10. The expression Thévoz uses is *écrits bruts.*

longer holds for her. For example, theft—far from being the uncontrollable consequence of her hormonal cycles—is for Sarrazin a question of free will: "I chose elsewhere, because I have a taste for risk" (p. 107); she also claims, "My theory of theft is not laziness but freedom, because of the heartbeat and the absolute independence" (p. 119). The American criminal Caryl Chessman, executed for rape and murder in the 1960s, becomes for Sarrazin emblematic of her belief in the individual's own determination of guilt and innocence: "I take the liberty, dear Chess, of giving you absolution.... A man who, for eleven years, has cried out that he had no part in a particular act becomes, in fact, a stranger to that act" (p. 165). The distance Chessman established between himself and his act, or between his felt and his imposed images of self, is what Sarrazin seeks. The *Journal* marks, however, not the accomplishment of that distancing, but the longing for it. It is Sarrazin's fiction that will convey the estrangement between author and prisoner, making "moral consciousness ... a projection of voluntary consciousness" (p. 165).

The final way Sarrazin, in her journal, twists the presumed cultural determinism of the past is by codifying her future persona, as if her will were the only determinant of her comportment. In a near oxymoron, she establishes the principle of a "spare personality" (p. 140) with which she will alter her behavior in her own terms, not those of her stigmatizing personality file. She also sets up a modus vivendi for life after her release: "Always being surrounded by pretty things ... making a debauch of harmony and beauty for my eyes and ears ... *taking care* of my appearance and everything I touch ... surrounding myself with objects and people I have *chosen*" (p. 125; her emphasis). This blueprint for herself not only counters views of social condticioning, it also undermines the goal of imprisonment itself, the "amendment" of the prisoner. Sarrazin's projection of herself—highly abstract and, as such, in defiance of the literal, unimaginative causality that characterized sociogenic theories—is seen as the reconciliation of her past acts with "a kind of as-yet-unclear renewal" (p. 129), as the preparation of her "future past" (p. 120). This quasi-mystical blending of time distinctions, which occurs throughout the journal in juxtapositions such as "infinite becoming" and "the eternal void," detaches Sarrazin's identity from the fixity of prison and of society. Instead, a vocabulary of energy and movement that the principal image of music fittingly expresses gives the *Journal* a fluidity that the author knows best transcribes her true identity.

Sarrazin's desire to be perceived as a writer, not a prisoner, finds its vehicle in *La Cavale*. As life outside the law necessitated anonymity, so writing will permit full expression of Sarrazin's being. Though the novel is set in prison and the narrative follows its daily events, the author ultimately uses that material to imaginatively transform confinement. *La Cavale* is at once directly concerned with prison and removed from it: it describes the process of creating a book about prison from within confinement itself. The heroine, Anick, effects a trade-off between her internal and external worlds and, at the same time, shifts her identity from inmate to author. She desires to attain the distance from her experience that will make that shift possible: "In the old days, I screamed, I broke things; I broke everything except the prison that watched me passively and confidently. Now I don't scream any more: it is I who watch the prison, I study the old contraption; I'm learning to detach the shouting part of myself, to peel it away without breaking the skin" (*La Cavale*, translated as *The Runaway*, p. 201). Later in the novel this process of "learning" becomes more an accomplished certainty: "I never 'realized' my prisons; I never saw them as anything but intervals, as pretexts for doing things that had no relation to them and to the purpose that had been assigned them" (p. 382).

The title's metaphor itself embodies the identity transformation that occurs in the book. The *cavale* image, representing at first the physical force that will make possible the mythic horse's escape from prison ("all these runaways in all directions, wild horses, phantom steeds that no one ever gets a leg over," p. 58), evolves into and is overtaken by the significance of imaginative power ("The runaway mare has quietly stretched out on its misty bed: am I not its master, have I not created it, do I not possess the right of life and death over it?" p. 462). Between Anick's first conception of a plot to gain physical freedom through a medical furlough—a double insistence on purely physical concerns—and her final affirmation of her mind's "gay, rich display put on for [her] alone, [her] secret break" (p. 480), there are stages of action and resignation. Anick plans to escape, first with her friend and fellow prisoner Maria, then, in her next prison, with Zizi (Julien); but this energy alternates with fatigue as "decisions... lose their reality" (p. 464) and fall immobile. For Anick comes to understand that the *cavale* is her own creation and so depends on her for sustenance. Instead of being an autonomous beast that will pulverize the prison walls, the horse can perform only when and as she wills it. Imaginative production thus supersedes physical destruction. This trade-off of physical liberty for the products of the mind is encapsulated in Anick's ambiguous term for her *cavale*: the French word *ouvrage*, or "work to be done/a piece of work or a book." Thus, the *cavale* allegory perfectly blends circumstance with imagination, making prison's constraints the very source and substance of Sarrazin's response.

Anick's development from an inmate planning her escape to a writer pondering her future creativity makes it clear that the novel responds most strongly to the loss of mental energy. With increasing frustration and anger, Sarrazin repeatedly deplores prison's numbing of the imagination:

> The banality of the days batters at me, penetrates me, blocks my pores; neither dangerous nor of any consequence, the routine rocks me and lulls me. (p. 181)
>
> In short, I'm going nuts, absolutely. A kind of tepid dopiness is taking hold of my mind, I'm barely simmering and I feel myself getting soft. (p. 198)
>
> How worthless the mind feels in the midst of all that motionless real matter! (p. 363)
>
> My mind is beginning to die of boredom. (p. 473)

Sarrazin takes the deprivations that deaden the spirit in prison and gives them narrative life through dramatization and humor. Thus, Anick (and Sarrazin) keeps her own intellect working, culminating in the book's final appreciation of the mind's gifts—of which the book *La Cavale* is itself the fruit.

In this triumphant quest for self-presentation that complements the *Journal*'s search for intimate truth, Sarrazin uses traditional novelistic conventions for her own ends. Attention to order and chronology, which she had repudiated in the journal, here becomes a narrative priority, established at the outset. The story is firmly situated in place and time: Anick is about to spend a "horribly definite period" (p. 9) in a setting whose details she describes precisely. The specific chronology in *La Cavale* is the one the prisoner lives by: the stages in her judicial process and, within prison, her successive losses and reactions. But this time frame is used not to affirm its validity—for the whole process is labeled "a lottery . . . luck . . . a circus" (p. 304)—but to further Sarrazin's progressive separation of herself from the prison. As Sarrazin traces the preliminary hearing, sentencing, and appeal, she is denying the very defense strategy used by Anick's lawyer: she rejects his claim of his client's symbolic "bold rebellion . . . in the name of all the prisoners in the world, what all prisoners dream of doing" (pp. 305–6), since Anick has no wish to be generalized or identified with other prisoners. Likewise, each step in prison's "modification" process is a chance for Anick to proclaim her uniqueness.

Thus, though Sarrazin offers *La Cavale* as a documentary of prison life, in reality she exploits that existence to reconstruct herself and others as she perceives them. Beginning with Anick's arrival, during which she is stripped successively of clothes, possessions, and identity, she watches herself being dispossessed. "I try to get my bearings" (p. 13), says Anick, thus acknowledging from the start her wish for control. She then describes the internal organization, collective or cellular, of each prison as her personal space is intruded upon. Here too control and self-affirmation win out, for Anick will succeed in putting her fellow prisoners "in their place." They are all antithetical to her image of herself and so, as was true for Roland and Steinheil in particular, constitute the basis of her strategy for maintaining dignity. The loss of professional identity—the women in prison sew nets and make feather boas—provides a further opportunity for self-definition: Anick refuses the mindless tasks of the workshop and makes writing her primary activity. And in response to the absence of a focus for sexual desire, Sarrazin introduces the character Zizi into the men's section of the same prison. Thus, unlike the other women, Anick has *within* her space of confinement the object of her erotic projections.

Because of this separation of Anick/Sarrazin from other prisoners, the structure of *La Cavale* is binary: it consists of two "characters" whose parallel daily lives, despite occasional interaction, evolve in detached spheres. Anick functions within the domain of her own mind, tracing her thoughts about others and, more important, her continued effort to write. The other women constitute a collective "character," called at one point "the ten-times-multiplied image of the Eternal Feminine" (p. 22) and elsewhere "a fat shrew fixed in her habits" (p. 82). This other character lives in the purely physical sphere made up of eating, sleeping, and seduction. Anick feels "quite uncomfortable among [her] little sisters in stir, who have their own way of reshaping society [within prison]" (p. 82). Although she must live and work with these women and their networks of relationships, Anick does so in the "calculated" way that ensures her peace of mind and its attendant intellectual freedom. That is, these women become a "unity . . . which is subject to constant interpretation by the inmate [Anick] as she perceives each situation from the point of view of her own interests."[23]

La Cavale represents the solipsistic focus of women's prison writing at its strongest. Sarrazin/Anick uses the other faceless entity as a foil whenever she wishes to demonstrate her superiority. Prison's bringing together "asocial" and "undersirable" women vindicates Sarrazin's self-aggrandizement. She says of these women, "They make me angry because they're greedy, because they're ugly, because their shabby outfits remind me that I'm wearing the same thing and that I too must be ugly" (p. 416). And with the stereotypically misogynist terms "eternal feminine" and "fat shrew" she denigrates others to elevate herself. Sarrazin uses the same technique—"the guiding rule of superior beings" (p. 67)—at the level of individual characters. Some are assigned deficiencies long attributed to women: low

---

[23]Giallombardo, *Society of Women*, 15.

intelligence (Lerouge, the dull-witted, exploited prison laundress); masochism (Simone, the alcoholic, abused peasant); and manipulativeness (Gina, the egocentric, combative bitch). They are also more subtly measured in relation to the norm—Anick—as possessing deformed versions of her qualities. For example, Simone's "love in the haystacks... if it could be called love to be laid once in a while" (p. 230) is really "the opposite(s) of love" (p. 264), a perversion of Anick's and Zizi's union. Gina's manipulativeness is a poor substitute for Anick's intelligence, for "her intelligence, her boldness, her promises amount to... they're worth nothing" (p. 71). And Jane's obedience, which earns administrative favor and an early release, seems to Anick "a good-luck token" (p. 165), that stems from weakness instead of choice.

Even the women with whom Anick develops special friendships are subjected to this comparison. The three prisoners in question, Maria, Nicole, and Christine, in contrast to the other women, all resemble Anick in some important way. Of Maria, Anick says, "From the first we shared the same sort of bad luck" (p. 56) as well as "the good luck, too, to know only the genuine side of life in a communal prison" (p. 56). Anick finds physical similarities, also, in their "constant straightening of the curve in [their] back" and even their "damned glasses" (p. 57). And, most critically, Maria had previously tried a *"cavale,"* thereby earning Anick's respect as well as foreshadowing her own escape attempt. Nicole, in keeping with the novel's general progression from physical to intellectual concerns, shares Anick's need for wit and subtlety: Anick knows, "Nicole too listens to me and enjoys it" (p. 262). And, like Anick, Nicole needs to communicate with her lover. Finally Christine is presented, toward the book's end, as a reincarnation of the young Anick: "Mere contact with Chris is enough to set me back ten years" (p. 423). Anick's integration of her past, present, and future identities, sparked by Chris, culminates in the writing of the novel, and she then "offer[s] [her] hand to this naughty, graceful kid [herself]" (p. 424). This healthy kind of narcissism, which coexists with the denigration of other women, is an essential parallel to the book's overall movement from loss to reconstruction, from defensive reaction to assertive control.

A final way Sarrazin transforms the effects of prison for her own purpose is her manipulation of the moral stigma felt by most criminal women. Julien/Zizi expresses this stigma at one point in the novel:

> Both of us are undesirable citizens, black as coal, said to be dangerous. . . . We're burglars, so there it is: the seed that grows into murder and social upheaval. (p. 335)

Women's usual sense of shame for the "unnatural" or "defeminized" behavior of crime, which Sarrazin answers in the *Journal* by extolling her traditionally "feminine" identity (heterosexual, intuitive, sensitive), in *La Cavale* is answered indirectly through humor and irony. The novel's opening sentence signals the author's perspective on her own experience: "I am really done up for my entrance into prison tonight: opossum and slacks" (p. 9). In this remark the author looks at herself with comic distance. But though the humor and irony are initially directed at herself, Anick soon turns them toward external targets:

> I no longer want to play around with either resignation or defiance; I shall withdraw into irony, if not into insolence. . . . Here, at night, I'll fashion complicated, lapidary phrases that I would hurl at the four corners of the cell in the dark; I'll hone my irony in the idleness and the quiet of the nights. (p. 400)

This ironic "targeting" of the people and systems that surround her has already been seen in Anick's caricature of the prison collectivity and in her derisive portrayal of others as distorted reflections of herself. And this use of caricature, seen in all the texts of imprisoned women, once again forms part of a larger theatrical image. *La Cavale*, like the prison works of past eras, reflects women's concern with seeing and being seen by making the penitentiary into a spectacle. Thus most of the inmates become one-dimensional characters performing before an unchanging backdrop in a judicial/penal "play" that is really a "circus."

There is a form of irony in *La Cavale* that, though no doubt unintentional, is inescapable. The novel's opening sentence poignantly shows Anick watching herself in a hopeless situation. She exercises "muscle" in the first of a series of tough, offhand expressions of strength. But the irony stems more from Anick's choice of language than from the impossibility of escape. For the language of *La Cavale* is frequently prison "argot," a "masculine creation,"[24] and bad French, both borrowed from the "underworld" and not Sarrazin's natural mode of discourse. Sarrazin's biographer, Josane Duranteau, describes this portion of the novel's language as "a foreign language . . . very thin, full of banal images and poor and lowly syntax."[25] Sarrazin herself becomes painfully aware of the insufficiency of this borrowed tongue:

> I forget the words that the beloved voice set, one by one, like jewels, into caresses; words, those silken outlets for the radiations of the heart, little words, big words, coarse words; for two months I have had a vocabulary composed entirely of formulae, of conventional phrases that I cling to to express sincerity, of shabby, run-down platitudes. (p. 473)

Passages addressed to Zizi—and these are almost always pieces taken from the *Journal*—usually are not spoken in the depersonalized voice of the "underworld." Otherwise Sarrazin frequently tries to appropriate the dominant male prison discourse. And, like Roland's Rousseauesque patterns or Huré's philosophical oratory, this usage points up the distance between the woman author and "virile" language. Sarrazin's ironic attempt to ascribe power to Anick appears in such sad and funny claims as, "In stir, the Bic is my piece" (p. 20), where hard-punching slang tries unsuccessfully to overcome circumstance.

But when Sarrazin does use discourse effectively in a conscious effort to affirm herself, her works are an important marker in female prison literature. For those before her had all operated within a lexical and intellectual framework that severely limited their discursive power. Roland's rationalistic and pre-Romantic lexicon, Cappelle-Lafarge's Romantic and positi-

---

[24] Marina Yaguello, *Les Mots et les femmes* (Paris: Payot, 1979), 34.
[25] Duranteau, "Preface," 51.

vistic patterns, Steinheil's aesthetic euphemisms, and Huré's abstract, philosophical locutions, though in each case exploited and undermined, all bespeak acceptance of literary constraints. These expressive frameworks, which reflected the moral and sometimes religious forces that impinged on literary conventions, made women's writing defensive and self-justifying. But Sarrazin "names" things in her text and thus imposes her authorial preferences. The *cavale* trope encapsulates imaginative strength and the dynamic mythology many women writers are now exploring.[26] It is true that single, explicit moral and lexical codes like those of earlier times no longer function, especially because of the plethora of coexisting sociological and literary currents, but Sarrazin also chooses to give precedence to her imaginative discoveries. In fictionalizing her experience rather than presenting a literal rendering of life in prison she attempts to legitimize herself not by reconstituting facts, but by transforming them. She thus weaves her critique of external views of herself into the fabric of her fictional universe. And by emphasizing invention she asserts the primacy of her role as writer. Her works are representative of a healthy change of focus among women prison writers from a negative and denial-oriented absorption with identity—necessary because, historically, deviant women lacked any positive, legitimate connection to society—to new, unmediated affirmations of self. These works reflect the direction that women's writing in general has taken. "Deviant women" are channeling their energies away from the struggle against moral and social stigma and toward insistence on their authorship.

A word of caution is necessary lest one think Sarrazin's affirmation of self transmits the unfettered optimism, the sense of infinite possibility and conquest of all mysteries that are now associated with imaginative power.[27] Her novel, even the title

---

[26]Simone de Beauvoir had analyzed the masculine fears that gave rise to Western mythologies in *Le Deuxième Sexe*, vol. 1 (Paris: Gallimard, 1949). Women's total absence from the imaginative elaboration of myths and the need for women to express new stories is presented forcefully and mimetically in Catherine Clément and Hélène Cixous, *La Jeune Née* (Paris: UGE 10/18, 1975).

[27]For the basis of this imaginative optimism, see, for example, Gabriel and Brigitte Veraldi, *Psychologie de la création* (Paris: Marabout, 1972).

itself, conveys ambivalence, since the *cavale* is, after all, a *fantasy* of triumph over circumstance. The beast, a dynamic creation and allegorical correlate to Sarrazin's faith in imaginative power, is nonetheless not an autonomous, transcendent creature; it is dependent on the author's vacillating feelings of both strength and inadequacy. As such it is not a symbol of pure revolt and destruction of prison walls. It is, rather, an analogue to real human possibility and to specifically female issues of power and vulnerability. With *La Cavale* Sarrazin proves that female criminals, by their understanding of limitation, are the antithesis of marginal "monsters": far from being antisocial and maladjusted, they are women in society, like all others.

Conclusion

There has been a curious hiatus in women's writing from confinement since the posthumous publication, in the 1970s, of Albertine Sarazin's journals and secret prison notes. One might have hoped that Sarazin's celebrity and the attention to prison it sparked would encourage other incarcerated women to tell their stories. One might also have supposed that the general burst of feminist theory and literature in the 1970s would foster self-expression by imprisoned women as well. But certain factors have complicated criminal women's situation in regard to writing.

Important texts have indeed come out of women's prisons in the past decade: the best known of these in France are Gabrielle Russier's *Lettres de prison* (1970), Nicole Gérard's testimony *Sept ans de pénitence* (1976), and the translated works of two Spanish authors, Lidia Falcón's prison commentary *Enfers* (1977) and Eva Forest's *Journal et lettres de prison* (1975) and her collection of personal testimonies, *Témoignages de lutte et de résistance* (1977). What these texts have in common, aside from their use of personal rather than fictional genres, is some degree of political consciousness—a sense of group as well as individual identity. Russier's letters, though basically individualistic in their description of her persecution and suffering, make connections between her experience and larger moral crises in society. Gérard brings a sense of sisterhood into the prison and frequently describes the events she lives through as shared by a collectivity of women. Both Falcón and Forest have strong ties to external movements in Spain—Forest, to a Basque liberation group and Falcón, to militant feminism as well as leftist activism. The popularity of these Spanish texts, adopted by many feminists, reflects a still-powerful tendency in contemporary French feminist thought—the integration of women's issues into a critique of "broader social problems."

Yet one wonders why no body of imaginative writings springing from prisoners' experience as women emerged in France in answer to the eloquent calls for women's autonomous self-expression. Such calls set off an explosion in women's literature in general that produced an array of strategies for expressing female lives and female selves. Numerous feminist periodicals, literary tracts, and manifestos have kept the question of women's writing and speaking in the public view. But why did this burst of creative inquiry not penetrate the walls of women's prisons?

Part of the reason is that much of this recent activity has been undertaken by highly trained and specialized intellectuals who write out of their conviction that gender inequities lie in the psyche—in the way we think. Women's issues are central to their writing, but their vital insights into psychosexual and historical-philosophical dynamics are often inaccessibly abstract. Imprisoned women, whose overall level of education is lower than that of their free sisters, are less prepared for such explorations.

Also, a climate of innovation now surrounds women's writing in France; it affects authors' motivations and their chances for publication and would also filter into prisons. Most women prisoners, interned for civil crimes, might well feel caught between the intensity and controversy of politically inspired writings and the abstruse intellectualism of experimental texts. As in women's literature in general, there is now little room for a traditional story with a conventionally individual presentation of self, particularly if, as in earlier prison works, the self is in part affirmed by denigrating other women.

It is also likely that the liberalizing of French prisons in the past decade may have contributed, paradoxically, to the absence of imaginative writings. Many institutions now publish internal newspapers that provide an expressive outlet for some women. When prisoners' writing was severely restricted in quantity and audience, women often snatched chances to write in secret. In addition, the new opportunities to study or to learn a profession in prison may occupy women who might otherwise turn to writing. As these women seek professional self-improvement—like women in general—they tend to direct their energies toward practical and applied activities rather than toward the theoretical or "creative."

The interruption in fiction from women's prisons and the appearance of private chronicles and journals that are far less confessional and more "political" signal a change in imprisoned women's conceptions of their lives, their stories, and themselves. Whatever their degree of awareness and intent, women writing from prison seem generally to associate their experience with events or people beyond their personal sphere. This change in perspective, which is occurring in women's writing overall, has also given rise to new definitions of female autobiography and to new critical approaches to women's stories. It is apparent that we need different methods of explaining the conditions for and techniques of writing women's experience. We must have new standards for reading and evaluation that embrace the refractoriness of women's responses in relation to accepted literary criteria.

Among the fresh approaches that can achieve richer appreciation of women's prison writing in particular is a cross-disciplinary feminist criticism. Such a reading, necessarily sociological because of the "feminist" concern with women in life as well as art, does not relate only to the text's internal workings. But when venturing onto political, historical, cultural, or economic terrain the feminist critic must first explore the presuppositions of these disciplines and see whether they apply to women's experience; those who uncritically adopt the traditional and "universalizing" views that often underlie such disciplines will continue to distort women's experience and undervalue women's writing.

A feminist approach to women's writing also uses the techniques and material of standard disciplines to challenge and extend these fields. Instead of perpetuating cultural myths—

such as the ones inherent in the specialized concepts of "biologically abnormal," "ethically inferior," or "socially maladjusted"—a cross-disciplinary criticism looks at the dynamic interchanges between the forces that affect women's lives. This approach focuses on the increasing personal and literary self-awareness with which female writers have reforged, for their own purposes, the unmalleable material of myths about women. It illuminates the reasons why women's texts, taken together, beyond being compelling works in themselves, complicate and contradict prevailing views about authorship.

Other archetypal methods for examining social and literary exchanges in women's works must be further developed and refined. I have sought to show that even those who are presumed to be most estranged from social systems and from thought and invention have performed the "alien" act of rejecting and subverting myths. Certainly all women authors have done so to some degree. And reading their stories not only can reveal new textual arrangements in known works, but also can recover valuable texts, like those of imprisoned women, that have been disregarded in the past.

Bibliography

General Issues

Albistur, Maïté, and Daniel Armogathe. *Histoire du féminisme français du Moyen Age à nos jours.* Paris, 1977.
Appignanesi, Lisa. *Femininity and the Creative Imagination: A Study of Henry James, Robert Musil and Marcel Proust.* New York, 1973.
Bachelard, Gaston. *The Poetics of Space.* Trans. Maria Jolas. New York, 1964.
Beauvoir, Simone de. *The Second Sex.* Trans. H. M. Parshley. New York, 1953.
Becker, Howard S. *Outsiders: Studies in the Sociology of Deviance.* New York, 1963.
Brée, Germaine. "French Women Writers: A Problematic Perspective." In *Beyond Intellectual Sexism: A New Woman, a New Society,* ed. Joan I. Roberts, 196–209. New York, 1976.
Brombert, Victor. *The Romantic Prison: The French Tradition.* Princeton, N.J., 1978.
Camus, Albert. *The Rebel: An Essay on Man in Revolt.* Trans. Anthony Bower. New York, 1967.
Clément, Catherine, and Hélène Cixous. *La Jeune Née.* Paris, 1975.
Eaubonne, Françoise d'. *Les Ecrivains en cage.* Paris, 1970.
Engelbarts, Rudolf. *Books in Stir: A Bibliographic Essay about Prison Libraries and about Books Written by Prisoners and Prison Employees.* New Jersey, 1972.
Erhel, Catherine, and Catherine Leguay. *Prisonnières.* Paris, 1977.
Fothergill, Robert A. *Private Chronicles: A Study of English Diaries.* London, 1974.

Foucault, Michel. *Discipline and Punish: The Birth of the Prison.* Trans. Alan Sheridan. New York, 1977.
Franklin, H. Bruce. *The Victim as Criminal and Artist: Literature from the American Prison.* New York, 1978.
Gelfand, Elissa. "Imprisoned Women: Toward a Socio-literary Feminist Analysis." *Yale French Studies* 62 (fall 1981):185–203.
———. "Women Prison Authors in France: Twice Criminal." *Modern Language Studies* 11, no. 1 (winter 1980–81):57–63.
Herrmann, Claudine. *Les Voleuses de langue.* Paris, 1976.
Horer, Suzanne, and Jeanne Socquet. *La Création étouffée.* Paris, 1973.
Jones, Ann. *Women Who Kill.* New York, 1980.
Kolodny, Annette. "Dancing through the Minefield: Some Observations on the Theory, Practice, and Politics of a Feminist Literary Criticism." *Feminist Studies* 6, no. 1 (spring 1980):1–25.
Makward, Christiane. "La Critique féministe: Eléments d'une problématique." *Revue des sciences humaines* (December 1977), 619–24.
Marks, Elaine. "Review Essay: Women and Literature in France." *Signs* 3, no. 4 (summer 1978): 832–42.
Moffat, Mary Jane, and Charlotte Painter, eds. *Revelations: Diaries of Women.* New York, 1974.
Sartre, Jean-Paul. *Imagination: A Psychological Critique.* Trans. Forrest Williams. Ann Arbor, Mich., 1962.
Simon, Rita James. *Women and Crime.* Lexington, Mass., 1975.
Smart, Carol. *Women, Crime and Criminology: A Feminist Critique.* London, 1976.
Spacks, Patricia Meyer. *The Female Imagination.* New York, 1975.
Sullerot, Evelyne, and Odette Thibault, eds., *Le Fait féminin: Qu'est-ce qu'une femme?* Paris, 1978.
Thévoz, Michel. *Le Language de la rupture.* Paris, 1978.
Trupin, James E., ed., *In Prison: Writings and Poems about the Prison Experience.* New York, 1975.
Williams, Raymond. *Marxism and Literature.* Oxford, 1977.
Woolf, Virginia. *A Room of One's Own.* New York, 1929.

Eighteenth Century

Texts by or Ascribed to Women Authors

Brinvilliers, la Marquise de. *Récit de ses derniers moments,* by Edme Pirot. Paris, 1883.
Duras, Duchesse de (Louise H.). "Memoirs." In *Prison Journals during the French Revolution,* trans. M. Carey. New York, 1891.

BIBLIOGRAPHY

Motte, la Comtesse de la (Jeanne de Valois). *Mémoires justificatifs de la Comtesse de Valois de la Motte écrits par elle-même.* 3d ed. Paris, 1886.
Pons, Mademoiselle de (Augustine). *Un Episode du temps de la Terreur.* Paris, 1857.
Roland, Madame. *Mémoires de Madame Roland.* Paris, 1966.
Staal, Madame de (Madame Delaunay). "Mémoires de Madame de Staal, écrits par elle-même." in *Oeuvres,* vol. 1. Paris, 1821.
———. *Une Idylle à la Bastille.* Paris, 1958.
Tencin, la Marquise de. "Les Mémoires du Comte de Comminges," "Le Siège de Calais," and "Lettres à M. de Richelieu." In *Oeuvres de Mesdames de Fontaines et de Tencin.* Paris, n.d.

Studies of These and Other Authors

"Dossier–Mancini (Hortense and Marie)," "Dossier–de la Motte," and "Dossier–Madame de Tencin," at the Bibliothèque Féministe Marguerite Durand, Paris 5ᵉ.
Funck-Brentano, Frantz. *La Marquise de Brinvilliers, d'après de nouveaux documents.* Paris, n.d.
Gelfand, Elissa. "A Response to the Void: Madame Roland's "Mémoires particuliers' and Her Imprisonment." *Romance Notes* (fall 1979), 75–80.
Kermina, Françoise. *Madame Roland, ou La Passion révolutionnaire.* Paris, 1976.
Lairtullier, E. "Madame Rolland." *Les Femmes célèbres de 1789 à 1795, et leur influence dans la Révolution.* Paris, 1840.
Ljungström, Angela. "Rôles féminins dans la révolution française de 1789: Marie-Jeanne Roland et Olympe de Gouges, l'antiféminisme et le féminisme." Thesis. Stockholm, 1977.
Masson, Pierre-Maurice. *Une Vie de femme au xviiᵉ siècle: Madame de Tencin.* Geneva, 1909.
May, Gita. *De Jean-Jacques Rousseau à Madame Roland: Essai sur la sensibilité préromantique et révolutionnaire.* Geneva, 1964.
———. *Madame Roland and the Age of Revolution.* New York, 1970.
Michelet, Jules. "Décadence morale du xviiᵉ siècle." *La Revue des deux mondes.* April 1, 1860.
Ravaisson, Fr. *Archives de la Bastille,* vol. 4. Paris, 1970.
Saint-Germain, Jacques. *Madame de Brinvilliers.* Paris, 1971.

Biological, Criminological, and Penal Contexts

Dauban, Charles-Aimé. *Les Prisons de Paris sous la Révolution, d'après les relations des contemporains.* Paris, 1870.

Roussel, Pierre. *Système physique et moral de la femme, suivi du système physique et moral de l'homme*. 6th ed. Paris, 1813.

Philosophical and Literary Contexts

Bretonne, Rétif de la. *Les Gynographes, ou Idées de deux honnêtes femmes sur un projet de règlement proposé à toute l'Europe, pour mettre les femmes à leur place, et opérer le bonheur des deux sexes*. 1777.
Poulain de la Barre. *De l'égalité des deux sexes*. 1673.
Rousseau, Jean Jacques. *Lettre à d'Alembert*, 1758; *La Nouvelle Héloïse*, 1761; Book 5 of *Emile*, 1762.
Sévigné, Madame de. *Letters of Madame de Sévigné to her Daughter and Her Friends*. New York, 1937.

Modern Studies

Abensour, Léon. *La Femme et le féminisme avant la Révolution*. Paris, 1923.
Castan, Nicole. "La Criminalité familiale dans le ressort du Parlement de Toulouse 1690–1730." *Cahier des Annales: Crimes et criminalité en France, xviie et xviiie siècles* 33 (1971): 91–107.
Delale, Alain. "Les Prostituées: De la maison close à la maison de correction." *Le Peuple français: Revue d'histoire populaire*, no. 24. (October–December 1976), 12–14.
Farge, Arlette. "Des femmes dans la société pré-révolutionnaire parisienne." In *L'Histoire sans qualités*, ed. Christiane Dufrancatel et al., 13–39. Paris, 1979.
Fauchery, Pierre. "La Destinée féminine dans le roman européen du xviiie siécle (1713–1807)." Thesis. Paris, 1970.
Fleischmann, Hector. *Les Femmes et la Terreur*. Paris, 1910.
Funck-Brentano, Frantz. *Légendes et archives de la Bastille*. Paris, 1902.
———. *Prisons d'autrefois*. Paris, 1935.
Hoffmann, Paul. "L'Héritage des lumières: Mythes et modèles de la féminité au xviiie siècle." *Romantisme: Mythes et représentations de la femme au xixe siècle* 13–14 (1976): 7–21.
Levy, Darline Gay, Harriet Branson Applewhite, and Mary Durham Johnson, eds., *Women in Revolutionary Paris 1789–1795: Selected Documents Translated with Notes and Commentary*. Urbana, Ill., 1979.
Mathiez, Albert. *La Révolution française: La Gironde et la Montagne*, vol. 2. 2d ed. Paris, 1927.
Miller, Nancy K. "Female Sexuality and Narrative Structure in 'La

Bibliography

Nouvelle Héloïse' and 'Les Liaisons dangereuses.'" *Signs* 1, no. 3 (spring 1976): 609–38.
Monglond, André. *Le Préromantisme français: Le Maître des âmes sensibles*, vol. 2. Grenoble, 1930.
Petitfils, Jean-Christian. "Les Femmes à la Bastille." In *La Vie quotidienne à la Bastille du Moyen Age à la Révolution*. Paris, 1975.
Thomas, Ruth P. "Montesquieu's Harem and Diderot's Convent: The Woman as Prisoner." *The French Review* 52 (October 1978): 36–45.
Trahard, Pierre. *La Sensibilité révolutionnaire: 1789–1794*. Paris, 1936.
Vincent-Cassy, Mireille. "Prison et châtiments à la fin du Moyen Age." In *Les Marginaux et les exclus dans l'histoire:* Cahiers Jussieu, no. 5, 262–74. Paris, 1979.

Nineteenth Century

Texts by or Ascribed to Women Authors

Bompard, Gabrielle. *Les Confessions secrètes de Gabrielle Bompard*. Dictated to and transcribed by Rémy de l'Aulnaye. Lille, 1890.
Cappelle, Marie. *Mémoires de Marie Cappelle (veuve Lafarge) écrits par elle-même*. 4 vols. Paris, 1841–42.
Lafarge, Madame. *Correspondance*. 2 vols. 2d ed. Paris, 1913.
———. (née Marie Cappelle). *Heures de prison*. 3 vols. Paris, 1854.

Studies of These Authors

"Dossier-Marie Lafarge," at the Bibliothèque Féministe Marguerite Durand, Paris 5ᵉ.
Gaultier, Jules de. *Madame Lafarge et la lutte contre les évidences*. Paris, 1934.
Gayot, André. "La Littérature de Madame Lafarge." *La Nouvelle Revue*, no. 17 (January 1, 1913), 18–30.
Hartman, Mary S. *Victorian Murderesses: A True History of Thirteen Respectable French and English Women Accused of Unspeakable Crimes*. New York, 1977.
Lhérisson, Fernande. *Madame Lafarge, écrivain romantique: Pages choisies précédées d'une étude sur sa vie et son oeuvre*. Bordeaux, 1934.
Locard, E. *La Malle sanglante de Millery: L'Affaire Gabrielle Bompard–Eyraud*. Paris, 1934.
Nadaud, Marcel, and André Fage. *Les Grands Drames passionnels de Casque d'Or à Mata-Hari* (Bompard). Paris, 1926.
Serval, Pierre. *Madame Lafarge*. Paris, 1959.

Imagination in Confinement

Criminological and Penal Contexts

Appert, B. *Rapport sur des prisons, des hospices, et des écoles des départements de l'Aisne, du Nord, du Pas-de-Calais, et de la Somme.* Paris, 1824.
Caignart de Mailly, M. P. *L'Evolution de l'idée au xixe siècle et ses conséquences.* Paris, 1898.
"Dossier–Criminalité" at the Bibliothèque Féministe Marguerite Durand, Paris 5e.
Frégier, H. A. *Des classes dangereuses de la population dans les grandes villes et des moyens de les rendre meilleures.* Paris, 1838.
Grandpré, Pauline de. *Les Condamnées de Saint-Lazare: Mémoires par Madame * * *.* Paris, 1869.
Joly, Henri. *La France criminelle.* Paris, 1889.
———. *Le Crime: Etude sociale.* 2d ed. Paris, 1888.
Lombroso, C., and G. Ferrero. *La Femme criminelle et la prostituée.* Trans. from the Italian by L. Meille. Paris, 1896.
Mallet, Joséphine. *Les Femmes en prison: Causes de leurs chutes, moyens de les relever.* 2d ed. Paris, 1845.
Parent-Duchâtelet, A. J. B. *De la prostitution dans la ville de Paris considérée sous le rapport de l'hygiène publique, de la morale et de l'administration.* Paris, 1857.
Ryckère, Raymond de. *La Femme en prison et devant la mort.* Paris, 1898.
Tarde, Gabriel. *La Criminalité comparée.* Paris, 1886.
Villermé, Louis-René. *Des prisons telles qu'elles sont et telles qu'elles devraient être.* Paris, 1820.

Philosophical and Literary Contexts (see also Twentieth Century)

Guillemin, Jules. *Les Oeuvres d'imagination: Essai d'esthétique littéraire.* Warsaw, 1882.
Joly, Henri. *L'Imagination: Etude psychologique.* Paris, 1883.
Ribot, Th. *Essai sur l'imagination créatrice.* Paris, 1900.
Tuke, D. Hack. *Le Corps et l'esprit: Action du moral et de l'imagination sur le physique.* Trans. from the English. Paris, 1886.

Modern Studies

Abensour, Léon. *Le Féminisme sous le règne de Louis Philippe et en 1848.* Paris, 1913.
Courtivron, Isabelle de. "Weak Men and Fatal Women: The Sand Image." In *Homosexualities and French Literature: Cultural Contexts/Critical Texts,* ed. George Stambolian and Elaine Marks, 210–27. Ithaca, N.Y. 1979.

BIBLIOGRAPHY

Devance, Louis. "Femme, famille, travail et morale sexuelle dans l'idéologie de 1848." *Romantisme: Mythes et représentations de la femme au xixe siècle* 13–14 (1976):79–104.
Dugas, L. *L'Imagination.* Paris, 1903.
Gaillac, Henri. *Les Maisons de correction 1830–1945.* Paris, 1971.
Granier, Camille. *La Femme criminelle.* Paris, 1906.
Guesde, Jules. *La Femme et la société bourgeoise.* Paris, 1923.
Hartman, Mary S. *Victorian Murderesses: A True History of Thirteen Respectable French and English Women Accused of Unspeakable Crimes.* New York, 1977.
Perrot, Michelle. "Delinquency and the Penitentiary System in Nineteenth-Century France." In *Deviants and the Abandoned in French Society: Selections from the Annales Economies, Sociétés, Civilisations,* vol. 4, ed. Robert Forster and Orest Ranum, 213–45. Trans. Elborg Forster and Patricia M. Ranum. Baltimore and London, 1978.
Wajeman, Gérard. "Psyché de la femme: Note sur l'hystérique au xixe siècle." *Romantisme: Mythes et représentations de la femme au xixe siècle* 13–14 (1976):57–66.

Twentieth Century

Texts by Women Authors

Falcón, Lidia. *Enfers.* Trans. from the Spanish by Françoise Campo. Paris, 1977.
Forest, Eva. *Journal et lettres de prison.* Bilingual ed. Paris, 1975.
——. *Témoignages de lutte et de résistance.* Trans. from the Spanish by Françoise Campo. Paris, 1977.
Gérard, Nicole. *Sept ans de pénitence.* Paris, 1976.
Hanau, Marthe. *Forces-Hebdomadaire.* Issues from December 1932 to March 1933. "Dossier–Marthe Hanau" at the Bibliothèque Féministe Marguerite Durand, Paris 5e.
Huré, Anne. *Descente en enfer.* Paris, 1966.
——. *Les Deux Moniales.* Paris, 1962.
——. *En prison.* Paris, 1963.
——. *Le Haut Chemin.* Paris, 1966.
——. *Le Péché sans merci.* Paris, 1964.
——. *Les Vendanges.* Paris, 1968.
Paul, Sylvie. *Ne me jugez pas!* Paris, 1962.
Russier, Gabrielle. *Lettres de prison.* Paris, 1970.
Sarrazin, Albertine. *L'Astragale.* Paris, 1964. Also published as *Astragal.* Trans. Patsy Southgate. New York, 1967.

Imagination in Confinement

———. *Biftons de prison.* Paris, 1977.
———. *La Cavale.* Paris, 1965. Also published as *The Runaway.* Trans. Charles Lam Markmann. New York, 1967.
———. *La Crèche.* Paris, 1973.
———. *Journal de prison 1959.* Paris, 1972.
———. *Lettres à Julien 1958–60.* Paris, 1971.
———. *Le Passe-peine 1949–1967.* Paris, 1976.
———. *Poèmes.* Paris, 1969.
———. *Romans, letters et poèmes.* Paris, 1967.
———. *La Traversière.* Paris, 1966.
Steinheil, Marguerite. *Mes mémoires.* Paris, app. 1911–12. Also published as *My Memoirs.* London, 1912.
Surany, Marguerite de. *Détenue politique à la Roquette.* Paris, 1964.
Valéry, Nicole. *Bénie sois-tu prison.* Paris, 1976.
Veiber, Paulette. *Mes dix-huit mois.* Paris, 1975.

Studies of These Authors

Albérès, R. M. "Des relations pas mondaines" (Sarrazin). *Nouvelles littéraires,* no. 2446 (August 1974), 4.
Baldick, Robert. "A Modern Goya in Prose" (Huré). *The Daily Telegraph,* December 23, 1965, 13.
Bourgeois, Michel. " 'Le Times' d'Albertine Sarrazin." *Combat,* July 6, 1972, 7.
Charasson, Henriette. "Une Romancière: Anne Huré." *Ecrits de Paris: Revue des questions actuelles,* December 1963, 86–94.
Cothran, Ann. "Narrative Structure as Expression of Self in Sarrazin's 'L'Astragale.' " *L'Esprit créateur* 19, no. 2 (summer 1979): 13–22.
Daix, Pierre. "La Taule et 'La Cavale.' " *Les Lettres françaises,* November 4, 1965, 5.
Decoin, Didier. "Sans âme ni conscience" (Gérard). *Les Nouvelles littéraires,* November 27, 1972, 4.
Desanti, Dominique. *La Banquière des années folles: Marthe Hanau.* Paris, 1968.
"Dossier–Henriette Caillaux," "Dossier–Marthe Hanau," "Dossier–Héra Mirtel (Madame Bessarabo)," and "Dossier–Gabrielle Russier" at the Bibliothèque Féministe Marguerite Durand, Paris 5e.
Duranteau, Josane. *Albertine Sarrazin.* Paris, 1971.
———. "Qui est Albertine Sarrazin?" *Combat,* October 7, 1965, 6.
Eaubonne, Françoise d'. "L'Evasion par l'écriture" (Sarrazin). *Magazine littéraire,* December 1972, 18–20.

BIBLIOGRAPHY

Floriot, René. *Deux femmes en Cour d'Assises: Madame Steinheil et Madame Caillaux.* Paris, 1966.
Ganne, Gilbert. "Le Féminin singulier" (Huré). *La Revue de Paris,* December 1964, 103–8.
Gelfand, Elissa. "Albertine Sarrazin: A Control Case for Feminity in Form." *The French Review* 51, no. 2 (December 1977): 245–51.
———. "Albertine Sarrazin: The Confined Imagination." *L'Esprit créateur* 19, no. 2 (summer 1979): 47–57.
Jardin, Claudine. "L'Enfer des prisons" (Gérard). *Le Figaro littéraire,* December 2, 1972, 114.
Kalda, Alexandra. "Anne Huré raconte ses prisons." *Arts,* September 25, 1963, 3.
Kanters, Robert. "Albertine, ou L'Art de la fugue." *Le Figaro littéraire,* November 11, 1965, 5.
Lacombe, Lia. "Vicime de la passion" (Huré). *Les Lettres françaises,* April 21, 1966, 5.
Mauriac, Claude. "L'Espèce de purification d'Albertine Sarrazin." *Le Figaro littéraire,* May 20, 1972, 14.
Mayne, Richard. "Kilroy Wasn't Here" (Huré). *New Statesman,* December 24, 1965, 1006.
Mithois, Marcel. "On m'a refusé le Goncourt parce que je sortais de prison" (Huré). *Réalités,* August 1963, 78–83.
Nadaud, Marcel, and André Fage. *Les Grand Drames passionnels* (Steinheil). Paris, 1926.
Nye, Robert. "Left Ear, Right Nose" (Huré). *The Guardian,* November 24, 1967, 11.
Piatier, Jacqueline. "Albertine, une figure de notre temps" (Sarrazin). *Le Monde,* August 22, 1974, 14.
Tavernier, René. *Madame Steinheil, ange ou démon: Favorite de la République.* Paris, 1976.
Villelaur, Anne. "Une si longue attente" (Sarrazin). *Lettres françaises,* January 1967, 6.
Wardle, Irving. "Closed Society" (Huré). *The Observer,* November 28, 1965, 28.

Criminological and Penal Contexts

Actes: Femmes, droit et justice, no. 16 (Autumn 1977).
Adler, Freda. *Sisters in Crime.* New York, 1975.
Alexander, Frantz, and Hugh Staub. "Id, Ego, and Superego." Taken from *The Criminal, the Judge and the Public.* Reproduced in *Law and*

the Lawless, ed. Gresham M. Sykes and Thomas E. Drabek, 168–80, New York, 1969.
Boucard, Robert. *Les Dessous des prisons de femmes.* Paris, 1930.
Bregeon, Mariette. "Approche criminologique et traitement de la criminalité féminine." Thesis. Rennes, 1967.
Buffard, Simone. *Le Froid pénitentiaire: L'Impossible réforme des prisons.* Paris, 1973.
Burkhart, Kathryn Watterson. *Women in Prison.* New York, 1973.
Carco, Francis. *Prisons de femmes.* Paris, 1930.
Cowie, J., V. Cowie, and E. Slater. *Delinquency in Girls.* London, 1968.
Dhavernas, Marie-Jo. "La Délinquance des femmes." *Questions féministes,* November 1978, 55–84.
"Dossier–Criminalité" (1900–1970s). Bibliothèque Féministe Marguerite Durand. Paris, 5e.
Erhel, Catherine, and Catherine Leguay. *Prisonnières.* Paris, 1977.
Faugeron, Claude, and Dominique Poggi. "Les Femmes, les infractions, la justice pénale: Une Analyse d'attitudes." *Revue de l'Institut de Sociologie,* no. 3–4. Brussels, 1975.
Gaillac, Henri. *Les Maisons de correction 1830–1945.* Paris, 1971.
Giallombardo, Rose. *Society of Women: A Study of a Women's Prison.* New York, 1966.
Goffman, Erving. "On the Characteristics of Total Institutions: The Inmate World." *Perspectives on Correction,* ed. Donal E. J. MacNamara and Edward Sagarin. New York, 1971.
Granier, Camille. *La Femme criminelle.* Paris, 1906.
Heffernan, Esther. *Making It in Prison: The Square, the Cool, and the Life.* New York, 1972.
Heuyer, Georges. *Les Troubles mentaux: Etude criminologique.* Paris, 1968.
Jones, Ann. *Women Who Kill.* New York, 1980.
Mikes, George. *Prison.* New York, 1964.
Mitford, Jessica. *Kind and Usual Punishment: The Prison Business.* New York, 1973.
Pollak, Otto. *The Criminality of Women.* New York, 1961.
Renaud, Jacqueline. "La Prison modifie pour toujours l'organisme." *Science et vie,* no. 685 (October 1974), 46–53, 154.
Schmelck, Robert, and Georges Picca. *Pénologie et droit pénitentiaire.* Paris, 1967.
Simon, Rita James. *Women and Crime.* Lexington, Mass., 1975.
Sliwowski, Georges. "La 'Sociologie du temps' et la peine privative de liberté." *Revue de science criminelle et de droit pénal comparé,* no. 2 (April–June 1974), 295–312.

BIBLIOGRAPHY

Smart, Carol. *Women, Crime and Criminology: A Feminist Critique.* London, 1976.
Sorcières, les femmes vivent: Prisonnières, no. 6, n.d.
Thomas, W. I. *The Unadjusted Girl.* New York, 1923.
Ward, David A., and Gene G. Kassebaum. *Women's Prison.* Chicago, 1965.
Wheeler, Stanton. "Socialization in Correctional Institutions." In *The Criminal in Confinement,* ed. Leon Radzinowicz and Marvin E. Wolfgang, 97–116. New York, 1971.

Philosophical and Literary Contexts

Chiari, Joseph. *Realism and Imagination.* London, 1960.
Cixous, Hélène. "Le Rire de la Méduse." *L'Arc,* 61 (1975): 39–54. Translated in *Signs* 1, no. 4 (summer 1976):875–93.
Cixous, Hélène, Madeleine Gagnon, and Annie Leclerc. *La Venue à l'écriture.* Paris, 1977.
Dugas, L. *L'Imagination.* Paris, 1903.
Herrmann, Claudine. *Les Voleuses de langue.* Paris, 1976.
Hoyack, L. *L'Intelligence créatrice.* Paris, 1931.
Husserl, Edmund. *Phenomenology and the Crisis of Philosophy.* New York, 1965.
Irigaray, Luce. *Ce sexe qui n'en est pas un.* Paris, 1977.
———. *Speculum de l'autre femme.* Paris, 1974.
Kristeva, Julia. "Pratique signifiante et mode de production." In *La Traversée des signes,* ed. Julia Kristeva et al. Paris, 1975.
———. "Le Texte clos." In *Sēmeiōtikē: Recherches pour une semanalyse.* Paris, 1969.
Laborit, Henri. *Eloge de la fuite.* Paris, 1976.
Sartre, Jean-Paul. *Imagination: A Psychological Critique.* Trans. Forrest Williams. Ann Arbor, Mich., 1962.
Shattuck, Roger. *The Banquet Years: The Origins of the Avant-Garde in France, 1885 to World War I.* Rev. ed. New York, 1968.
Thévoz, Michel. *Le Language de la rupture.* Paris, 1978.
Veraldi, Gabriel, and Brigitte Veraldi. *Psychologie de la création.* Paris, 1972.
Yaguello, Marina. *Les Mots et les femmes.* Paris, 1979.

Index

Abbaye, L' (prison), 70
Adler, Freda, 60
Aggression, 40–41, 60
Animist medicine, 45–46, 87, 141–43
Balzac, Honoré de, 46–47, 115, 159
Barrot, Odilon, 153
Bastille, La (prison), 64–65, 111
Baudelaire, Charles, 20, 125–26
Beauvoir, Simone de, 48, 117, 214
Belle époque, 117, 176–87, 194. *See also* Steinheil, Marguerite
Bergson, Henri, 180
Bompard, Gabrielle, 34, 74–75, 120, 179
Boudard, Alphonse, 61, 106, 126
Brée, Germaine, 24
Brinvilliers, Marquise de, 34, 43–46, 56, 66–67, 86, 119–20
Brives (jail), 73–74, 163
Brombert, Victor, *La Prison romantique* of, 20, 90, 100, 115–16, 125
Buffard, Simone, 79

Caignart de Mailly, M. P., 52
Caillaux, Henriette, 34, 75–76, 176, 181, 186, 192
Camus, Albert, *L'Homme révolté* of, 15, 20–21, 97, 99, 208

Canon, prison, 15–16, 84, 98–110; authors in, 15–16, 100–110; contestation in, 20–21, 29, 99–100, 110, 209; criteria of, 19–20, 128; legitimization of, 35. *See also entries for individual authors*
Cappelle-Lafarge, Marie, 47–48, 56, 71–74, 95, 115–16, 121–23, 126–27, 153–75, 207, 211, 219, 224, 236–37; accusations against, 156, 162–63, 168; critical judgments of, 122, 171–72; *Heures de prison* of, 31, 48, 124–25, 155–75; life of, 31, 156, 174; *Mémoires* of, 31, 48, 89–91, 115–16, 121, 155–75; positivism and, 155–59, 164, 168–70; religiosity of, 160, 165–66, 175; Romanticism and, 155, 168, 170; trial of, 156–57; truth and, 157, 169. *See also entries for individual works*
Cavale, La (Sarrazin), 33, 97, 117–18, 216–22, 230–38; effects of prison on, 81–82, 219–22, 231–32, 235; genre choice of, 232, 237; language in, 223, 236–37; presentation of self in, 217, 230–38; title of, 97, 230–31, 237–38; the visible in, 126, 220, 235–36. *See also* Sarrazin, Albertine

255

INDEX

Chénier, André, 102–3, 109, 151
Chessman, Caryl, 229
Cixous, Hélène, 22, 83, 86, 119
Colette, 117
Collège du Plessis, Le (prison), 69
Confessional writing, 68, 96, 111, 119–24, 155, 217. *See also* Female tradition, prison
Convents, 17, 63–64, 68, 72, 95, 161, 197
Corporal punishment, 17–18, 65–68, 151–52, 175
Criminality, female: biological and sexual emphasis in, 42–49, 58–60, 132–33, 141–44, 179, 199–200, 205, 218, 220–21, 224–26; eighteenth-century views of, 42–46, 131–33, 141–44; nineteenth-century views of, 46–54, 153–63, 175; positivistic descriptions of, 41–42, 50–51; psychological emphasis in, 54–57, 74, 178–94, 199–201, 205, 217, 221–22; sadism in, 49–51, 161–62, 190; sociological emphasis in, 52, 57–58, 77, 178, 189, 200, 218, 228–30; statistics for, 39–41, 46; twentieth-century views of, 54–62, 176–81, 183–90, 193, 199–203, 205, 210, 217–19. *See also entries for individual criminologists and prison works*
Criminals, female: marginality of, 24; well-known, 34–35. *See also* Criminality, female; Female tradition, prison; Women writers; *entries for individual women*
Criminology. *See* Criminality, female

Descartes, René, 85, 201
Diderot, Denis: *La Religieuse* of, 68, 112. *See also philosophes*
Dreyfus affair, 185
Dumas, Alexandre, 161, 172
Duras, Duchesse de (Louise), 43, 46, 64, 69–70, 113
Duras, Marguerite, 117, 119, 214

Eaubonne, Françoise d': *Les Ecrivains en cage* of, 21–22
En prison (Huré), 33, 98, 117–18, 195–213; classicism in, 205–9, 212–13; effects of prison on, 195–96, 199, 201–5, 207, 210–11; genre choice of, 196–97, 212; philosophical and spiritual preoccupations in, 197–205, 207–8, 211–12; presentation of self in, 196–201, 206, 209. *See also* Huré, Anne
Erhel, Catherine and Catherine Leguay: *Prisonnières* of, 78–81

Falcón, Lidia, 239–40
Farge, Arlette, 42
Faure, Félix, 32, 75, 182–83, 185
Female tradition, prison, 23, 110–28; eighteenth century, 110–14, 123; genres of, 82, 95–97, 111–14, 117–24, 134, 148–49, 173–74, 196–97, 212, 217; narrative structures in 113, 115–16, 119; nineteenth century, 114–16; search for identity in, 28–29, 82, 110, 124–27, 209, 217; subversion in, 26, 28–30, 110, 127–28; themes in, 111, 117–18, 125–26; twentieth century, 116–19; the visible in, 125. *See also* Confessional writing; Novels, prison; *entries for individual authors and works*
Feminist inquiry, 19, 25–26, 62, 195, 215–16, 239–52; language and women in, 25–26, 83, 118, 195, 212; socio-literary analysis in, 23, 26–27, 241–42
Fiction, prison. *See* Female tradition, prison; Novels, prison
Forest, Eva, 239–40
Foucault, Michel, 61; social control and, 17–19; *Surveiller et punir* of, 16–19, 67, 74, 114, 139, 153, 161, 201
Franklin, H. Bruce: *The Victim as Criminal and Artist* of, 16–17, 111

INDEX

Frégier, H. A., 46–47
Freud, Sigmund, 54–55, 96, 180, 218

Genet, Jean, 20–22, 61, 104, 106–110
Gérard, Nicole, 34, 61, 78, 126, 239–40
Gide, André, 194, 201, 204, 209
Goffman, Erving, 78–79
Grandpré, Pauline de, 48

Haguenau (prison), 76–77, 195, 198, 201, 203, 208, 211
Hartman, Mary, 53
Herrmann, Claudine, 28, 94
Heures de prison (Cappelle-Lafarge), 31, 48, 73, 124–25, 155–75, 211; effects of prison on, 163–67; genre choice in, 173–74; presentation of self in, 165–67; stylistic devices in, 170–71. *See also* Cappelle-Lafarge, Marie
Heuyer, Georges, 59–60, 77, 218
Hoffmann, Paul, 86–88; 141
Homme révolté, L' (Camus), 15, 20–21, 97, 99, 208
Hoyack, L., 96–97
Huré, Anne, 61, 81, 95–96, 98, 119, 125, 127, 195–213, 214, 219, 224, 237; conservatism of, 195, 212–13; *En prison* of, 33, 98, 117–18, 195–213; life of, 32–33, 78, 195–96, 204; trial of, 204. *See also entries for individual works*
Husserl, Edmund, 96, 195, 202–3
Hysteria, 54–57, 74–76, 87, 91, 162–63, 179, 187–88, 192, 217

Identity, search for. *See* Female tradition, prison; *entries for individual works*
Imagination: definitions of, 83–98; eighteenth century, 86–89; nineteenth century, 89–94; seventeenth century, 84–86, 180; twentieth century, 94–98, 237–38. *See also* Mind-body relation
Imagination, L' (Sartre), 85, 92, 99, 107, 180
Imprisonment. *See* Prisons
Irigaray, Luce, 22, 83, 86, 125

Joly, Henri, 52, 91–93, 159–60
Jones, Ann, 41
Journal de prison 1959 (Sarrazin), 23, 97–98, 119, 123, 216–17, 222–30, 232, 235–36; effects of prison on, 222–23, 227–28, 235; form of, 217, 223, 225–28; presentation of self in, 217, 223–30; themes in, 217, 225, 228; truth in, 224. *See also* Sarrazin, Albertine
Journals and diaries, prison. *See* Confessional writing; Female tradition, prison

Kolodny, Annette, 19, 22
Kristeva, Julia, 83

La Bruyère, Jean de, 201, 205–6
Lacenaire, 47, 115
Lafarge, Marie. *See* Cappelle-Lafarge, Marie
Language, and women. *See* Feminist inquiry
Leduc, Violette, 118, 212
Leguay, Catherine and Catherine Erhel: *Prisonnières* of, 78–81
Leibniz, Gottfried Wilhelm, 86
Lombroso, Cesare, 46, 48–56, 92, 158–61, 178–79, 192

Male prison tradition. *See* Canon, prison
Mallet, Joséphine, 50, 158
Marxism and Literature (Williams), 27, 83, 91
Mathiez, Albert, 150
May, Gita, 88, 151
Mémoires (Cappelle-Lafarge), 3, 48, 73, 89–91, 115–16, 121, 155–75;

257

INDEX

critical judgments of, 122; effects of prison on, 163–67; genre choice in, 173–74; presentation of self in, 165–67, 172; stylistic devices in, 170–71, 173; the visible in, 167–70. See also Cappelle-Lafarge, Marie

Mémoires (Roland), 31, 69–70, 88–89, 138–52; critical judgments of, 150–51; effects of prison on, 137–41; genre choice of, 134, 148–49; narrative structure in, 113; 134–36; 143–44; presentation of self in, 136–47; social importance of, 147–48, 151–52; stylistic devices in, 135, 149–50; truth in, 133–34; the visible in, 144–46. See also Roland, Madame

Més mémoires (Steinheil), 31–32, 94, 116–17, 176–94; effects of prison on, 189, 191–93; genre choice in, 182–83, 194; presentation of self in, 183–91; search for literary effect in, 178, 182, 187, 191, 193–94. See also Steinheil, Marguerite

Mind-body relation, 17–22, 84–85, 164–66, 174–75. See also Imagination

Monglond, André, 134, 150

Moniteur universel, Le, 88, 132

Monstrousness, 15, 31, 34–35; 131–32, 135–36, 141–42, 153, 158, 212, 238; biological, 39–62; intellectual, 83–128; social, 63–82

Montesquieu, Baron de, 113

Montpellier (prison), 74, 163

Motte, Comtesse de la (Jeanne de Valois), 34, 43, 65–66, 142

Myths (about women), 23–26, 242

Novels, prison, 82, 95–97, 99, 111, 114, 118–19, 196–97, 217, 232, 237. See also Female tradition, prison; *entries for individual works*

Pascal, Blaise, 85, 201, 204
Paul, Sylvie, 34, 57–58, 76–77, 192
Père Duchesne, Le, 133, 144
Perrot, Michelle, 39, 47, 63
Personality dossiers, 76–77, 192, 205–6, 221–22
Philosphes, Les, 86–87, 112. See also *entries for individual authors*
Phlipon, Manon. See Roland, Madame
Pirot, Edme. See Brinvilliers, Marquise de
Pollak, Otto, 58, 218
Pons, Mademoiselle de, 43, 69–70
Portraiture. See *entries for individual works*
Positivism, 90–94, 155–59, 164–70, 180. See also Criminality, female
Poulain de la Barre, 85
Prison romantique, La (Brombert), 20, 90, 100, 115–16, 125
Prisonnières (Erhel and Leguay), 78–81
Prisons: concept of, 15–18, 76–77; conditions in, 63–82, 240–41; effects of, 16, 69, 71–72, 78–82, 137–38, 163–67, 191, 195–96, 199, 201–5, 207, 210–11, 218–23, 227–28, 231–32, 235, 240–41; eighteenth century, 17–18, 64–70, 137–38; inmate adaptive systems in, 81–82, 210, 222; nineteenth century, 18, 70–75, 163–67; revolts in, 62, 78; twentieth century, 75–82, 178, 191, 199, 201–5, 207, 219–23. See also *entries for individual prisons and prison works*

Rétif de la Bretonne, 44–45
Revolts (prison), 62, 78
Revolution (1789), 43, 64, 131, 151. See also Criminality, female; Prisons
Ribot, Th., 91–93, 180
Robespierre, Maximilien de, 134, 140

INDEX

Rochefort, Christiane, 117–18, 214
Roland, Madame, 19, 91, 95, 120–23, 127, 131–52, 211, 219, 224, 236; accusations against, 131–34, 151–52; life of, 30–31, 43–46, 64; *Mémoires* of 31, 69–70, 88–89, 113, 133–52; trial of, 131. *See also entries for individual works*
Romanticism, 89–90, 115–16, 120, 125, 155, 168, 170, 205. *See also* Brombert, Victor; Cappelle-Lafarge, Marie
Roquette, la (prison), 195, 197–98, 206
Rousseau, Jean-Jacques, 43–44, 86, 88–89, 127, 134, 139, 141, 147
Roussel, Pierre: *Système physique et moral de la femme, suivi du système physique et moral l'homme* of, 45–46, 48–49, 65, 69–70, 87–89, 92, 141–42. *See also* Animist medicine; Criminality, female
Russier, Gabrielle, 34, 78, 239

Sade, Marquis de, 103–5, 109
Saint-Lazare (prison), 76, 178, 186, 191
Sainte-Pélagie (prison), 70, 137
Sand, George, 89–90, 115–16, 160–61, 173
Sarraute, Natalie, 117–119
Sarrazin, Albertine, 61, 96–98, 121–22, 127–28, 207, 212–13, 214–38, 239; *La Cavale* of, 33, 81–82, 97, 117–18, 126, 216–22, 230–38; *Journal de prison 1959* of, 33, 97–98, 119, 123, 216–17, 222–30, 232, 235–36; life of, 19, 33, 78, 216. *See also entries for individual works*
Sartre, Jean-Paul, 118, 207, 210; *L'Imagination* of, 85, 92, 99, 107, 180; *Saint Genet* of, 15, 107–8
Schmelck, Robert, 77
Self-presentation, women's. *See entries for individual works;* Female tradition, prison
Sévigné, Madame de, 66–67
Smart, Carol, 39, 60
Social control. *See* Foucault, Michel
Spacks, Patricia Meyer, 21, 97
Staal-Delaunay, Madame de, 34, 43, 64–65, 112–13, 120, 126
Staël, Madame de, 89, 115–16
Steinheil, Marguerite, 75–76, 94–96, 121–22, 127, 176–94, 199, 207, 211–12, 217, 219, 224; 237; accusations against, 185, 187, 190, 193; *belle époque* aesthetics and, 176–87; 194; life of, 32, 176–82, 188–89; *Mes mémoires* of, 31–32, 57, 94, 116–17, 178–94; trial of, 176, 181–83, 185, 188–89, 192–93; the visible in, 178–81, 184–87. *See also entries for individual works*
Subversion, women's. *See* Female tradition, prison
Surveiller et punir (Foucault). *See* Foucault, Michel

Tarde, Gabriel, 52
Tencin, Claudine de, 34, 111–13, 121
Terror, the, 30, 65, 68–69, 131–33, 136, 139, 143. *See also* Roland, Madame
Thomas, W. I., 58–59, 218
Trahard, Pierre, 150
Tuke, D. Hack, 92–93
Tulle (prison), 73–74, 163

Veraldi, Brigitte and Gabriel, 97
Verlaine, Paul, 105–7, 109
Villermé, Louis-René, 70
Villon, François, 22, 100–106, 109, 111, 120

Weiss, Madame, 34, 53–54, 56
Wilde, Oscar, 61, 106
Williams, Raymond: *Marxism and Literature* of, 27, 83, 91

259

INDEX

Women writers: criminal, 24, 27–33, 43, 64–66, 75–77, 110–28, 239–42; noncriminal, 24, 113, 115–19, 214, 237, 241–42. *See also* Female tradition, prison; *entries for individual authors*

Women's writings. *See* Female tradition, prison; *entries for individual authors and works*

Woolf, Virginia, 21

Zola, Emile, 187

Library of Congress Cataloging in Publication Data

Gelfand, Elissa D., 1949–
 Imagination in confinement.

 Bibliography: p.
 Includes index.
 1. French literature—Women authors—History and criticism. 2. Prisoners' writings, French—History and criticism. 3. Women authors, French—Biography. 4. Women prisoners—France—Biography. 5. Female offenders—France—Biography. 6. Feminism and literature. I. Title.
 PQ149.G47 1983   840'.9'9287   83-7191
 ISBN 0-8014-1543-8